THE
CHINESE HOROSCOPES
GUIDE TO RELATIONSHIPS

The Chinese Horoscopes Guide to Relationships

Love and Marriage, Friendship and Business

THEODORA LAU

*Illustrations and Calligraphy
by Kenneth Lau*

Broadway Books

New York

BROADWAY

A previous edition of this book was published in 1997 by Doubleday, a division of Random House, Inc. It is here reprinted by arrangement with Doubleday.

For convenience and brevity, the personalities of the earth branch or lunar signs have generally been referred to in this book as "he." Unless otherwise indicated, the information should be taken to apply to both sexes.

First published 1995 by Souvenir Press Ltd
43 Great Russell Street, London WC1B 3PA
and simultaneously in Canada

Broadway Books titles may be purchased for business or promotional use or for special sales. For information, please write to: Special Markets Department, Random House, Inc., 280 Park Avenue, New York, NY 10017.

PRINTED IN THE UNITED STATES OF AMERICA

BROADWAY BOOKS and its logo, a letter B bisected on the diagonal, are trademarks of Broadway Books, a division of Random House, Inc.

Visit our website at www. broadwaybooks.com

First Broadway Books trade paperback edition published 2002.

The Library of Congress Cataloging-in-Publication Data
has cataloged the Doubleday edition as:
Lau, Theodora.
The Chinese horoscopes guide to relationships: love and marriage,
friendship and business / Theodora Lau ; illustrations and
calligraphy by Kenneth Lau.
p. cm.
"Main Street books."
Previously published; London: Souvenir Press, 1995.
1. Astrology, Chinese.   2. Interpersonal relations—Miscellanea.
I. Title.
BF1714.C5L37   1997
133.5′9251—dc21   97-9643
CIP

ISBN 0-385-48640-5

15 14 13 12 11 10

Contents

THE TWELVE EARTH BRANCHES IN THE
RELATIONSHIP TREE

The branches are many, but the root is One.
Chinese proverb

INTRODUCTION

The
Twelve Earth Branches

THE TWELVE EARTH BRANCHES

Most people in the West today are familiar with the twelve animal signs of Chinese astrology, each governing a lunar year and bringing to it, and to the people born in that year, its own individual personality. What is not so widely known is that these animal names were a later addition, dating from the time of the Lord Buddha who, according to legend, assigned a year to each of the twelve animals who came to bid him farewell on his departure from Earth.

In ancient Chinese astrological lore, however, which is now 4,692 years old, the study of horoscopes were based primarily on the theory of the Twelve Earth Branches governed by the twelve-year lunar cycle. Before each year had been given an animal name, these were identified by their earth branches only. In this book I have used the proper branch terms as well as the animal names to identify and classify twelve basic character types, and because the study of human interaction lies at the core of Chinese horoscopes, I have shown the twelve branches in their associated groupings on the Relationship Tree, as a simple way of illustrating how the different personalities relate to and react against one another. Interaction between the earth branches or lunar animal signs is comprehensively explained in every-day terms and examples. By learning how to identify yourself with the correct earth branch you will automatically remember the rank-ing order and the branch number, which is hard to do when using only the animal names.

For example, if I were to say simply that you are a Dragon, you would not know immediately that the Dragon is actually another name for the fifth earth branch, called *Chen*. In Chinese astrology and numerology, the position and order of each branch play a sig-nificant role and in the Chinese almanac and historical treatise of astrology lunar signs are referred to by their earth branches, not by their colourful mythical animal names. After reading this book you will know that the fifth earth branch (the Dragon) is most compatible with the first (the Rat) and the ninth (the Monkey) branches and that these three form the First Triangle of Affinity. Furthermore, the fifth branch is in conflict with the eleventh branch (the Dog) which is located opposite it in the Circle of Conflict. In this circle, an odd number is ranged against another odd number directly facing it, while an even-numbered branch will likewise find the most difficulty with another even-numbered branch, 180 degrees away.

Special sets of characteristics are found in each of the twelve types according to its earth branch. These interact with one another in a myriad ways and degrees of intensity. Optimum ways to get desired results, defuse antagonism or discover the most workable approach when dealing with one or more lunar personality types are suggested here.

Don't be surprised if you find that you possess the characteristics of several of the earth branches. This is normal, as few of us are pure signs. In addition to our year signs, we all carry the traits of our ascendant signs which rule our birth hours, as well as our per-sonal month's sign governed by the Twenty-Four Segments. The twenty-four segments are synchronised with all the Western Zodiac signs so it is easy to identify which of the twelve earth branches your Western sign belongs to. For instance, Sagittarius is the first earth branch, Capricorn is the second, Aquarius is linked with the third branch and so on, with Scorpio as the twelfth and last earth branch.

To discover the ruling Earth branch of your Western astrological sign based on the month of your birth, please refer to the following chart. This third 'branch', after the year of birth and the time of birth, also plays a significant role in shaping our personalities and relationships. It is relevant to point out that the segments coincide to the exact day of the Western astrological signs and were marked by Chinese festivals to establish their importance further.

THE EARTH BRANCHES IN THE TWENTY-FOUR SEGMENTS OF THE CHINESE ALMANAC

Earth branch	Western sign	Dates
1st = Rat	Sagittarius	November 22 to December 21
2nd = Ox	Capricorn	December 22 to January 20
3rd = Tiger	Aquarius	January 21 to February 19
4th = Rabbit	Pisces	February 20 to March 20
5th = Dragon	Aries	March 21 to April 19
6th = Snake	Taurus	April 20 to May 20
7th = Horse	Gemini	May 21 to June 21
8th = Sheep	Cancer	June 22 to July 21
9th = Monkey	Leo	July 22 to August 21
10th = Rooster	Virgo	August 22 to September 22
11th = Dog	Libra	September 23 to October 22
12th = Boar	Scorpio	October 23 to November 21

You will find four sets of triangles in the Chinese cycle of Twelve Earth Branches. These are Triangles of Affinity and they are made up as follows:

1   Triangle of the Doers: Rat—first; Dragon—fifth; Monkey—ninth.
2   Triangle of the Thinkers: Ox—second; Snake—sixth; Rooster—tenth.
3   Triangle of the Protectors: Tiger—third; Horse—seventh; Dog—eleventh.

4 Triangle of the Catalysts: Rabbit—fourth; Sheep—eighth; Boar—twelfth.

These four sets of triangles and the resulting interpersonal relationships woven by their interaction will give more insight into the different personality types as revealed by Chinese astrology.

Chinese culture is in itself a most colourful fabric of intricate relationships. Finely woven in brilliant hues and exquisite designs, everything is based on interaction among groups or individuals likely to have the best chance of success. Working on tried and true principles which would produce the highest ratio of affinity or the least amount of discord was the goal of civilised Chinese society.

Success was considered synonymous with good working relationships, the ability and perseverance to make profitable use of the right contacts. Everyone had to possess or develop *guan xi* which were the special channels for getting things done. *Guan xi* was indispensable. Politically, militarily, personally and commercially, these interlocking relations lubricated the wheels of everyone's life. The careful cultivation of relationships created influential ties that bound and nurtured, and gave birth to opportunities where none existed before.

Of course, present-day *guan xi* is a polluted word in China and is also used to refer to corruption, bribery or undue influence (going by the 'back door'). However, the essential meaning of *guan xi* is that it matters greatly to have the right connections in the right places. *Guan xi* is only valued when used, so it is an art to know how to recognise and exploit the opportunities available, and the human ties that result must be acknowledged and honoured. It is a system of favours for favours, information for information and mutual exchanges of special treatment. It is the eastern equivalent of clout.

To the realistic Chinese, there are no short cuts in forming and maintaining relationships. People go to painstaking lengths to make the proper links and realise that alliances are never permanent or total—situations could change with the weather. As a rule, nothing is in writing and does not need to be. The links may be as tough and malleable as a fine strand of steel or as transitory as blowing straw. Needs and wants must be carefully evaluated and one must frequently be prepared to ask or accept trade-offs not to one's liking. Time limits are loosely adhered to and can stretch into the next generation if family ties are involved. All relationships bring mutual obligations and are often graded according to the degree of involvement required. In Chinese culture, human interaction is an essential exercise in any sphere of society and must be studied in order to achieve the skills necessary to make relationships work.

This ageless tradition has not changed. Relationships open doors for us. Relationships bring us in contact with people who can effect changes in our lives or make us part of a bigger, better team. Relationships foster synergy and symbiotic bonds. Relationships help us manage what we find unmanageable. Relationships bring influence and control over what was previously not within our grasp. It may sound simplistic, but in the end, everything boils down to good, workable relationships. Society cannot exist without them and we must accept that we are all social animals trying to co-exist harmoniously.

Modern MBAs have created all kinds of new names for relationships. It is now called 'networking' or being part of the 'loop'. People have to 'bond' through sports, common interests, special clubs or experiences in life. Joining up with the right party or parties is the main aim. The link-up of a network is essential to making it in today's world—both personally and in business.

We are all encouraged to send emissaries to sound out the competition and check out their influence. Before any decisions can be made, we must have feedback of how they are linked with other players. News travels through special 'information corridors' or 'highways'. When relations break down or disagreements ensue, we need arbitrators to work out our differences and hopefully patch things up before it is too late. Mediation is highly sought after. Whether we are busy mending broken fences of friendship or romance, building new bridges of communication, making connections to other networks or simply expanding our sphere of influence, we are employing the basic principles of finding and making good relationships.

In this book I shall explain the positive and negative attributes of each earth branch and show how to understand and work with each of the twelve basic personalities of the lunar cycle. Perhaps once you learn to recognise individual traits in yourself and in others, you will be able to deal rationally and objectively with problems that may arise. If one distances oneself, it is easier to observe the subject with a better perspective and thus find or create a workable solution.

You may want to come back to this introduction after reading other chapters in the book, as the charts and tables are provided here for easy reference should you become sidetracked or confused. The brief but comprehensive summary given here can be likened to attending a dinner party where one meets twelve guests for the first time. At first it is difficult to remember all the names of so many new people, but once the preliminaries are over we can get to know each personality better as one chapter is devoted to each of them. Then the introductory part becomes clearer and more comprehensible the second time round.

The Relationship Tree of the Twelve Earth Branches, used throughout this book, was conceived as a symbolic, living home to express the unity of the twelve lunar personality types. The cycle of the Twelve Earth Branches, also referred to as the lunar animal signs, has always been presented in linear form in Chinese horoscopes. I first divided the twelve signs into four independent groups of three signs each and called them 'Triangles of Affinity' in my previous book, *The Handbook of Chinese Horoscopes.*

Each of the residents of the four triangles possesses similar traits and a common outlook. The signs within each cluster of affinity will band together and work with each other amicably. Their numerical values are based on the Yang or active male attributes for the odd numbers, versus the Yin or feminine attributes for the even numbers. The first and third triangles are made up of odd-numbered branches while the second and the fourth triangles are made up of the even-numbered branches. Since there are equal pairs of even and odd numbers, everything balances out in the end, there is no strength and no weakness. Like the Tai Ch'i, the ultimate principle of all matter, the goal is to achieve equilibrium. When there is equilibrium or 'give and take' in a relationship, we can truly say there is harmony.

To show that in unity there is also diversity, each branch has its own individual traits and has been assigned its own personality name.

CHARACTERISTICS OF THE TWELVE EARTH BRANCHES

Branch name	Animal name	Personality type	
1st = Zi	Rat	*Initiator*	'I do'
2nd = Chou	Ox	*Enforcer*	'I will'

3rd = Yin	Tiger	*Idealist*	'I feel'
4th = Mao	Rabbit	*Conformist*	'I comply'
5th = Chen	Dragon	*Visionary*	'I see'
6th = Si	Snake	*Strategist*	'I plan'
7th = Wu	Horse	*Adventurer*	'I act'
8th = Wei	Sheep	*Peacemaker*	'I love'
9th = Shen	Monkey	*Innovator*	'I think'
10th = You	Rooster	*Administrator*	'I count'
11th = Xu	Dog	*Guardian*	'I watch'
12th = Hai	Boar	*Unifier*	'I join'

Long before psychologists came on the scene, put name tags on the different types of personality and classified us according to groups, the ancient Chinese did a great deal of research and typecasting of their own, based on carefully kept records of arranged marriages, choice of mentors, unions of clansmen, business enterprises, partnerships and conglomerates. This whole intriguing science could simply be defined as 'knowing people'. My interpretations of the descriptions and interactions between the Twelve Earth Branches are but a humble attempt at summarising this complex and intricate relationship system based on Chinese horoscopes. Common patterns of behaviour, thought processes, affinity, incompatibility and predictable reactions of each personality type defined in this book were developed through my study of the Chinese zodiac to bring new light in building the best possible personal and business relationships.

ASCENDANTS

The twenty-four hours of the day are divided into twelve segments and each of these is governed by one of the earth branches. Based on our time of birth, we have a second personality which will blend with the year of our birth. If a person has the same ascendant sign as the birth year sign, then that person is considered a 'pure sign' and has a very strong personality type that is consistent with the earth branch he or she represents. Most of us, however, will display uncharacteristic traits now and then or could be dominated by our ascendant sign if it is a stronger sign than our birth sign or branch.

For instance, a person who is born in the year of the Sheep (the eighth branch) may appear soft-spoken and docile on the exterior, but since he has a Dragon ascendant (he was born between 7 a.m.

and 9 a.m.), he may have an indomitable spirit and can be formidable when challenged. On the other hand, a person of the exacting Rooster branch (tenth) may be happy-go-lucky and quite irresponsible but extremely charming and outgoing because her ascendant is ruled by the colourful Tiger hours (3 a.m. to 5 a.m.) at her birth.

Our ascendant's characteristics play a large role in our total make-up and may sometimes not immediately be recognised in our personality. This is more the case if we are influenced by strong early relationships within the family. Let's say that a person born in the first branch (Rat) during the hours ruled by the sixth branch, or that of the Snake, has a mother also born in the year of the Rat. If this person has close bonds with his mother, his Rat characteristics governed by the first branch may be stronger and more visible. His Snake-ascendant personality is still present, however, but may not come to the fore until he leaves home, marries or asserts himself ambitiously in pursuing a political career.

Hence, friends may be surprised by the emergence of his ascendant's personality, and remarks such as 'I didn't know you had it in you' are quite common when a repressed ascendant makes new relationships, selects new partners or shows a different side of its nature.

THE TWELVE EARTH BRANCHES AND THEIR ASCENDANT HOURS

1st branch	11 p.m. to 1 a.m.	(Rat)
2nd branch	1 a.m. to 3 a.m.	(Ox)
3rd branch	3 a.m. to 5 a.m.	(Tiger)
4th branch	5 a.m. to 7 a.m.	(Rabbit)
5th branch	7 a.m. to 9 a.m.	(Dragon)
6th branch	9 a.m. to 11 a.m.	(Snake)
7th branch	11 a.m. to 1 p.m.	(Horse)
8th branch	1 p.m. to 3 p.m.	(Sheep)
9th branch	3 p.m. to 5 p.m.	(Monkey)
10th branch	5 p.m. to 7 p.m.	(Rooster)
11th branch	7 p.m. to 9 p.m.	(Dog)
12th branch	9 p.m. to 11 p.m.	(Boar)

TRIANGLES OF AFFINITY

You will find four sets of triangles in the Chinese cycle of twelve branches, which are grouped as follows:

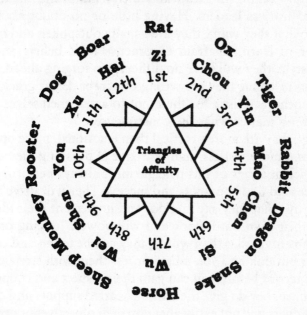

The Doers

The first triangle is composed of the Doers. They are made up of the first, fifth and ninth branches or, respectively, the Rat, Dragon and Monkey. These personality types are hands-on people who love

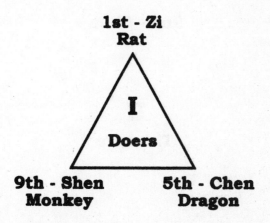

taking the initiative and are self-starters needing little or no motivation from others.

Innovative and positive in their way of thinking, the members of this trio enjoy taking the lead and their enthusiasm makes them capable and fearless leaders. Having little or no doubt about their abilities or what they want, they are usually outspoken and opinionated. Eager to learn, unafraid to practise their beliefs and high-spirited in style, they will have no difficulty in forging ahead. Do not expect them to admit they are wrong or accept defeat graciously. It would be uncharacteristic for them not to assert themselves and try the untried, no matter what the consequences.

Generally, they are more practical than emotional, more optimistic than wise and more restless than reflective in pursuing their dreams. The three personalities of this triangle must always perform and act out their ideas to find happiness and success. They will strive to make their mark by what they say and do; and implement their ideas into reality by their own hard work and will-power. Judging others by accomplishments rather than words, they can be tough and competitive in their outlook and you must impress them with strength and a good track record before you can gain their respect and cooperation. However, once they do give their wholehearted support and commitment, these doers will not easily abandon their objectives or principles.

The Thinkers

The second triangle of affinity is made up of three pragmatic earth branches called the Thinkers. They are the second, sixth and tenth branches, known respectively as the Ox, Snake and Rooster.

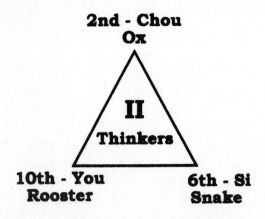

2nd - Chou
Ox

II
Thinkers

10th - You   **6th - Si**
Rooster   **Snake**

People of this trio are purposeful and reflective in their thinking and value intellectual prowess and didactic thinking. Gifted with superior intelligence and the ability to sort things out calmly, they are the planners and schemers who plot the course for others to follow.

The personalities of the second triangle are noted for their patience, thoroughness and steadfast dedication. Their perseverance and self-sacrifice will inspire others to perform above their ability. As the visionaries of the cycle, they are confident in their own analytical powers and will have a strong perception of how things could and should be done. Unswayed by public opinion, they are known to be unyielding and resolute in outlook and will outwit or outmanoeuvre their opponents with their calm but formidable powers. They are the most determined thinkers who will slowly but surely reach their goals by unwavering tenacity and constancy of purpose. To work with them, one must learn to appreciate their analytical and cerebral abilities and appeal to their intelligence and practical side. Show them how they will benefit in a rational, systematic, well thought-out plan. All contingencies must be addressed and provided for as these are great believers in having other options and do not like surprises or sudden changes. Because of their strong dislike of failure or weakness, they can be ruthless when thwarted or misled. Be careful to explain all issues before embarking on any enterprise, as these personalities will not forgive you if you leave loose ends or fail to anticipate all the possibilities. In the end, they will depend on their own astute assessment of facts, and in decision-making they will opt to follow their heads rather than their hearts.

The Protectors

The third triangle of affinity is composed of the third, seventh and eleventh branches, also known as, the Tiger, Horse and Dog personalities. The Protectors are fiery, emotional and subjective types. Guided by compassion, they seek to serve humanity and promote understanding. They can be the impulsive, self-appointed defenders of justice and morals in the world. Although they are extroverts and unselfish by nature, they can also be unorthodox in their approach and views. These individuals are often aggressive and defiant when challenged. True to their beliefs and conscience, they react emotionally and have volatile tempers. Occupants of the third triangle are most likely to be militant and passionate in defence of their causes

**3rd - Yin
Tiger**

**III
Protectors**

**11th - Xu
Dog**

**7th - Wu
Horse**

and they will not hesitate to act independently to attain their objectives and protect their rights.

Basically, they are sociable and democratic but can be combative and commanding when called upon to defend themselves or those they love. Selfless, protective and, above all, loyal, this staunch group will not retreat from a fight or stand silently by and endure injustice. They are reputed for their courage but are also known to be rebellious and obstinate when they are negative.

To work well with these three personalities, you should appeal to their innate sense of honour and fair play. If they feel they can do something for the good of all, they will readily put aside their wishes for the benefit of the majority. Honest and open in their dealings, they do expect others to behave in like manner. The occupants of this triangle believe in personal contact, so if you would like to develop strong bonds with any one of them, it would be wise to meet them on a one-to-one basis and have a heart-to-heart talk. This way, they can look you in the eye and make up their minds immediately whether they like you or not. Guided by their emotions, they can assess a situation accurately by instinct, and more often than not their first impressions are correct. The Protectors are most likely to have magnetic and colourful personalities that are attractive to the public at large, and consequently they get projected into the limelight of the stage, cinema or politics.

The Catalysts

The fourth triangle of affinity is ruled by the fourth, eighth and twelfth branches, also identified as the Rabbit, the Sheep and the Boar. This group of catalysts is composed of the intuitive, sympathetic and cooperative personality types who bring about changes in others without changing themselves. Supportive, sincere and generous, people who occupy the fourth triangle are not only keen observers but also skilled in self-preservation. Artistic, impressionable and creative, they are the guardians of the visual arts, experts in communication, computers, broadcasting, the movie industry and the music world. Acting as movers and shapers behind the scenes, this trio have their fingers on the pulse of all segments of society and know how to make things happen for their own benefit, consciously or unconsciously.

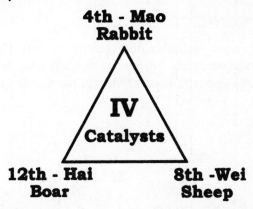

Often they may be too sensitive to changes or negative influences from others, so that they change their minds easily or have feelings of insecurity. They tend to be inconsistent and dependent on others to effect the changes they desire. In dealing with the occupants of the Catalysts triangle, one must not expect unconditional support and unwavering loyalty. Remember, they seek to bring people together in the universal spirit of cooperation. They will be able to introduce you to all the right people and make connections one would not dream possible; but they cannot and will not force relationships, nor should you expect them to stay and hold your hand through thick and thin. These personalities are not famous for their constancy and tend to indulge themselves when given the opportunity. They have no inclination for long, painful battles of wills and do not provoke or start fights even when they have just cause. True to their peaceful natures, they make good arbitrators and referees. Because they find it easy to understand and identify with others and are not too competitive or combative in their approach, they are most likely to succeed in getting everyone to join forces with them.

Approachable, obliging and diplomatic, they know how to make friends and appease enemies to the best of their advantage. Anyone who wants to work with this group of catalysts should emphasise the virtues of compromise instead of confrontation and the benefits of negotiation instead of open conflict. These indispensable experts of 'give and take' will be successful in working out their problems and the problems of others in their own special way.

CIRCLE OF CONFLICT

In each chapter you will also find the sign or personality type most likely to be incompatible with your branch and this sign will be located directly opposite your branch in the Circle of Conflict.

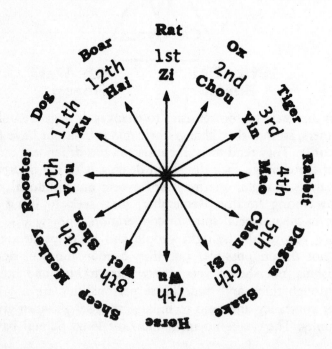

	Branch			Branch
1st	Rat	opposes	7th	Horse
2nd	Ox	opposes	8th	Sheep
3rd	Tiger	opposes	9th	Monkey
4th	Rabbit	opposes	10th	Rooster
5th	Dragon	opposes	11th	Dog
6th	Snake	opposes	12th	Boar
7th	Horse	opposes	1st	Rat
8th	Sheep	opposes	2nd	Ox
9th	Monkey	opposes	3rd	Tiger
10th	Rooster	opposes	4th	Rabbit
11th	Dog	opposes	5th	Dragon
12th	Boar	opposes	6th	Snake

RELATIONSHIPS

The cornerstone of workable relationships is found in the art of listening. Learning to listen and understand is a difficult but rewarding task. It was a tribal custom of native Americans to cultivate listening by the use of a 'talking stick'. During councils of war, important discussions, negotiations or disagreements, the person holding the talking stick was allowed to speak without interruption for an indefinite period, but before the opposition was given a chance to reply, he had to be able to repeat everything the holder of the stick had said, to the satisfaction of the first speaker. Only when the person in possession of the talking stick was satisfied that his opponent fully comprehended his position would he pass the stick on to that person. Then it would be his turn to listen patiently to what the other was saying, with the same purpose of being able to repeat what was said.

This simple but ingenious method cleared disputes and misunderstandings quickly and effectively because both sides learned to pay attention to what was being said. If we know where someone is coming from or why he is troubled, it will be easier for us to resolve matters. This does not mean we must agree with what others say, think or do. It simply means learning to hear and acknowledge different points of view without prejudice and without forming an opinion prematurely.

In the following twelve chapters we shall deal with what to expect of each sign and how it views life in general. Once we are able to comprehend how a certain type of person thinks and reacts, we shall be able to establish some sort of relationship, no matter how weak or fleeting. People who fear commitments or relationships are living under the misconception that they are heavy burdens that must be borne stolidly, like crosses or millstones around the neck. Once made, these shackles cannot be cast off. Thus, the fear of relationships is real and dreaded by many. Perhaps, after reading this book with an open heart and mind, you will be better able to define the type of relationship you are having or want to have. Misconceptions can be corrected when we realise that there are multitudes of relationships and that it is up to each and every one of us to determine and analyse the kind of relationships involved and why they do or do not work well.

It is interesting to note that current business management seminars and best-selling books now tout working relationships by establishing teams. The team members are all aware of their duties and responsibilities and know that, once their mission is accomplished, their relationship will terminate. Statistics prove that everyone performs better and is able to weather personality clashes when they know they are not going to be imprisoned by the relationship. We can see just how common this practice is when we observe how pre-school children play. One child usually brings his toy over to a friend's place, and when they have finished playing he takes his toy and goes home. Should a fight or disagreement ensue, the owner of the toy will terminate the game and leave earlier. However, if he really wants to resume the relationship, he will be back the next day to play again, with a slight change in the rules. If children can accept relationships for what they really are, then perhaps we should learn from them and not complicate our lives needlessly by fearing relationships instead of forming them.

Ten Types of Relationship

As children, if we belong to a family of two or more siblings, we all know how to make the favoured child approach the parent to ask for something. If we are the only child, we still obtain the assistance of an ally in working on our parents if we feel a good word from the right person will tip the scales in our favour. The teacher's favourite in school will usually be utilised to get or give information that could prove valuable to the interests of the class. It is simply part of our nature to make things easier for ourselves, to get what we want with the least amount of resistance or opposition. When we are young and uninhibited, we think nothing of using someone else's relationship to further our own cause. It is the quickest and simplest way to turn a 'no' or a 'maybe' into a definite 'yes'.

As we grow older we begin to cultivate our own relationships or bond with those we choose. We also become more inhibited and selfconscious and do not form close relationships so naturally. As our lives become more complicated, relationships grow more involved and intricate.

Yet most of us do not lose the knack of identifying the best person to send as our ambassador to a figure of authority: someone who knows how to present the request in a good light and say the right thing at the right time. In other words, the emissary is chosen for his chances of success. We pin our hopes on his skills and his ability to use the right approach for our benefit. To be perfectly honest, we establish relationships because they are going to be useful in one way or another. People who fail to develop or build relationships are often without allies and are usually left by the wayside, more pitied than shunned.

There are some basic rules to remember when establishing relationships. The first and foremost is that relationships are not forever. But neither must they be terminated just because we think we no longer need the connection. We all have relationships that are placed on hold or have been dormant for many years simply because we have moved on or are no longer in the same circles. However, when our paths cross again we resume the relationship just as if there had never been any interruption. There is a certain strength and resilience in such bonds that do not break but are still intact after a long time and can be so easily renewed. These are our best, long-term, permanent and voluntary relationships, ones we can slip comfortably in and out of. They are tucked away in our hearts and do not make stressful demands on us or tug at our conscience because they carry certain responsibilities.

Learning to classify every relationship helps us cope with everyday functions and prevents us from being overwhelmed. We will not feel unnecessarily obligated or confused if we can compartmentalise things and know confidently where we stand. The Chinese teach children at a tender age to know their place. This does not mean that a child must be seen and not heard to have impeccable manners, but that he must learn to discover where and how he fits in before making any move. One's invisible rank is always taken into account, so one must know how to act accordingly. Careful observation is indispensable to develop that skill of 'knowing one's place', which is looked upon as a great advantage to possess. It could take an entire lifetime for some people to learn what to say, when to say it and, more importantly, whom to address it to, while others can do it by instinct and have no trouble fitting in. They may not always establish deep or long-lasting relationships but they are always cordial and able to get along with everyone amicably. These are the ten kinds of relationship by which we can classify all human contact:

1   *Permanent or long-term*
Such relationships are usually with parents, siblings, relatives and spouses. They may or may not be voluntary since we cannot choose family members, and contacts are usually obligatory with, no doubt, a certain amount of love and hate as we weigh the many responsibilities that come with each of them and the intensity we feel.
— Persons belonging to the triangles of the Thinkers and Catalysts are usually less resistant to permanent relationships and even need long-term associations to which they can anchor their emotions.
— Persons identified as Doers and Protectors do not take permanent relationships so seriously and may need to break away once in a while to enjoy their freedom.

2   *Essential*
These are mutual contacts that may work for a long time, or equally important but short-term relationships with people such as doctors, lawyers and other professionals of our own choice, with whom we feel we have good rapport and who are essential in our lives. When you telephone an essential relation, that person will not have to ask what you want or why you are calling, it is usually understood. Your doctor will assume you need his services, your accountant will assume you have a financial question or problem and not some other matter. These relationships are generally voluntary as we can cut the bonds if we no longer require them, but they may also be combined with some other type of relationship and are then not so clearly defined.

— Doers and Protectors are quick and competent in this type of relationship and do not have any problems in using or terminating essential relationships to their advantage.

— Thinkers and Catalysts tend to be slow in warming up to essential relationships and just as reluctant to terminate them as they do not like change in their lives. At times, they may become possessive and too demanding, which is detrimental to the effectiveness of this type of contact.

3 *Conducive*

We need these to build up our confidence and encourage us to perform certain tasks or help us to achieve our goals. They are helpful relationships with people such as our teachers, pastor, advisers, mentors, sponsors and other superiors who may gain little from the association for themselves. These are useful relationships which help us grow and prosper.

— Doers relish such conducive contacts and will usually quickly establish excellent rapport.

— Thinkers tend to be more independent and strong-willed and may not readily concede that they need conducive relationships. They could be inhibited or aloof in the beginning but once their resistance evaporates will usually realise that they need help from their superiors.

— Protectors not only work well in such relationships but are excellent when they are the mentors, advisers, teachers and sponsors. Whether in the role of the person being helped or the one who is helpful, Protectors will unselfishly give all they have to this type of association.

— Catalysts love being helped, advised and catered for. They are more dependent on the opinions and views of their superiors and will thrive in such associations. Since Catalysts excel in the art of communication, they have no problem in making their needs known to anyone who can help them achieve their goals.

4 *Competitive*

These relationships are ones we usually choose to participate in, fully aware that we are vying for a prize or superiority, but sometimes they may be forced upon us, as in contests, examinations, sports, games and professional tendering for projects or business opportunities. We try to learn as much as possible about our rivals so that we can successively triumph over their shortcomings and emerge victorious. Anyone who does not recognise the nature of this type of relationship from the onset will diminish his chances of success or may even contribute to his own failure. Of course, one is not obliged to be nice but one should show some courtesy and sportsmanship if the contact is to be called civilised.

— Doers and Protectors take to such competitive relationships like ducks to water. They usually ask no quarter and will give none in return. Yet they maintain a spirit of fair play and have a lively sense of humour that helps them keep their perspective.

— Thinkers and Catalysts do not enjoy too much competition and will do what they can to have the odds in their favour before joining in. Thinkers are analytical and will ask for guarantees where none are possible, while Catalysts pray for a win-win situation instead of ruthlessly pursuing the objective. These two groups also tend to be bad losers.

5   *Controlling*

This type of relationship covers situations where you are the superior or in a supervisory position to direct others. Whether one is the controller or the controlled, the fact remains that the narrower the scope of this functional relationship, the more workable it will be. For instance, if someone only controls a small portion of your job performance or your time, you will be able to conform with more tolerance than if a controlling association restricts you on a large scale. Such relationships become difficult once the controlling party tries to expand his authority or stray into other areas where he should not be. Strife and stress are sure to follow when this happens and we must act quickly to narrow the scope or shorten the time involved back to what existed in the first place.

— Doers and Protectors tend to approach such relationships with their eyes wide open and will not suffer abuse without quick retaliation or rebellion. They are difficult to handle and do not like to back down once they feel oppressed. If treated with respect they will respond well and give their full cooperation.

— Thinkers and Catalysts are not as democratic as Doers and Protectors and tend to be less outspoken and more set in their ways. Yet, as controllers, these two groups tend to overstep the bounds and may be found guilty of the very faults of which they may accuse others. Thinkers are authoritarians and Catalysts are over-possessive, so both groups have the tendency to be unreasonable in positions of power.

6 *Destructive or adversarial*

These associations result in antagonistic clashes that are negative from the onset. They are not the same as competitive relationships which may not be destructive if they are conducted in the spirit of a friendly vying for supremacy. In a competitive relationship you may win one football match and lose the next, but in a destructive relationship both sides lose, even if they refuse to admit it.

When someone is out to destroy you, you will usually be the first to know. Somehow you will have a premonition that things are not well. Often, right from our initial contact, we are guided by intuition or first impressions in our dislike of someone. The more you seek to appease your foe or sort out a destructive relationship by yourself, the more difficult it will be to show strength and not weakness. Messages tend to be most misconstrued in this type of contact. These are the types of relationship that need a go-between or mediator who must deal with both sides. Only through the efforts of an impartial intermediary could such relationships have any hope of being made productive or neutralised. The use of Chinese horoscopes could prove helpful in destructive or antagonistic relationships by finding the right person or persons to act as mediators.

— Doers are not shy about what and whom they love or hate. You will know immediately if a Doer person is out to get you as he will not hide his feelings or intent.

— Thinkers are more secretive and reflective. You may never know they dislike you or want to destroy you. Thinkers will bide their time and could be subversive in their efforts to undermine their so-called enemies. They find it hard to trust mediators, too, so one has to find a way to crack their defence shields in order to establish some kind of communication.

— Protectors, like Doers, are outspoken and bold. Unafraid to follow their convictions or show their feelings, Protectors make bad but visible opponents. Usually they do not like to resort to underhand methods and may be persuaded to work things out with the help of a suitable mediator.

— Catalysts are unpredictable adversaries because they tend to be suspicious by nature and do not like to reveal their true feelings when they are angry or hurt. Anger tends to build up in Catalyst personalities until they explode like pressure cookers. However, Catalysts are usually optimists when it comes to resolving conflicts and will welcome intermediaries with open arms if they feel assured that an adversarial situation can be neutralised.

7   Obligatory

These are relationships based on commitments which we feel we must honour due to some form of responsibility. Usually this type is involuntary and occurs out of a sense of duty. So long as we know we are performing our promise or promises, we tend to be obliging and force ourselves to be happy. One usually rationalises a great deal when involved in a perfunctory relationship and makes the best of a dutiful commitment. Charitable functions to raise money, family reunions, weddings and social functions to please others or just to keep the peace are good examples of obligatory relationships.

— Doers and Protectors perform such obligations cheerfully but may not always be depended upon to show up or be on time. Perhaps because they are aware of how obligatory relationships are forced upon them, they try to do as little as possible.
— Thinkers and Catalysts will perform their obligations faithfully but will demand concessions and negotiate terms to their satisfaction. They tend to trade favour for favour such as: If I come to your party, you must come to my fund-raising event, and so forth. However, they are dependable and consistent.

8   Voluntary

These are types in which we make a conscious choice and may or may not assign a time limit. When one is involved in a voluntary relationship, it is advisable to decide right from the beginning how much involvement is needed and how far we will go. Say we join a rota of parents to fetch children from school. If we make a schedule right from the start and stick to it as well as lay down the rules about how many times each person will fetch the children during a term, there will be less chance of misunderstandings as time goes on.

— Doers and Protectors will usually call the shots in such arrangements and be decisive and proactive in their approach. These

personalities tend to volunteer their time and energy readily and do not feel hemmed in by voluntary relationships. However, they will also be the first to break such commitments if they no longer want them.
— Thinkers and Catalysts are more conscious of their obligations and more reserved in speaking out, even when they should. Consequently, they usually feel taken advantage of and may harbour resentment and find it hard to terminate voluntary relationships when they no longer work.

9 *Temporary or short-term*

These are contacts we make as a necessity of life. The postman, the sales assistant, the delivery man, the receptionists and the many other people who come into contact with us in our daily life are all part of a maze of temporary relationships we unconsciously cultivate. Usually, we are civil but quick and to the point. We state what we need or want and the relationship terminates as soon as we are served or have served the other person. These temporary and short-term relationships are very important as people do judge us by the way we handle these short-term contacts. It is wise always to remember that these 'friends of the road' could well turn into 'friends of the heart'.
— Doers are outgoing and thrive on casual, short-term relationships. They have natural styles and make good impressions on people they come in contact with because they are open, easy to please and uncomplicated.
— Thinkers are perfectionists, hard to please, and find difficulty in dealing with strangers who do not know what they like or how to please them. However, they can be polite yet distant. They will also be the ones who insist on calling one's attention to mistakes they find and will not allow exceptions to the rules.
— Protectors are generous and flexible. They tend not to be demanding but can be impatient and in too much of a hurry. Otherwise, they are affable and easy to work with. They know how to charm their way around and will make exceptions to the rules to accommodate others.
— Catalyst personalities are kind and sociable but they tend to be picky and may complain or sulk if things are not done to their satisfaction. They do not like being rushed or forced into making

quick decisions and may procrastinate or change their minds several times. On the positive side, they can be understanding and patient in dealing with others, especially with children and animals.

10   *Mixed or Converted Relationships*

These are combinations of the other nine relationships as well as overlapping ones that have changed from one initial type into another as the relationship progressed or deteriorated. Because we are all complicated and diverse in the way we act, react and interact, we all have many of these mixed relationships. Again, learning to sort them out and see them for what they really are sets our minds and hearts at ease. Once we have decided what type or types of relationship we are having with a particular individual, we can make conscious choices about what we want from this association. Our decision may upgrade or downgrade the relationship, but once we make up our minds, the concurring adjustments tend to come naturally. Usually, a change in the status of a relationship is evident in our attitude and often reflected in our body language or tone of voice. There is little use in feeling too much guilt or regret. Relationships are never stagnant, and although we sometimes mourn the death of a good relationship, we must accept the fact that they tend to take on a life of their own. Because all relationships are elastic, we find ourselves adjusting into our comfort zones and could move closer to or away from someone at will.

Like plants and flowers, relationships must be fed, cultivated and watered. Even so, they still do not all turn out alike. Certain plants blossom only when well watered and need a great deal of care, while others, like cacti, do not need much nurturing and can be prickly to the touch. Others may go dormant only to come alive in the spring, while evergreens maintain their youth forever. But all the while we live and learn by all our interactions, doing better each time at identifying, forming and establishing good relationships.

HOW TO USE THIS BOOK

In order to read about your own personality and those of other people with whom you are involved, you need to know which earth branch or lunar sign rules their year of birth. The listing of lunar years on the following pages will help you identify their sign, and you can then turn straight to the appropriate chapter.

THE EXACT LUNAR YEARS FROM 1900 TO 2007

Sign		*The Earth Branches*	
Rat	January 31, 1900 to February 18, 1901	1st	Zi
Ox	February 19, 1901 to February 7, 1902	2nd	Chou
Tiger	February 8, 1902 to January 28, 1903	3rd	Yin
Rabbit	January 29, 1903 to February 15, 1904	4th	Mao
Dragon	February 16, 1904 to February 3, 1905	5th	Chen
Snake	February 4, 1905 to January 24, 1906	6th	Si
Horse	January 25, 1906 to February 12, 1907	7th	Wu
Sheep	February 13, 1907 to February 1, 1908	8th	Wei
Monkey	February 2, 1908 to January 21, 1909	9th	Shen
Rooster	January 22, 1909 to February 9, 1910	10th	You
Dog	February 10, 1910 to January 29, 1911	11th	Xu
Boar	January 30, 1911 to February 17, 1912	12th	Hai
Rat	February 18, 1912 to February 5, 1913	1st	Zi
Ox	February 6, 1913 to January 25, 1914	2nd	Chou
Tiger	January 26, 1914 to February 13, 1915	3rd	Yin
Rabbit	February 14, 1915 to February 2, 1916	4th	Mao
Dragon	February 3, 1916 to January 22, 1917	5th	Chen
Snake	January 23, 1917 to February 10, 1918	6th	Si
Horse	February 11, 1918 to January 31, 1919	7th	Wu
Sheep	February 1, 1919 to February 19, 1920	8th	Wei
Monkey	February 20, 1920 to February 7, 1921	9th	Shen
Rooster	February 8, 1921 to January 27, 1922	10th	You
Dog	January 28, 1922 to February 15, 1923	11th	Xu
Boar	February 16, 1923 to February 4, 1924	12th	Hai
Rat	February 5, 1924 to January 24, 1925	1st	Zi
Ox	January 25, 1925 to February 12, 1926	2nd	Chou
Tiger	February 13, 1926 to February 1, 1927	3rd	Yin
Rabbit	February 2, 1927 to January 22, 1928	4th	Mao
Dragon	January 23, 1928 to February 9, 1929	5th	Chen
Snake	February 10, 1929 to January 29, 1930	6th	Si
Horse	January 30, 1930 to February 16, 1931	7th	Wu
Sheep	February 17, 1931 to February 5, 1932	8th	Wei
Monkey	February 6, 1932 to January 25, 1933	9th	Shen
Rooster	January 26, 1933 to February 13, 1934	10th	You

| Dog | February 14, 1934 to February 3, 1935 | 11th | Xu |
| Boar | February 4, 1935 to January 23, 1936 | 12th | Hai |

Rat	January 24, 1936 to February 10, 1937	1st	Zi
Ox	February 11, 1937 to January 30, 1938	2nd	Chou
Tiger	January 31, 1938 to February 18, 1939	3rd	Yin
Rabbit	February 19, 1939 to February 7, 1940	4th	Mao
Dragon	February 8, 1940 to January 26, 1941	5th	Chen
Snake	January 27, 1941 to February 14, 1942	6th	Si
Horse	February 15, 1942 to February 4, 1943	7th	Wu
Sheep	February 5, 1943 to January 24, 1944	8th	Wei
Monkey	January 25, 1944 to February 12, 1945	9th	Shen
Rooster	February 13, 1945 to February 1, 1946	10th	You
Dog	February 2, 1946 to January 21, 1947	11th	Xu
Boar	January 22, 1947 to February 9, 1948	12th	Hai

Rat	February 10, 1948 to January 28, 1949	1st	Zi
Ox	January 29, 1949 to February 16, 1950	2nd	Chou
Tiger	February 17, 1950 to February 5, 1951	3rd	Yin
Rabbit	February 6, 1951 to January 26, 1952	4th	Mao
Dragon	January 27, 1952 to February 13, 1953	5th	Chen
Snake	February 14, 1953 to February 2, 1954	6th	Si
Horse	February 3, 1954 to January 23, 1955	7th	Wu
Sheep	January 24, 1955 to February 11, 1956	8th	Wei
Monkey	February 12, 1956 to January 30, 1957	9th	Shen
Rooster	January 31, 1957 to February 17, 1958	10th	You
Dog	February 18, 1958 to February 7, 1959	11th	Xu
Boar	February 8, 1959 to January 27, 1960	12th	Hai

Rat	January 28, 1960 to February 14, 1961	1st	Zi
Ox	February 15, 1961 to February 4, 1962	2nd	Chou
Tiger	February 5, 1962 to January 24, 1963	3rd	Yin
Rabbit	January 25, 1963 to February 12, 1964	4th	Mao
Dragon	February 13, 1964 to February 1, 1965	5th	Chen
Snake	February 2, 1965 to January 20, 1966	6th	Si
Horse	January 21, 1966 to February 8, 1967	7th	Wu
Sheep	February 9, 1967 to January 29, 1968	8th	Wei
Monkey	January 30, 1968 to February 16, 1969	9th	Shen
Rooster	February 17, 1969 to February 5, 1970	10th	You
Dog	February 6, 1970 to January 26, 1971	11th	Xu
Boar	January 27, 1971 to February 15, 1972	12th	Hai

Rat	February 16, 1972 to February 2, 1973	1st	Zi
Ox	February 3, 1973 to January 22, 1974	2nd	Chou
Tiger	January 23, 1974 to February 10, 1975	3rd	Yin
Rabbit	February 11, 1975 to January 30, 1976	4th	Mao
Dragon	January 31, 1976 to February 17, 1977	5th	Chen
Snake	February 18, 1977 to February 6, 1978	6th	Si
Horse	February 7, 1978 to January 27, 1979	7th	Wu
Sheep	January 28, 1979 to February 15, 1980	8th	Wei
Monkey	February 16, 1980 to February 4, 1981	9th	Shen
Rooster	February 5, 1981 to January 24, 1982	10th	You
Dog	January 25, 1982 to February 12, 1983	11th	Xu
Boar	February 13, 1983 to February 1, 1984	12th	Hai
Rat	February 2, 1984 to February 19, 1985	1st	Zi
Ox	February 20, 1985 to February 8, 1986	2nd	Chou
Tiger	February 9, 1986 to January 28, 1987	3rd	Yin
Rabbit	January 29, 1987 to February 16, 1988	4th	Mao
Dragon	February 17, 1988 to February 5, 1989	5th	Chen
Snake	February 6, 1989 to January 26, 1990	6th	Si
Horse	January 27, 1990 to February 14, 1991	7th	Wu
Sheep	February 15, 1991 to February 3, 1992	8th	Wei
Monkey	February 4, 1992 to January 22, 1993	9th	Shen
Rooster	January 23, 1993 to February 9, 1994	10th	You
Dog	February 10, 1994 to January 30, 1995	11th	Xu
Boar	January 31, 1995 to February 18, 1996	12th	Hai
Rat	February 19, 1996 to February 6, 1997	1st	Zi
Ox	February 7, 1997 to January 27, 1998	2nd	Chou
Tiger	January 28, 1998 to February 15, 1999	3rd	Yin
Rabbit	February 16, 1999 to February 4, 2000	4th	Mao
Dragon	February 5, 2000 to January 23, 2001	5th	Chen
Snake	January 24, 2001 to February 11, 2002	6th	Si
Horse	February 12, 2002 to January 31, 2003	7th	Wu
Sheep	February 1, 2003 to January 21, 2004	8th	Wei
Monkey	January 22, 2004 to February 8, 2005	9th	Shen
Rooster	February 9, 2005 to January 28, 2006	10th	You
Dog	January 29, 2006 to February 17, 2007	11th	Xu
Boar	February 18, 2007 to February 6, 2008	12th	Hai

Dates taken from the Chinese Perpetual (Ten Thousand Years) Lunar Almanac.

1
THE ZI BRANCH
FIRST LUNAR SIGN

The Initiator's Song

I am the self-contained initiator
I serve as a link yet I function as
a complete unit.
I aim at encompassing heights
and strike my target
straight and true.
Life is one joyous journey for me.
Each search must end with a new quest.
I am progress, exploration and insight.
I am the womb of activity —
the 'seed' from which life must spring.

I am Zi, the Initiator

Theodora Lau

THE FIRST EARTH BRANCH: ZI
THE SIGN OF THE RAT

THE ASSIGNED LUNAR YEARS OF THE RAT

January 31, 1900	to	February 18, 1901
February 18, 1912	to	February 5, 1913
February 5, 1924	to	January 23, 1925
January 24, 1936	to	February 10, 1937
February 10, 1948	to	January 28, 1949
January 28, 1960	to	February 14, 1961
February 15, 1972	to	February 2, 1973
February 2, 1984	to	February 19, 1985
February 19, 1996	to	February 6, 1997

If you are born on the day before the start of a lunar year, e.g. January 23, 1936, you belong to the previous earth branch or animal sign, which is the twelfth branch (the Boar).

If you were born on the day after a lunar year ends, e.g. February 11, 1937, you belong to the next earth branch or animal sign, which is the second branch (the Ox).

THE FIRST EARTH BRANCH
THE SIGN OF THE RAT

The first character profile of the twelve earth branches is that of the Rat. He is called *Zi* in Chinese and symbolises a 'seed' or a beginning. The Rat personality views his environment as a domain to be investigated, mapped out and controlled. He is the leader, the innovator and instigator, who pokes his nose everywhere – especially in places where it often does not belong. The more you seek to hide something from him, the more curious and suspicious he will be. He will not rest until he solves the mystery or uncovers the secret. The Rat delights in solving riddles; they are irresistible challenges to his nature. This type of person is a plotter, schemer, investor, speculator and motivator. The Rat, as you must have gathered, is the most inquisitive of the twelve. Being the first also makes him a pioneer who loves to open new roads and discover new ways of doing things. The Rat sees himself as a vital link and one can be sure he knows the value of networking or connecting all the links of a chain.

This personality type is extremely sociable and active. He loves to be in the thick of things; to be part of a vast and influential network. Able to understand at an early age how to compromise, negotiate and generally 'make a deal', the Rat person is usually charming, articulate and able to express and put his ideas across expertly. Communication is his forte and he is always in touch with his environment. Information flows freely to and from the Rat and he is able to shift through all the bits and pieces and come up with the data he wants.

In any relationship, a person of this first earth branch can be very giving and affectionate. He or she is gifted with a keen understanding of how to handle others and can be extremely intuitive. Consequently, the solicitous Rat person can get himself into influential circles and positions of importance. He will know how to flatter the object of his admiration and cannot do enough for a person he loves or admires. No amount of adoration is sufficient to shower upon someone he likes when he is infatuated or in desperate need of something. He is easily enamoured and will like to make a strong impression on the object of his interest, publicly if possible, to show his high esteem. The Rat type reveres his parents, dotes on his spouse, spoils his children and will make all kinds of excuses for his favourite relatives, employees and friends when they do something wrong. While he can be the most destructive critic of his enemies, he will be fiercely protective of his own interests and loved ones. An industrious soul, this type has a huge capacity for work and involvement. A tireless, progress-orientated innovator, the Rat personality is always busy with some project—raising money, meeting deadlines, spreading the latest word, campaigning and getting the votes in. Easily agitated and given to voicing his displeasure, he is not known for his patience. He tends to nag or become petty and manipulative when not given his way or left out of something. He can become indiscreet when he is upset and will be spiteful and power-hungry when he is negative.

Demonstrative, ardent and attentive, the efficient Rat type may come on too strong for some people. He is usually not aware of his aggressive and controlling ways. His enemies may call it manipulation and even blackmail but he just feels he needs to take control of the situation before things get out of hand. It is not unwise to follow the Rat's lead as he is well informed and given to checking out all the options before taking a stand. Often, his suspicions are justified and worth taking a second look at. If one cannot stand too much togetherness, then it would not be a good idea to have a Rat personality as one's best friend. Being clannish and sentimental in his ability to establish close ties, this person overvalues relationships and has trouble letting go once a friendship or affair is terminated.

He tends to rehash and examine things under a microscope and needle others into exasperation. Perhaps this is an uncontrollable reaction for him when he feels he is losing or has lost control. An embattled person of this first type can be quite a force to reckon with when he feels the reins of power slipping from his grasp, as he is a bad loser and a relentless foe.

Before one can hope to deal successfully with a Rat personality, one must understand his peculiar traits and way of thinking. To try to negotiate prematurely is to lessen one's chances of success. This type of person likes to approach his problems by first knowing all about them. Details and the fine print intrigue him. A self-starter, he can be shrewd, calculating and greedy at times—it is the accumulative and hoarding instinct in his nature. At times he is self-centred like an only child but does not mean to offend or intentionally harm anyone. Naturally, he will be looking out for Number One—he doesn't know how to do otherwise. Constantly on the look-out for new opportunities, ways to better himself and make more money, this person will gravitate towards success or people who have the same interests and goals as he does. He takes his time to nurture both long- and short-term relationships. He is forever planning trips and picnics, organising meetings, reunions with long-lost relations or schoolmates, charting of family trees, getting signatures on some petition and the like. One cannot fault the Rat for not trying, for not knocking on every door, turning over every stone and exploring every option. The problem may be that he often tries too hard—like trying to flog a dead horse back to life. He does not give people the room they may need to catch their breath or get back their wind once they have been knocked down. Trying to patch up things that are hopelessly broken is almost as bad as fixing something that is not broken at all. The Rat personality has a myopic perspective when it comes to his emotions or his finances. He often throws good money after bad in trying to save a hopeless situation because he simply cannot accept defeat.

However, once he can bring himself to face defeat or realise that something is definitely over, he is able to reconcile and recover quickly after he has vented his anger and frustration. Then he is all caught up reorganising his company, getting a brand new life or love and moving on—a wiser, better and bigger person.

The Rat personality is a pursuer of clout. He will see the importance of joining the right clubs and organisations and affiliating himself with people who matter. No matter what he says, he is impressed by money, fame or power. By getting close to the source he hopes to better his own situation, to acquire some of what he sees as important (perhaps some of it will rub off on him). He tends to select friends, associates, even spouses with the same criteria and judges people and things by how he can use them. The practical Rat type is not averse to taking the easy way out when he is cornered. This does not mean that this personality is an evil opportunist or sycophant. Rather, it proves his superior instincts for finding and identifying what he wants; the ultimate recipe for success.

The Rat personality bases his worth on performance and progress. He rates himself as knowledgeable and reliable and is usually pleased when others come to him for help or advice. He prides himself as a storehouse of information and connections, and possibly he does have the keys to the databank of all the gossip in town. This is an aggressive male or positive sign in Chinese reckoning and with his Yang character is able to fend for himself because he is rarely in doubt about what he wants. Persistent and hardworking, he feels he should be well rewarded for his efforts and is not above taking his just due if he feels he will be short-changed or cheated in any way. He is frugal and cost-conscious, always comparing and bargaining to get the best possible deal. Whenever he does some favour for you, he will want to be compensated—maybe not immediately, but consciously or unconsciously, he will keep tabs. This goes for both his business and personal relationships, but more so in business transactions. Alert and intelligent, he is always ready and receptive to ideas and new approaches.

This type of person tends to carry his frugality to extremes and insists all the time on saving time, effort, manpower, material and money. He hates waste and could be just as parsimonious on himself, too. Sometimes, stingy, Scrooge-like types use money as a compensation for love or as a means to exercise control over others. Just try to requisition supplies or ask the Rat-type boss for his signature to buy an expensive item and he could turn into a vicious interrogator. You'll be sorry you opened your mouth.

The Rat personality is just as demanding of himself and sets himself high standards to meet. He tends to prepare fastidiously for the future; applying to the good schools, saving up enough money for a large purchase, working diligently at combining many little outlets into one big organisation and worthy endeavours that require careful planning and much foresight and tenacity. He can be unrelenting, excitable and anxiety-ridden when he is putting together one of his projects. This captivating person is likely to be highly strung and outspoken. When he is edgy or unhappy, it will be hard for him to hide his emotions. He will want those close to him to question him about what is bothering him. If you don't, he will feel that you don't love him and couldn't care less about his welfare. To help dissipate his bottled feelings, one would do well to listen to him without interruption. After he gets everything off his chest, he can be more rational, have a better assessment of the situation, and be more likely to listen to explanations or take advice. In other words, he may cure his own problem through self-analysis. He just needs a sounding board at times to work out his frustrations. This personality does not believe in sulking. You can be sure he will let you know if you have offended or irritated him in any way. Refusing to be coy about anything, he would rather make a long list of all your faults and shortcomings and discuss each of them with you down to the last petty detail. Don't try the same technique on him, however, because it won't work. Not that he will deny any of his own faults, but he will welcome so much the opportunity to talk about himself that in the end you will regret bringing up the subject at all, unless of course you are a psychologist and being paid to listen to all his woes.

The person of the first branch is not a gambler at heart but, let's face it, he is never quite satisfied. Constantly drawn to bargains, foreclosures, giveaways, sacrifice sales and other games or schemes in which he thinks he could benefit, he assumes that others are not as clever as he is and that he will be able to get something for nothing. Consequently, his decisions are based on getting the most by giving up the least. An experienced negotiator, he can haggle and chisel the competition to the bone. Bargaining is a form of entertainment to him and he could get caught up in it. He may end up with con-tainerloads of obsolete merchandise just because he got it cheap. In the end, the storage costs alone may exceed the worth of the goods themselves. His most important lesson in life is knowing when to stop and in not underestimating others. Luck and being in the right place can only carry one so far.

If one is in business with this type, one must help him learn when to let go and cut the losses. We cannot win them all and the wisest thing to do in a bad situation is to get out while the going is still good. The Rat type needs strong associates who can force him to accept reality, regroup his resources and start anew. Be prepared for a big struggle as this type will never concede defeat easily; he will resist taking any losses and may harp and complain to no end. A good solution would be immediately to draw his attention to a new project or business opportunity to which he can devote his energies. He cannot be left idle!

Fortunately, this personality will know the value of compromise and working with others when he has no choice. Never too stubborn or inflexible to listen to sensible advice, he can compete with the best minds in the world. And, when the odds are stacked against him, you can be sure he will try to find an ingenius way out of his predicament. Gifted with a shrewd, razor-sharp mind, he never forgets what he is after and will know when to ask for the maximum that an opportunity can allow. He rarely takes NO for an answer and will try again and again from different angles until he succeeds. This type is a formidable business person and will make his presence felt in whatever field he is playing. Because he always has his eye on something bigger or better, he has the habit of comparing, competing, trading up and wishing for more. If he is unable to control this flaw in his character, he will be easily given to envy, dissatisfaction and crying foul when he is not able to win the game.

Aside from his love of turning a profit to show his skill at making a good investment, the Rat personality has a strong need for affection and security. Money may be used as his security blanket and also become his undoing. He has a tendency to gather all he considers essential to his happiness close to his bosom and he could well suffocate the object of his affections in his tight-knit circle of family and friends. Money is a weapon to this type and he will not hesitate to use it. Too late he learns that a weapon knows no master and his intricate plans may often misfire or backfire. This undesirable quality is something he must learn to curb and he must control the instinct to become obsessive and possessive of people and things he loves. Flowers blossom when they are given more space in which to grow.

The maxim of the Zi type, as the Initiator of the cycle, is: 'I do'.

TRIANGLE OF AFFINITY

The Rat or Zi type is the first player in the First Triangle of Affinity which produces a group of three positive Doers of the Twelve Earth Branches. There are four Triangles of Affinity in which the personality types are grouped. There is one Circle of Conflict in which all opposite branches are incompatible. In the First Triangle, we have the Rat, Dragon and Monkey—respectively the first, fifth and ninth branches.

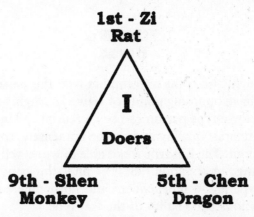

1st - Zi
Rat

I

Doers

9th - Shen   **5th - Chen**
Monkey   **Dragon**

The trio who make up the First Triangle of Affinity are a group of positive people who are identified as Doers. They like hands-on activity and are performance and progress orientated, adept at handling matters with initiative and innovation. These three players prefer to initiate action, clear their paths of uncertainty and obstacles and do not hesitate to forge ahead. Restless or short-tempered when hindered or unoccupied, they are fuelled by dynamic energy and ambition. The occupants of the first triangle are the ones who produce revolutionary ideas and like to make great things happen. They can team up beautifully as they have a common way of understanding and doing things and will certainly appreciate each other's way of thinking.

CIRCLE OF CONFLICT

The first earth branch will encounter his strongest opposition and personality clashes from persons belonging to the seventh branch or natives of the Horse sign. Anyone with his ascendant in the hours

**1st - Zi
Rat**

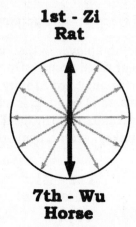

**7th - Wu
Horse**

of the Horse will also come into conflict with this personality type—they tend to have opposing points of view. The highly intelligent and flamboyant Horse-type person can be mercurial and inconsistent. He tends to lost interest quickly and can be immensely irresponsible and stubborn to boot. The Rat type is not able to work well with someone who will change or abandon him if he finds things not to his liking. The Horse type is too independent and hot-tempered to please the security-conscious personality of the Rat type.

RELATIONSHIPS WITH THE FIRST EARTH BRANCH—THE RAT

Within the Family

The Rat type as a child or parent is affectionate, thoughtful and very family orientated. This personality thrives in the nucleus of his family and will care greatly for his parents and forgive them all their shortcomings. He is most likely to have his parents, siblings and even grandparents living with him in their old age and he will not willingly turn anyone from his family away. In spite of grumbling and petty arguments regarding expenses and inconveniences, the Rat personality clings to the warmth of his family ties. Some Rat types go into the medical profession or nursing just to be useful in taking care of sickly parents or siblings. They will even turn the home into a hospital to make sure their loved ones are well cared for and comfortable.

Involved in and concerned about the welfare of his family members, he can also be found doing things for his loved ones such

as organising reunions, birthday parties, anniversaries and all sorts
of festivals. The sentimental and sociable Rat person enjoys human
contact, remembers all special events and is usually proud of his
family.

As a parent, this person will dote on his children and be protective
and manipulative at the same time. He will bond early with his
children and plan all the details for their progress and success in life.
A Rat mother will also remember everyone's favourite dish and use
food as a bribe or reward for good behaviour and as her expression
of love. A Rat parent places great emphasis on a good education and
will advise offsprings on the importance of meeting the right people,
having influential contacts and even marrying well. You can be sure
this type will check the credentials of all his or her children's friends.
The Rat person will be ready to make great sacrifices for his children
but is equally demanding in expecting children to spend time with
him and give him respect, or to care for him in his old age. He can
be mean and critical when he feels neglected or unappreciated, but
within his own family, he does not keep tabs and on the whole will
be generous and forgiving. Often blinded by his unconditional love
for his family, he does not want to see or hear about their faults. He
needs to be needed and will reciprocate with love and consideration
for his relations. Basking in the warmth of his family circle, the Rat
type is most relaxed, congenial and himself at home.

As a Teacher

The charming Rat personality enjoys teaching and helping others.
This gives him a chance to show how very clever and well informed
he is. Inquisitive children or students are never rebuked by the talkative Rat who likes to debate, discuss or digress on different subjects.
But the Rat also demands complete attention and initiative. Not only
will he encourage his favourite students but he will know how to
motivate all his students in innovative and challenging ways. If someone does not apply himself after all the Rat teacher's efforts, he can
and will be mercilessly dropped, but not before a severe scolding
from the Rat about his lazy and ungrateful ways. The Rat teacher
will also skilfully use peers to embarrass other students into working
harder. With his innate sarcasm and sharp tongue, an angry Rat
teacher can be very harsh and salty. There is also the possibility that
he may be sparing in giving high grades or praise and will never be

quite satisfied with the progress or performance of the class. He sets very high standards and expects a lot from his students.

Of course, this type will play favourites and it will be easy for the right people to charm the Rat teacher into being lenient and more considerate. His favoured ones will usually get him to believe that he, the teacher, is wise and in control. They will negotiate by asking for more than they want and then surrendering ground to show that their teacher is winning. The Rat teacher just needs to know that he has the upper hand. Once he is assured he is in control, he will be able to relax and be more amicable.

As a Lover and Spouse

The Rat personality is as affectionate, considerate and sentimental in love as he is calculating in business. However, he expects the feelings to be mutual and reciprocated—no lukewarm relationships for him. At times he is like a self-centred child who needs constant feedback about his worth. Never able to get enough confirmation, this type must be reassured by a hundred little gestures that he is loved and respected. On his part, he is never grudging to people he holds in high regard and will be the most thoughtful and loving partner one could find. Birthdays, anniversaries and all memorable events will be carefully observed by the Rat personality. He collects souvenirs of the heart as well as memorabilia that mark all special events in his life. With his excellent memory, he will remember your favourite ice cream, flower, colour, film or song and have reservations at your favourite restaurant ready for your surprise party. He will go out of his way to show you how much he loves you in many original ways.

A person on this first lunar branch will love to share the secrets in his life with his loved ones. This way you could both put your heads together and be united against the opposition, a sort of 'you and me against the world' theme. Plots and intrigue spice up and bond him with his love. Talkative and outgoing, he will love to share all his ideas and dreams with the object of his devotion. He loves togetherness.

You are truly loved if this type brings you home to meet his family or invites you to a family gathering. He will require his family's stamp of approval before he makes lasting commitments. Romantic and sociable by nature, he can have deep and intense emotions and makes an excellent lover or spouse for the Dragon (fifth) and Monkey (ninth) signs. Together they will pursue the pleasures of life passionately and wholeheartedly. This personality is an uninhibited and demonstrative lover and spouse. Not likely to be shy or too reserved, he will always make the effort to keep the love fires burning and can be relied upon to take the initiative in tender affairs of the heart.

As a Business Partner

A person of the first earth branch makes on the whole a good and astute business partner. He is alert for opportunities, hardworking and frugal. Although calculating and conniving at times, he will work diligently to promote or increase business. He is a real go-getter and will not need to be pushed to do his part. When it comes to sharing the pie, he may be a bit selfish and demand a larger share. But this should be addressed early on in the game so that the Rat-type person knows his limitations and does not seek to take advantage of the other partner or partners when the time comes to share the profits or dividends. This personality can be possessive of his authority and will tend to interfere (with good intentions, of course) in the affairs of other departments. Often he feels he can improve efficiency or production with his suggestions or recommendations. His good will and natural entrepreneurial abilities must be given a lot of consideration when weighed against his negative traits. When he is compatible with his business partners the company will prosper under his guidance, but when he is not, there will be a lot of petty bickering and criticism that is counterproductive to the interests of all. Check with the Affinity Triangles and Circle of Conflict before embarking on any business relationships. The exception may be in the ascendants, too. If you have a Rat ascendant but belong to an earth branch incompatible with the Rat, you could still work out a workable partnership with this personality type. Sometimes your Rat partner may have the same ascendant as yours and this is most helpful to relations. Say you are a Horse with a Rat ascendant and your business partner is a Rat with a Horse ascendant, you may both find more things in common than in conflict and your relationship will be good if you can divide areas of responsibility right from the beginning of your association—for example, the Rat could take care of the books and purchasing while the Horse could do the advertising and marketing.

As a Boss

'Keep busy, look busy' may be the best advice to give to someone who works for a boss of this earth branch. The Rat boss will care a lot about his employees' welfare and be solicitous of their health and working conditions, but he does tend to meddle in personal affairs and can be indiscreet at times. He also plays favourites and may unconsciously be more helpful to those who flatter him. Inquisitive and at times controlling, he does not like anyone to usurp his powers and wants to be involved in all decision-making. If you consult him and ask him for advice, he will be very attentive and sympathetic to your ideas, but if you assume you have his approval because you are doing something positive for the company as a whole, he could feel you are trying to undermine his authority. He may also have trouble delegating tasks and tends to have things piled up because, due to his insecurities, he does not assign the work to others. Often, he complains he has to do everything himself. If you can understand his fears and his way of handling problems, you will be able to work well with him instead of against him.

As a Friend and Colleague

The Rat-type personality makes a warm and caring friend as he genuinely wants to get to know people well. He has no trouble communicating and may be too talkative as a result, but he does try to please and he will remember all the little things that you like and celebrate special events in a meaningful way. Charming and with a lively sense of humour, the Rat type is popular, captivating and sociable. On the negative side, he may also be clannish and tend to discriminate against others who may not have the same views as he does. He expects you to band together with him in criticising or ostracising dissenters. When he does not get his way, he can also be manipulative and scheming. However, if you know how to appeal to the soft side of his nature and help him to be rational and fair in his dealings, he will be able to overcome his negative instincts and value the relationship even more.

Don't worry about his argumentative nature, he just loves controversy now and then and thinks it adds spice to the relationship. He won't mind if you nag him as much as he nags you—it's all part of the game. The one thing he cannot tolerate is apathy and indifference.

As an Opponent

This personality type can be a formidable opponent. He is shrewd, devious and unrelenting in his criticism of his foes. Spreading rumours, bits of gossip and other disquieting news may be his speciality. Skilful at arguing and nit-picking, he could exasperate even the most seasoned fighters. Armed with cartloads of information to back up his case, the Rat type can be persistent and vindictive when he goes into battle. He will also make affiliations to further his cause— some big names or heavyweight supporters to tip the balance in his favour. The best way to deal with a Rat opponent is to play your cards close to your chest and not give him more ammunition than he already has. Never cut off communications as he will always have an ear open for a possible settlement or a way out. The native of this branch is too clever to close all his routes or self-destruct. You must study your opponent very carefully and the Rat personality must be baited with extreme finesse. He sees himself as a master of the game and will be very shrewd at making deals to his advantage. Let him think he is winning before you play your ace. Above all, offer him a way out and allow him to save face when the odds are in your favour.

As the Mediator

The native of the first branch is an excellent mediator who will work untiringly with both sides until he gets some resolution. He is progress-orientated and performance-minded and will be a good arbitrator if he does not let the details get in his way. His biggest difficulty may be remaining completely impartial and not letting his feelings or personal opinions cloud his judgement. If he gets side-tracked because he establishes better rapport with one side versus the other, he will lose his effectiveness. He functions well when he focuses only on the facts and presents the whole picture to find a workable solution from both sides. This type can be a very convincing emissary and will be more than able to go back and forth, bringing messages, offers and counteroffers until he finds a mutually acceptable solution. His initiative and crafty persistence will be beneficial in difficult negotiations. He works best with the Dragon (fifth branch) and Monkey (ninth branch) and will be valuable dealing with all the other branches with the exception of the Horse where he could be more detrimental than helpful. Do not send the Rat personality as mediator for a Horse, Tiger or Dog type, as the message may not be presented or received in the proper spirit. But, generally, the clever native of the Rat type knows when and how to make the best of a situation and will only give concessions that he has to make. If he has a stake or if there is a reward at the successful conclusion of a deal or settlement, you can be sure this type will try doubly hard when he is motivated, even if he swears he wants nothing for himself.

RELATIONS WITH OTHER BRANCHES

With another Rat—First Branch

There is bound to be a lot of togetherness in such a partnership—whispering, plotting, planning and pooling of resources. Being of the same branch, they will both need large doses of affection and attention. Activities will be centred around the home, family and making money—or at least, novel ways of pinching the pennies. In love as well as in business, they tend to have friendly competitions trying to outdo each other. Their joint cumulative urges may be intense and they will never willingly discard anything they consider useful (which is practically everything). In the end, these two calculating personalities may suffer from overexposure as they keep seeing their own traits, good and bad, reflected in their business partner or mate. The female tends to be fussier and more critical, while the male is more aggressive and intimidating; however, if they join forces to protect their mutual territory or possessions, they can be fierce and ruthless. Their common goal is a need for security and recognition.

With an Ox—Second Branch

This could be a good and workable partnership because the Ox type is devoted, hard-working and a good listener. Guess who will do all the talking! Such a partnership enhances the abilities of both parties because the strength and endurance of the Ox type appeals to the enterprising Rat personality. Both will strive to do more than their share to achieve success. The Rat does not seem to mind the Ox's slow, methodical pace so long as they both share the same purpose and objective, while the Ox could use the shrewd Rat's innovative abilities to his advantage and benefit from his resourcefulness. Both are definitely achievement-conscious and will measure their compatibility by the yardstick of financial success. The Rat person will naturally be the spokesperson for this team.

With a Tiger—Third Branch

In this partnership the Rat is progress-orientated and cannot stand waste or extravagance, in which the colourful personality of the third branch will love to indulge. If the Rat can harness the many sterling qualities of the Tiger type, he or she may be the manager and promoter—guiding, advising and cautioning the Tiger into more conventional behaviour. No doubt, the generous but idealistic Tiger will reward the crafty Rat for sticking with him. However, sparks could fly if they both display quick tempers and refuse to compromise on small issues. Both personalities here are charming and extroverted, although the Rat tends to be stingy where the Tiger may be loud and accusing if he feels cheated or left out. In the end, both must realise that they should put positive energy into this relationship. The question is how they will choose to direct their energies and who will be at the controls. There could be minor skirmishes or major battles depending on their ascendants.

With a Rabbit—Fourth Branch

This match has advantages but also some major disadvantages, and may not bring out the best in both personalities. They could be on good terms and share mutual interests, but fall short where real commitment is required. In reality, they are both calculating in different ways and will want guarantees before forging a close relationship. This underlying shrewdness could be the main reason why their relationship may not work out well, since expectations are too high and will create a strain for the parties concerned. The Rat is the more affectionate and demonstrative of this pair, while the Rabbit person could be indulgent and aloof. The more the sensitive Rabbit tries to establish his independence and space, the more the Rat will try to control or restrict him.

With a Dragon—Fifth Branch

Both members of this team belong to the same Triangle of Affinity, so the Rat type will be naturally drawn to the vitality and energy of the dynamic Dragon. Likewise, the Dragon will find the Rat enthusiastically sharing his ideas and showing great resourcefulness.

Together they will create good synergy and have a successful union. This relationship gives assurance to both sides that their talents will be utilised and bring them extra benefits. The Dragon needs believers in order to weave his magic, while the Rat will see the Dragon's potential without any difficulty and know how to manage the Dragon's power and vitality. They both have enough self-confidence to trust the other party and make the commitments required. In spite of their equally demanding natures, they will enjoy a gratifying partnership if their mutual admiration and support for each other does not waver. Luckily, the magnanimous Dragon person is not calculating and may leave all the nasty details to the crafty Rat, who will excel in taking care of their interests.

With a Snake—Sixth Branch

In this combination, both personalities are intelligent and clever, but in very different ways. They tend to be equally possessive and ambitious and will work tirelessly to achieve their goals. However, the Snake has difficulty confiding in others and may find the Rat no exception, especially when the Rat tries to pry the secrets out of him. Both are well matched in tenacity, but the Snake type is basically a thinker, a schemer and a loner, while the Rat is an aggressive Doer who responds well to discussion, openness and a mutual exchange of ideas. If they find a common cause to which they can devote their energies, they could find happiness or a workable relationship. There are adjustments to be made on both sides, but if the prize is worthy they will both be reasonable and adaptable, simply because they are materialistic and practical when it comes to getting what they want out of any relationship.

With a Horse—Seventh Branch

The independent and adventurous personality of the seventh branch will not appeal to the security-conscious, possessive, stay-close-to-home Rat type. Both personalities are also active, Yang (masculine) branches and do not like to take a back seat in any relationship. The Horse type is quick-witted and impulsive but will find negotiating and bargaining with the inquisitive and calculating Rat not to his liking. Likewise, the Rat is careful but easily agitated by the Horse's carefree and restless nature. In a relationship, they will move at different speeds and see things from different perspectives. Unless they share a common ascendant, they will bicker for control and end up on opposing sides. In attempting to resolve their difficulties, they must put aside their own selfish agendas and learn to listen. If they find a good mediator, they will see that their views are not that far apart, but first they must simply suppress their egos and be objective.

With a Sheep—Eighth Branch
There is not likely to be great attraction for either side of these two branches unless they have the same ascendant which could establish a strong bond. Both types need affection and validation and tend to be possessive. But the Rat's aggression frightens the peace-loving Sheep who really does not need the Rat's anxiety and criticism in heavy doses. These two types have to get their priorities right and not let their emotions take over. The Rat personality will seek to save and exploit resources to the maximum, while the Sheep may spend lavishly to advertise, get attention and justify his worth, to the dismay of the thrifty Rat. On the whole, the Rat type is analytical and astute while the kindly Sheep is creative and sociable. They have need of each other's expertise and could link up successfully if they are willing to compromise and understand the basic differences in their make-up.

With a Monkey—Ninth Branch
These two Doers are strongly compatible because they share the same values and positive attitude that will make them winners. Besides belonging to the same Triangle of Affinity, the Monkey's ingenuity never fails to impress the Rat, while the Rat's intelligence appeals to the clever Monkey. Both are willing to contribute their share to forge a great relationship and can overlook each other's faults when they weigh the positive benefits of their union. In business or in love they work well together because both are open to constructive criticism and have a good sense of humour. Energetic, performance-orientated and enterprising, these two will complement each other and cheer one another on to greater heights of achievement.

With a Rooster—Tenth Branch
In this particular combination there may be a lot of rhetoric and debate on whose way is better, but very little done in a merger between these two branches. Their detailed assessments and careful

appraisals are too critical and intense to find a acceptance with either side. They may miss a lot of opportunities while they argue about who is smarter, faster and/or more informed. However, if they have mutual obligations, they will not want to be found lacking and can learn to be efficient if they are forced to. Problems are usually caused because neither side likes to relinquish control and both enjoy magnifying small issues. If they share a common ascendant, they could enjoy working together because these two types have hard-working natures and are skilful in managing money or a business.

With a Dog—Eleventh Branch

The Rat type respects the Dog's competence and respect for authority. Both types in such a partnership like to perform diligently and responsibly. The Dog is warm and affectionate and will find the Rat's personality responsive. However, the crafty Rat is the more astute of the two and the loyal Dog may find the Rat's practical solutions self-serving at times. In the end, the Dog will seek to be loyal to his ideals and question the Rat's motives, which the Rat may resent. But if these two are honourable and learn to trust each other, they could achieve much together and work beautifully as a team.

With a Boar—Twelfth Branch

In this team are two positive and optimistic people who could develop strong social as well as emotional ties. The Boar is generous where the Rat type is thrifty and resourceful. They will work hard to cultivate friends and influence important people to further their careers or ambitions. Public-minded, honest and obliging, the Boar will find the clever and well-connected Rat a great asset as a partner or spouse. The Rat, however, may find it hard to control both the Boar's appetite and his spending. Fortunately, the Boar is too thick-skinned to be hurt by the Rat's nagging and will make a lot of allowance for the frugal Rat to do his cost-cutting and financial planning. The Boar rarely sticks to the budget, while the Rat cannot live with the anxiety caused by the Boar's expansive and indulgent ways. To succeed in this partnership, the Rat must control the purse strings and curtail the Boar's spending. The Boar will thank the Rat in the end for exploiting their mutual talents and saving for that rainy day.

2

THE CHOU BRANCH

SECOND LUNAR SIGN

The Enforcer's Song

Mine is the stabilising force
that perpetuates the cycle of life.
I stand immobile against the
tests of adversity,
resolute and unimpeachable.
I seek to serve integrity,
to bear the burdens of righteousness.
I abide by the laws of nature
patiently pushing the wheels of Fate.
Thus, I shall shape my own destiny.

I am Chou, the Enforcer

Theodora Lau

THE SECOND EARTH BRANCH: CHOU
THE SIGN OF THE OX

THE ASSIGNED LUNAR YEARS OF THE OX

February 19, 1901	to	February 7, 1902
February 6, 1913	to	January 25, 1914
January 24, 1925	to	February 12, 1926
February 11, 1937	to	January 30, 1938
January 29, 1949	to	February 16, 1950
February 15, 1961	to	February 4, 1962
February 3, 1973	to	January 22, 1974
February 20, 1985	to	February 8, 1986
February 7, 1997	to	January 27, 1998

If you were born on the day before the lunar year of the Ox, e.g. February 14, 1961, you belong to the previous earth branch or animal sign, which is the first branch (the Rat).

If you were born on the day after a lunar year ends, e.g. February 5, 1962, you belong to the next earth branch or animal sign, which is the third branch (the Tiger).

THE SECOND EARTH BRANCH
THE SIGN OF THE OX

The second character profile of the twelve earth branches is that of the Ox. He is called *Chou* in Chinese and symbolises strength through unity and obedience. The Chou or Ox personality surveys his world and sees it only through his own perspective. Life for him is not a popularity contest; he needs to exercise complete autonomy over his territory—otherwise he cannot exist or function. He learns early in life that the source of his strength is his ability to endure and persevere. This type of person is a study in fortitude. Whatever he possesses, one can be sure he obtained through his own efforts and hard work. He conquers through his own merits and for this reason may often be entrusted with positions of authority and given extra responsibilities. The Ox type is not one to shrink from duty, shouldering his burdens admirably and performing well under pressure. Not one to complain or explain, he is often criticised for being unapproachable and inflexible.

This personality is the first of the Thinkers in his Triangle of Affinity. He cannot be rushed into making decisions or acting without an approved plan. Like the other two signs that occupy his triangle, the Snake (the Strategist) and the Rooster (the Administrator), this type is strong, silent and principled. He is governed by stringent rules that he sets for himself (never mind if they are right or wrong) and he won't change these easily. Gifted with a resolute and logical mind, he is analytical in his intelligence and only influenced by proven facts. If you wish to impress him, have all the figures ready and stress the excellent track record; point out the tried and tested results and the reliability of the product. Insurance protection, warranties and unconditional guarantees appeal to him. Be systematic, methodical and conservative in your approach. Allow him to digest the information and make up his own mind, in his own time.

Be forewarned that he is not receptive to new ideas. He does not like to try out new things and must be prodded to allow changes in his life. He is a creature of habit and is often too programmed to act spontaneously. When he holds himself up as the ultimate example to be followed, he can be masochistic in proving his unbeatable capacity to endure suffering. However, he is admired for his firmness in mind, his ability to weather whatever storms life brings and his dedication to his commitments.

On the reverse side of the coin, the Chou type of the Second Branch is often stingy with affection and approval; afraid these would be interpreted as signs of weakness. He detests uncertainty, excuses and lack of resolution. He toes the line without question and expects everyone else to have the same stamina and dedication. When he is angry or disappointed he is openly hostile and does not hide his disapproval. Although he is the most dependable and conscientious of people, he cannot be expected to make many allowances for lesser mortals who break the rules. He does tend to have a long memory and nurtures hurts and grievances for too long. This is because his exacting nature cannot tolerate forgiving someone without some proper retribution or punishment. Others may tend to compromise or wipe the slate clean, but you can count on this type to want a final accounting of how each penny was spent. He'll want compensation plus interest on all late payments and your promise in writing that you have learnt your lesson and will never, ever break the rules again.

To work effectively with this type of personality, one must bond with his beliefs, associate with his close group of friends, agree with his schedule and subscribe to the same goals as he does. At least there is never any pretence that he will make major changes in his outlook or his life to gain a new friend. A traditionalist at heart, he is set in his ways and makes little secret of it. His idea of networking is to chain himself to the career or business he chooses and succeed by sheer willpower and tenacity. Don't expect him to come courting with lavish gifts and flattery. He has too much pride ever to grovel. Rather, you will know of his many talents and contributions through others who value him and hold him in high esteem. His reputation will usually be sterling and unblemished. There will be more than enough people to sing his praises and endorse his trustworthiness. He pays his bills on time and would rather do without something if he cannot afford it.

Although he is one who will diligently plough back his profits into his business and attain a firm footing for his financial status, the personality of this earth branch is not a particularly good messenger or negotiator. The only thing one can rely on is that he will not make any changes or moves abruptly. At times, he is decidedly inflexible and in negotiations that could be like walking into a brick wall. I am familiar with a very well-known leader of industry who belongs to this branch and is feared by his colleagues and employees because he will not allow anyone to use the bathroom once a meeting or negotiation has begun. He, of course, may have the world's strongest bladder, but after twelve hours or more of negotiating, his friends and foes have a newfound respect for his endurance and usually surrender without too much resistance. This type will excel in military manoeuvres and is recognised as a fearless leader because of his unbending and stoical ways. He will never tolerate insubordination or disrespect.

The personality of the Chou branch does not easily relinquish control. He would actually like never to give up any control if he can help it and is often reluctant to admit when matters are above his head. If he could accept help from others and be more willing to get the job done by sharing responsibility, he would have an easier life and many more friends. But, as a prominent twentieth-century architect born under this earth branch once said in a rare interview, he had the choice early in his career to live with either 'hypocritical modesty or honest arrogance'. He chose honest arrogance. The rest is history. His architectural creations endure as testimonials to his talent and skill and his arrogant refusal to compromise his standards even by a single iota.

The Ox type is basically performance-orientated and industrious but not a pursuer of power. Power comes to him naturally because of his inborn dedication and industriousness. He worships discipline and self-control and is always willing to go the full distance, and even beyond if necessary. Clout and fame are natural outcomes of his ability to accomplish difficult tasks or roles that require patience and steadfast resolution. One thing that he is not caught doing is hedging his bets or sitting on the fence—not taking one side or another for fear of making enemies. The Chou type is anything but ambivalent. He knows his own mind and is not afraid of speaking it when he has to. Although he may hide his ability and intelligence under an undemonstrative or cold front, he still makes sure that others are aware of his criteria. He can be very particular and unyielding in his demands and will not hesitate to refuse flatly to compromise with anything below his standards. It is this authoritarian outlook that makes him a poor negotiator or mediator.

A good example is a former neighbour of mine born under this sign. She was a well-respected hospital administrator and had a job with important responsibilities. Everything was fine until another neighbour wanted to replace a rickety fence between their properties. It is surprising how fast things escalate when people start to disagree, and the situation went from bad to worse, with the police coming out every week to address another of their complaints. Their police file was already a few inches thick when I offered to act as mediator. The situation bordered on the ridiculous, with both sides totally polarised in their positions. They did not do things by half-measure. The husbands were pitted against each other, the wives got into shouting matches, the children fought and even their dogs disliked each other with great intensity—over the fence. When I volunteered for the unenviable task of mediator, I learned that they no longer had a disagreement only on what kind of fence they wanted or how much they wanted to spend. It was a question of how high this barrier must be in order for the two parties not to see each other or any part of the other's house or garden. The council regulations gave a maximum of two metres, but apparently that was not high enough to separate them. At any rate, I asked what each side really wanted and proceeded to make a list of the grievances and possible solutions or suggestions. Every time I took up an issue with the Ox neighbour, she would shake her head and say in a determined voice that that issue was: non-negotiable. While stressing that she had become physically ill as a result of the problems caused by the unreasonable behaviour of the other neighbour; she was puzzled by their unco-operative attitude and refusal to compromise. I was beginning to feel sorry for the people who worked with her as her own rigidity was so invisible to her that she could not see how she had trapped every-one into a cemented role.

Fortunately, about this time, the other neighbour decided to plant a whole row of fast-growing trees along the fence. The Ox-type woman immediately accused her neighbour of planting those trees because he knew her children were allergic to the flowers they bore in spring, and furthermore, the evil neighbour knew the wind would blow from a certain direction, making sure the leaves would fall on her side of the fence come autumn. In the end, after three years of conflict, both neighbours had put up their own fences. The Ox-type personality erected a block wall that was expensive and solid. The neighbour who had planted the row of trees put up a wooden 'spite' fence that was about seven centimetres taller than the block wall and stuck out here and there like tufts of unruly hair. As for myself, I learned never to volunteer to assist people of this second branch out of conflict because in their minds they already have the solution (even if they do not know it or are ready to admit it) and they will do what they have made up their mind to do come what may; no matter how long it takes. He or she can outstare and outlast the competition.

In a confrontation with anyone of this branch, it would be more advisable to work from behind the scenes and not lock horns immedi-ately. Find out what the law says or what are the documented prac-tices and rules. Present only one alternative to the Ox person. Do not allow him choices. It will hasten a decision if he has only one or two options to work with. Don't worry about intimidating him: he rules by intimidation, consciously or unconsciously, and will not go like a lamb to the slaughter anyway. His rigidity of purpose is admirable and could be called his saving grace. People find his calm-ness and consistency very reassuring. He inspires confidence by the strength of his convictions and impregnability.

The Chou branch is actually a feminine sign and belongs to the passive or Yin side of the balance. This means that any aggression contained in this sign is always hidden and internal. One only finds out the extent of this person's strength after one has engaged in a struggle or combat. He may not be the aggressor but he will certainly triumph as the resister. Endurance is his middle name and he will not be the first to blink in a confrontation. He may not blink at all!

This type of person does not like to take advantage of others and may even be rather meek at times in asserting himself. But once he gets fired up, then he cannot or will not back down. Generally, he creates his own luck or opportunity by hard work and perseverance. Practical and conservative, he does not expect or demand immediate results. Carefully, slowly and methodically, he toils unceasingly to reach his goals. Once he has captured ground he will not surrender his hard-earned position. The Chou personality is not mean or petty. Fair and honest in his dealings, he also hates owing anyone favours and is therefore afraid of asking for help. Trying to go it alone makes him seem aloof and hostile at times, but this is usually caused by his fear of showing any weakness or his extreme dread of failure or rejection.

His main problem in life will be his inability to communicate and, often, his miscommunication with others. He can be a fierce sulker and has the tendency to clam up when he is unhappy. Prising information out of him is always a difficult, even impossible task. Given to few words, he does not know how to help his own case by giving his reasons for acting in a certain way. Instead, he stonewalls and makes matters worse by digging in and resisting all efforts to meet others halfway. On such occasions he turns his very strength into his own undoing. If he could cultivate the art of listening and the ability to communicate without first making a judgement (as he often does), he would be able to eliminate most of the disagreements he encounters. His shortcomings are few and not irreparable, but he does often take the long, hard route instead of the proverbial short cut. He is also the person who will most likely opt to be cruel only to be kind, the one who will give you the bad news without adornment because there is no other way, in his opinion, for you to face the facts. Don't ever expect him to lie and spare your feelings. He considers that foolish and pitiful and would think unkindly of you if you ever tried to put sugar on his medicine either.

In business relations with this type of person, it would be wise to have everything down in writing—always. He is a particular and conscientious worker and a very reliable partner, but he will always work to a schedule and with a fixed plan. He hates short notice, changes or surprises. Associates must be able to live by his rules, which may be just a few, such as never being late for an appointment, or borrowing his personal belongings, or forgetting to switch off the light. He will stick to his old habits like a religious fanatic. While he is predictable and unassuming at times, he has a will of iron. Hard work and challenges invigorate him and he is often unshaken by bad news or setbacks. He tends to regroup his forces like an able general and forge ahead. Industry, manufacturing and commerce would be lost without the steadfast and conscientious entrepreneurial talents of this type of personality.

However, because he is a basic Thinker and not a Doer, Protector or Catalyst, he may be as good a follower as a leader. As a matter of fact, he would sometimes like others to point him in the right direction, identify the goals and make all the right introductions. He needs good PR and front men to polish his often austere and authoritarian image. Being taciturn by nature, he is never generous with praise or encouragement. Suffice to say that he knows how to reward those who are hardworking and loyal, and does not expect accolades and awards for himself. It will be reward enough for him to know he did his best. In the final analysis, he will confirm his own worth and does not seek approval from others. Strict, unyielding and sometimes curt and tactless, he suffers quietly and with dignity, always putting up that brave front. The solemn people of the Chou branch are renowned for their ability to succeed against great odds. Two excellent examples are the late former US President Richard M. Nixon and former British Prime Minister Margaret Thatcher, who both belong to the Ox or Chou branch.

In his personal and business life the Ox personality will be efficient and organised. He loves to plan ahead and will have his objectives carefully mapped out in his own mind. Not one to mind other people's business, he will keep to himself. However, if his judgement or opinion is sought, he can be very forthright and impartial. If he is in charge, he likes to keep a tight rein on the controls and resents anyone questioning his authority. Dissenters and critics may be harshly dealt with, especially if they are troublemakers who have nothing positive to contribute. Irritated by idleness, waste and petty gossip or bickering, he is often a pillar of hope and energy in times of crisis.

Unfortunately, he often fails to appreciate the value of compromise. His pride also impedes his ability to bow to the wishes of the majority if he has to live with some small injustice to keep the peace.

Although he has great staying power, he tends to be too analytical in dealing with his problems and does not take into consideration the human frailties and emotions that may be involved. He needs associates and capable go-betweens who have the skill to present his ideas in innovative ways or to package and sell his valuable skills in a more attractive manner. On his own, he may be bland, unimaginative and distant, hiding his light under a bushel. A disciplined and obedient follower, he can be left to finish tasks by himself. If he owns a business, one can be sure he will be on hand to open the store bright and early and lock up at night. He will not baulk at dirtying his hands or toiling at menial jobs if that sets a good example and proves his ability to start from the ground up.

The key words of the Chou type as the Enforcer of the cycle are: 'I will'.

TRIANGLE OF AFFINITY

The Ox or Chou personality is the first member of the Second Triangle of Affinity which produces a group of three introspective Thinkers of the Twelve Earth Branches. There are four Triangles of Affinity in which the personality types are grouped. There is one Circle of Conflict in which all opposite branches are incompatible. In the Second Triangle, we have the Ox, Snake and Rooster—respectively, the second, sixth and tenth branches.

This trio who occupy the Second Triangle of Affinity are a group of purposeful Thinkers who like quietly to compose their thoughts and strategy before taking any action. They are the planners, the schemers and the meticulous decision-makers who base things on

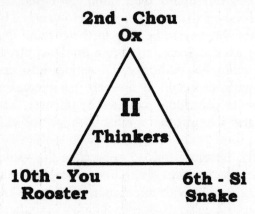

statistics and information. Unlikely to need the approval of others once they have made up their minds, these personalities only need their own validation that they are doing the right things, following the plotted course. These players prefer to observe, ponder and investigate before making any judgement. They will check out the facts, look into details and generally like to have all available options thoroughly explained before making their move.

The three Thinkers tend to have introspective and egoistic characters. Secretive, reserved and often stoical, they are also consistent, tenacious and gifted with foresight and fortitude. They will be recognised for their dedication to duty, patience and ability to inspire others by their example. Able to outwit and outthink the competition, the Ox, Snake and Rooster personalities are able to reach their goals through calm resolution and determination.

To work well with them, one must be able to have the facts and figures ready and appeal to their superior intelligence and analytical capabilities. Explain how they will benefit both in the long and short term. Plough back the profits. Show how things will pay off in stages and how they will profit slowly but surely. They tend to avoid taking risks and dislike gambling or speculative ventures. They can be ruthless in their quest for power and will not hesitate to eliminate those who block their path. This is because power translates into control. Intelligent, practical and calculating, they are systematic in dealing with their problems and with their enemies. Cautious, deliberate and industrious, they will follow their intellect instead of their emotions. Always careful to address all issues before making a decision, they are hard on themselves and their partners when an enterprise or business venture stumbles or fails. These are very business-minded personalities, who will always be out to turn a profit or reap some reward for their efforts. Great believers in their own innate capabilities, they will work tirelessly at something until they succeed or their efforts bear fruit. Others tend to rely on them to be the visionaries of the future and will hitch a ride with this stalwart trio to new heights of success.

The three performers of the Second Triangle of Affinity will be able to get along fabulously in love and business. Working as a team is easy and beneficial for them as they appreciate each other's way of thinking. As marriage and business partners, they will find understanding and will work productively towards common goals. They value stability and long-term relationships and will have the endurance and confidence to support one another in their endeavours.

People with their ascendant signs belonging to this Second Triangle of Affinity will also be able to establish close ties with the natives of this group and find much in common.

CIRCLE OF CONFLICT

The Ox personality of the Chou branch will encounter his biggest clashes and opposition from people belonging to the eighth branch or a native of the Sheep sign. The Sheep personality finds the Ox much too serious and rather dull. He feels that the Ox never learns how to enjoy life, and constantly looks at the dark and pessimistic side of things. The Ox is the fact-finder while the Sheep tends to be guided by instinct.

2nd - Chou
Ox

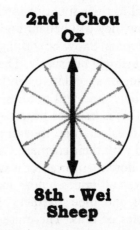

8th - Wei
Sheep

From the Ox's perspective the Sheep is frivolous, short-sighted, whining, dependent and, most of all, irresponsible. In the Ox personality's eyes, people of the eighth branch never seemed to be worried about anything in life, yet are the first to complain and bleat about unimportant matters. Actually, both of them are worriers. The Sheep type agonises over what to wear, how to act, what to say to make a good impression or where to go for a holiday. The Ox considers all these things silly—there are too many grave issues that will occupy his mind and energy. The Ox worries about the rise in the basic rate, his bank loan, tax returns and current stock market trends.

The Sheep type considers it life-threatening if he cannot get a reservation in the best restaurants and is not invited to a popular party. He lives in a different sort of world and moves in elegant circles. The Sheep usually makes his living doing the exact opposite of what the Ox would consider. The Ox will spend his time in the garden, repairing his home or central heating before the onset of winter and invests his spare cash in stocks and shares. He will not spend a lot of money on such fripperies as expensive clothes, jewellery and gourmet meals in fancy restaurants. In most cases, the Chou personality prefers to lead a modest life and eat simple fare.

RELATIONSHIPS WITH THE SECOND EARTH BRANCH— THE OX

Within the Family

The Ox type as a child or parent is dutiful. Family-orientated and responsible in outlook, he tends to show his love in terms of how hard he can work for the people he loves. He treasures his family and will stick by them through thick and thin. Often, he does not express his feelings in words but will make up for it by his deeds. He can be dominant without appearing domineering. Soft-spoken and kind-hearted, he will carry many of the burdens without complaint. Because the Ox has a basic fear that he is not doing enough or not doing his fair share for his precious family, family members often take advantage of him and his guilt complex. They may load him with more responsibilities than a normal person could handle and expect him to carry them on his strong back. Although he is outwardly a tower of strength, inwardly he may be lonely, misunderstood and insecure. Introspective and at times withdrawn and uncommunicative, he can also be difficult to relate to. Other family members may fail to include him in activities, thinking that he does not like to have fun or go on holiday, when in fact the Ox lives to be with the ones he loves and would desperately want to share happy times and experiences with them. When it comes to comfort and luxury, the Ox finds it easy to deny himself enjoyment, or squandering money as he sees it. Other family members may interpret this as being parsimonious and austere, but this type can only feel secure when he has something stashed away for that rainy day that is sure to come.

As a parent, this type can be demanding and authoritarian. He makes the rules and woe to anyone who breaks them. This may be because he feels protective and paternal but it may also be because he enjoys his position of dominance. He hates having his rules questioned and can be unforgiving to those who go against his wishes. Sometimes he is too much of a disciplinarian and his children tend to be afraid of displeasing him. If he cannot temper his rule with kindness and understanding, he will have difficulty establishing close relationships with other family members.

As a child, a person of the second branch is obedient, self-reliant and responsible. Eager to please his elders, he will perform well and willingly. As a student he will assimilate his lessons well, idolise his teachers and conform to the rules and standards of his school. Proud and stubborn, he will not like to admit failure or defeat and will show tenacity and determination in pursuing his interests. He is likely to be good at sports as he is competitive and unyielding by nature. A conservative at heart, he will not be rebellious or outlandish in behaviour. He is not a trouble-maker or a rebel. He abhors controversy and does not like to be drawn into fights or debates. If he has a choice, he prefers to work alone and be held accountable only for his own actions. When he is judged on his own merits, he feels he is in charge of his own destiny and will perform better than when given a small part in a team effort.

As a Teacher

The stoical personality of the second branch is a natural teacher and mentor. His sternness belies a sharp and intelligent mind and even a kind of dry wit. He can be amusing and sarcastic at the same time. His sense of humour hides under his undemonstrative front, only to emerge when things are at their bleakest. Bad news and tough circumstances bring out the best in him and he will gather his forces to face the challenges. Famous for his authoritarian rule, deadlines and regimented curriculum, the personality of the Ox can also be generous and supportive to his students. Like an immovable force shielding his pupils, he can move heaven and earth for their benefit and will be a great inspiration to those who are lucky enough to be under his guidance. In spite of his seemingly unbending outlook and love of convention, he will always be available to his students if they should need his help. This is the kind of professor who will remember you and your little faults twenty years later and still keep a record of your missing homework. But in his eyes you will see the twinkle of genuine affection and know that although he will never let you get away with any transgression, he will always be there for you and give you his unwavering support and attention.

As a Lover and Spouse

The Ox or Chou-type person is not the most demonstrative of lovers and spouses, but this is not to say that he cannot be intense and totally devoted to those he cares deeply about. This person sees a loving relationship as one based on trust and reliability. He may not show his love openly, with flowery words and expensive gifts, but you can rely on his broad shoulders to shelter the ones he loves. Being ruled by habit, he can be predictable and often criticised as unimaginative. You must be specific in informing him about your wishes or he may be a bit 'dense'. Don't expect him to guess what you want by your subtle hints; he does not catch nuances or know how to read between the lines. Often, he is at a loss to know why others may be upset with him. If he asks you what is wrong, tell him. Do not be coy or pretentious, for he does not have the skill to draw out secret hurts from those he loves. If one is not candid with him, he will assume all is well and go on with his usual schedule without knowing what he has done wrong. In love and marriage, this type looks for stability and harmony. He can be selfless and deeply bonded to those he can identify with. Usually, he picks partners who can read him and anticipate his wishes, yet he expects these same partners to boss him around a bit, remind him of every little thing and, yes, adhere to his inflexible schedule. Secretly, natives of the second branch love it when people fuss over them, although they may never admit it openly. Don't ever think he does not appreciate the special way you wrap his sandwich or when you give him an extra biscuit on his plate. You'll never know he cares until the day you forget that tiny endearment and he will lament in disbelief that you don't love him any more. He can be rather clumsy in affairs of the heart and his shyness and tongue-tied ways will tend to lead him to have long courtships. However, the good part of this is that one becomes his friend and confidant before love blooms, and this careful nurturing may produce a warm and lasting partnership.

Perhaps it would be safe to say that although the Ox personality is modest and gifted with inner strength, he is sometimes guilty of taking those he loves for granted. He rarely shares his emotions and opinions and expects a lot from those he is involved with, often not realising that he must express his love in visible ways and not expect others to know everything that is going on inside him. In love he may find a handful of close associates or only one true love for his entire life. This will be enough to sustain him. He forms deep and very close relationships, and when he finds his soulmate, he will have very little doubt and will allow nothing to stand in his way.

As a Business Partner

A native of the second branch does not form partnerships easily. For him to work with anyone on a long-term basis (and he will insist on long-term), he must know all there is to know about that person. He would like to establish a rapport based on mutual respect and preferences. The ground rules will be carefully laid out and the business plan crafted for every possible contingency. The Ox personality has a good head on his shoulders and will not let emotions or friendships influence his decision-making ability. He expects his business partners to tighten their collective belts and work hard during the initial stages and then plough back the profits to build up the business. Security and viability are key words in his mind and he can be extremely able in running a commercial venture or establishing a corporation.

Honest, hardworking and dedicated, he will have the stamina and determination to make whatever venture he undertakes a success. Although he may not appear aggressive, he has great will-power and a lot of endurance. He will not tolerate setbacks or failure for long. One can depend on him to pull his own weight and concentrate on doing all in his power to make the business prosper.

His most compatible business partners will be the Snake and the Rooster types or those born with ascendants belonging to his branch. The conventional and steadfast Ox personality can identify easily with these people and form strong ties when embarking on any enterprise. Persons born under the other nine branches will be good partners but to a lesser degree. Naturally, it would be advisable for the Ox type to avoid having a partnership with the Sheep personality as they will have different outlooks and opposing goals. Unless a Sheep person has a strong Ox ascendant, he will not have the consistency and formidable dedication required and demanded by the regimental

Ox type. The Sheep personality will be unhappy and feel oppressed by the dominance of the particular and controlling native of the second earth branch, while the Ox will only invite frustration when he links up with the emotional Sheep.

As a Boss

The Ox personality makes a good boss because of his leadership qualities. He will be fair and honest in his assessment although he will not turn a blind eye to slacking. With the Ox boss, one learns from the beginning how one is expected to perform and behave. Rules are rules and he will not like his subordinates to break or bend any of them. Unlike the Rat of the first branch, the Chou or Ox person does not practise favouritism and will resent those who expect him to grant them special treatment. Instead, he will set the stage for the proper behaviour by being a shining example for all to follow.

Sparing with praise but practical and generous with rewards for a job well done, the Ox boss is predictable and reliable to a fault. He may not often criticise (a frown of disapproval should prove quite enough), but when he does make a point, it would be advisable to take it. Performance-orientated and industrious, he would like to achieve tasks ahead of schedule instead of just being on time. Methodical and careful, he will do one thing at a time, but do it well. Persons who work for him will never be left in the dark about what is the goal of a certain job or how they are to achieve it.

As a Friend and Colleague

The Chou or Ox person is very selective as a friend or confidant. He would rather be alone than with people he does not care for. He will not go out of his way to be 'nice' just so that others will have a better opinion of him. Instead, he may be cordial, helpful and conscientious without ever being close. This is because he needs time to bond with others and does not make friends easily. Unlikely to confide in others, he will always try to project a strong and capable image—one that does not need help or pity.

Yet, as a friend and co-worker, one could not ask for a more loyal and protective ally than a Chou-type person. He usually supports his friends and team-mates with unwavering determination. Above all, he is a good listener. Although he is one who rarely gives advice and suggestions, when he does, he is always sincere and trustworthy.

You can be sure that an Ox friend will never desert you in your hour of need.

As an Opponent

This personality type can be a relentless and merciless foe. Unable to tolerate defeat or failure, he has an immense capacity for battle. A bad loser, the Ox type is not gracious or forgiving in defeat. One can always identify him in sports events as the one with the most dejected and angry face when his team loses. It could take days to cheer him up.

When one has this personality type as an opponent, one must never show any weakness or indecision. He does not ask for quarter and expects none. Do what you must and to the best of your ability. The only thing that you could get from him would be his respect or grudging approval for a game well played, a battle well fought. Make no excuses for your defeat if you lose and no explanations for your victory if you win. With the Ox person, there will be no need.

As the Mediator

The native of the second earth branch is not a good mediator. True, he can be most impartial and analytical, almost to the point of brutality, but he fails to sense nuances, is impervious to subtle hints and in general does not read people well. As a judge he would excel, but as a go-between, his own sense of righteousness and unbending adherence to the rules may work against the interests of the parties he is trying to bring together—he may not settle for anything less than total control, total obedience and total justice. Unable or even unwilling to look for a 'win-win' solution, this personality tends to see all things in black and white even when they are really in many shades of grey.

Mediators often do not have the power to enforce their decisions or suggestions and this could irritate the Ox personality because the parties may not take his advice or value his assistance and resolve their differences. If the arbitration that this type performs is binding, then it would be more beneficial and successful as he is above all a very fair-minded person and can assess situations with his own kind of clarity and sense of duty. In a position of authority, he could put the fear of God into opposing parties and force them to see reason and accept their respective responsibilities.

He works best with Snakes (sixth branch) and Roosters (tenth branch) and will be able to convince or sternly bully other signs into some sort of compromise in order to restore the peace and order that he loves. When this person is given the task of mediator, he will take his mission seriously and go beyond the call of duty to resolve matters in whatever way he can, sometimes in a high-handed manner. Do not send this personality type to mediate for the over-sensitive Sheep (eighth branch) as his efforts may not be received in the spirit in which they are meant. The Sheep person requires a lot of sympathy and personal attention and in this the Ox may be found lacking.

RELATIONS WITH OTHER BRANCHES

With a Rat—First Branch

This could be a compatible partnership, excellent for marriage and business. Both are realists, practical and hard-working. The Rat tends to be outspoken and bossy but always has a soft spot in his or her heart for the devoted and sincere Ox type who does not mind making sacrifices for the team. The Ox is stubborn and set in his ways, but the charming and affectionate Rat will know how to handle the Ox in his sullen moods and persuade him to be more open-minded and flexible. In the end, both will benefit from their association. The more sociable Rat will draw out the Ox, while the steady Ox will stay the course and be very down-to-earth in any relationship.

With another Ox—Second Branch

This could be a very solid, all-work-and-no-play duo with no deep understanding or close bonds. Thinkers are not good communicators and unlike Doers, Protectors and Catalyst types, do not like to take the initiative in making the first move. Ox types are also ruled by habit and may not find it easy to adjust, especially to someone who is just as strong-willed or inflexible. Necessity may tie these two together, but once they get a job done they may find they have nothing else in common. Both parties in this union are too serious and like-minded, and although they perform their responsibilities without any complaints or problems, they could suffer from a lack of closeness and real involvement that is vital to a lasting relationship.

With a Tiger—Third Branch

Here, the disciplinarian comes face to face with the errant rebel who delights in creating controversy just to get attention. The Ox does not have great imagination or good humour when it comes to the antics of the theatrical Tiger, and unless these two share a common ascendant it will not be easy for them to bond. The Ox is slow to anger, but he likes to stick by the rules at all costs, while the Tiger is not one to shy away from confrontation or thumbing his nose at authority when things are not to his liking. There could be fierce battles between these two formidable combatants. However, if the Ox is able to set the pace and is allowed to exercise his authority and the Tiger can be brought under control without too much resistance, this team will enjoy considerable success and attract supporters, because they can bring out the best in other people with their different approaches.

With a Rabbit—Fourth Branch

The Ox is strong, authoritative and capable of great sacrifice and endurance, while the Rabbit type is refined, indulgent and sagacious but will not volunteer for anything that requires too much effort on his part. They may have mutual intellectual interests, but the Rabbit is likely to see the Ox as inflexible and a bit of a pessimist in outlook. There could be sulking matches when they are both angry and their resentment affects their cooperation. The Rabbit type is quick to spot an opportunity and very adept at handling public relations which the cautious but able Ox may find beneficial in this partnership. However, if the Rabbit is unable to work amicably with the Ox, he will not hesitate to go his own way, as he would rather switch than fight anyway. There will be no strong clashes of will, just quiet resignation and cold realisation if things don't work out. Neither may go out of his way to please the other, so that the relationship may be just cordial and not deep.

With a Dragon—Fifth Branch

The Ox is the realist while the Dragon is the idealist in this combination. Both are duty bound and take their responsibilities seriously. But whereas the Dragon must lead and follow his dreams, the methodical Ox could plot a very steady course and be a loyal and level-headed supporter. Even in the background, the Ox could be the quiet power behind the throne. If these two are able to depend on each other, they could make a formidable team. If not, they could both be destructive and fight for dominance. Most of the time, however, there is a mutual respect as Ox and Dragon are both achievement-conscious and would rather get things done than bicker over small issues.

With a Snake—Sixth Branch

These two will make a good and lasting partnership as they both bring more than their fair share to the relationship. The dependable Ox will provide the ambitious Snake type with invaluable support and together they will exploit their resources to the limit. Both are realistic, although the Snake may have a stronger influence on the Ox than the other way round. Yet the Ox loves being needed and will not mind the Snake's eccentric ways so long as he is made to feel worthy and part of the Snake's well-devised plans. Both are willing and able to lay a strong foundation before starting anything and their objectives are usually long-term. Therefore they will find no difficulty setting goals and following them through.

With a Horse—Seventh Branch

These two earth branches move and think at different levels not conducive to good communications. The Ox is careful and patient where the Horse person can be quick-witted but impulsive. There may not be a meeting of minds if the Ox favours tradition and wants to travel on the well-trodden path, while the Horse may wish to try a risky new short cut. Like dancing partners out of step, both may want to lead and blame the other for failing to follow. The Ox and the Horse have much to offer each other, but first they have to agree on the route and the rules of the game. In the end, if they do decide to play together, the game may be short or aborted unless they share the same ascendant. The one thing they will both need is tolerance and if they do not have this ingredient in their relationship, the union may not survive the strain.

With a Sheep—Eighth Branch

A great difference in priorities may be the main contention in a relationship between the Ox and the Sheep. The Ox has too many priorities while the Sheep type has practically none. One is always punctual and on schedule while the other cannot keep track of time and refuses to be hurried. One is regimented and disciplined while the other is creative and emotional. Opposites may attract, but in this case, the poor Ox type will be exasperated by the petulant Sheep who is kind and lovable but totally unsuited to the no-nonsense Ox person. The sheep achieves through negotiation, communication and by being especially understanding and cooperative with those who recognise his skills and many gifts. The Ox does not like to depend on others. He will carry his own load, succeed by his own merits and accomplish much through his own dedication and hard work. Neither can appreciate the outlook of the other type and may not wish to work in the same circles or associate much with each other.

With a Monkey—Ninth Branch

The Monkey can and will cooperate with anyone and everyone if it is to his benefit. But the Ox often cannot comprehend the Monkey's intricate schemes and distrusts his unconventional ways of getting round problems. To the inventive Monkey type, who firmly believes nothing is impossible, the Ox will seem unimaginative and overcautious. The Monkey, being an optimist, may wish to harness the Ox's strength and put it to good use. Whether the Ox is willing to cooperate with the clever but audacious Monkey type is another matter. To have a good, working relationship, these two must feel comfortable with each other and learn to rely on one another. The problem may be that the Ox has reservations about the Monkey's too-good-to-be-true ideas and will not be able to give his complete trust or support.

With a Rooster—Tenth Branch

The Rooster type and the Ox type will find harmony as they are both extremely well organised and love routine, planning and order in their lives. Although the Rooster may be the more verbal or fastidious of the two, the patient Ox understands the industrious but meticulous Rooster through and through. While the Ox is always quietly confident of his own ability and worth, the Rooster can be opinionated and controlling in a relationship. Thankfully, the Ox is not opposed to guidance from the high-flying Rooster and may even benefit from the latter's exemplary administrative skills. Their partnership will be fruitful and long-term as these two like to stick to what they know and who they know and do not go for frivolous or short-term associations.

With a Dog—Eleventh Branch

A Dog person will work well with the Ox type if they are both aware of their respective roles. The honourable Dog respects authority and has no struggle with the Ox who can be fair, reliable and honest in his dealings. Likewise, the Ox finds the Dog realistic and faithful to the same goals. However, the Dog may also find the Ox inflexible and uncompromising at times and this may lead to unhappy confrontations. The Dog can be tough and unyielding when challenged, and unless these two decide to champion a common cause they may be on opposite sides of the fence. However, there is no large struggle for dominance in such a union as neither of these two types will go out of his way to look for trouble. They are more concerned with protecting their own territory and minding their own business.

With a Boar—Twelfth Branch

The popular Boar type usually makes every effort to be nice and helpful to everyone, but the stern Ox may not care to be one of his best friends. The supportive and unselfish Boar may find an acceptable union with the domineering but soft-spoken Ox but may suffer in the bargain because the Ox type can be very demanding. The Ox needs to plan and control and may not be amused by the Boar's easygoing and spendthrift lifestyle. The Boar is not as careful with his finances nor as discriminating with his selection of associates— much to the irritation of the Ox, who prefers everything to be well defined right from the start. The Boar also enjoys lavish events and celebrates every occasion with a large gathering of friends. The spartan Ox is frugal, preferring work to play, and will not endorse spending money frivolously—no matter how many supporters the Boar can gain.

3

THE YIN BRANCH
THIRD LUNAR SIGN

The Idealist's Song

I am a delightful puzzle.
All the world is my stage.
I set new trails ablaze,
I seek the unattainable,
try the untried.
I dance to life's music
in spirited abandon.
Come with me on my carousel rides.
Bathe in the myriad colours,
the flickering lights.
All hail me the unparalleled performer.

I am Yin, the Idealist

Theodora Lau

THE THIRD EARTH BRANCH: YIN
THE SIGN OF THE TIGER

THE ASSIGNED LUNAR YEARS OF THE TIGER

February 8, 1902	to	January 28, 1903
January 26, 1914	to	February 13, 1915
February 13, 1926	to	February 1, 1927
January 31, 1938	to	February 18, 1939
February 17, 1950	to	February 5, 1951
February 5, 1962	to	January 24, 1963
January 23, 1974	to	February 10, 1975
February 9, 1986	to	January 28, 1987
January 28, 1998	to	February 15, 1999

If you were born on the day before the lunar year of the Tiger, e.g. February 16, 1950, you belong to the previous earth branch or animal sign, which is the second branch (the Ox).

If you were born on the day after a lunar year ends, e.g. February 6, 1951, you belong to the next earth branch or animal sign, which is the fourth branch (the Rabbit).

THE THIRD EARTH BRANCH
THE SIGN OF THE TIGER

The third character profile of the twelve earth branches is that of the Tiger. He is called *Yin* in Chinese and symbolises passion and integrity. The Yin or Tiger personality surveys his world and sees it through the eyes of an idealist. Life is a gigantic stage to him, on which he will no doubt be playing many leading roles. Competitive, outspoken and courageous, he will take on any and all comers with a positive 'never say die' attitude.

His primary goal in life is to be involved with something that makes a difference in the world—preferably, a huge difference. A humanitarian at heart, he will always try to support a worthy cause, champion the rights of the underdog and fight for those, like children or animals, who cannot defend themselves. Not one who shrinks from controversy, he tends to be a rebel or an activist if he feels his views are being ignored.

Colourful, unpredictable and commanding, the Yin person provokes a reaction wherever he goes and in whatever he does or says. Extremely charming, playful and outgoing at his best, he can also be annoyingly suspicious, accusing and ill-tempered at his worst. He may act rashly at one moment and then hesitate to deliver the final blow when the time comes. He has a soft heart and, for all his fireworks, is not half as vicious or ruthless as he would like others to believe. He often gives the wrong impression to lesser mortals who do not understand or fail to appreciate his flair for the dramatic. This impulsive person is bound to say or do in a moment of anger things that he will later regret.

The Tiger of the Yin branch is the first of the Protectors in his Triangle of Affinity. He, like the other two residents of his triangle, the Horse (seventh branch) and the Dog (eleventh branch) are guided by their emotions. Compassionate and armed with noble intentions, they are society's self-appointed defenders of justice, ideals and standards. The trio of the Protectors' circle are unselfish, extroverted and energetic in pursuing their goals. At times they may be opinionated and unorthodox in their methods (bordering on extreme measures when they feel the necessity). Aggressive and defiant when challenged, these people simply do not back down under pressure or opposition. Those who are more highly strung may even relish confrontation. But in general, a native of this group is true to his conscience and reacts swiftly in response to his feelings. Above all, personalities of this group are renowned for their courage and convictions.

To get along with the Tiger one must understand his sense of honour and equality. If he is convinced he is doing something for the benefit of all, he is always willing to make the necessary sacrifices. He is honest and open in his dealings, although at times too brash when he is optimistic. To work well with the Tiger-Yin person, direct contact is necessary. One must be able to be on the same wavelength as he is and provide the stimuli to make him react positively. He tends to work by instincts and whatever vibrations he picks up are often on the mark. His uncanny ability to gravitate towards the heart of the matter and home in on the source of the trouble is difficult to explain but easy to observe. First impressions and gut feelings mean a lot to the Tiger and he will be able to assess people and situations with one look. Guided by emotions, he is likely to have a magnetic and colourful personality. A forceful speaker and irrepressible performer, he will often be at the centre of controversy or public attention, whether or not he deliberately planned to become so involved.

The personality type of the third branch is not very interested in planning. He has the drive and enthusiasm for spur of the moment inspirations, but would prefer to leave the details and scheduling to others. Don't spoil his fun with all the dreary facts and figures and the warnings on the label. This person often needs special protection from himself as his obstinacy and undisciplined attitude could make him his own worst enemy. On the other hand, it will be surprising how many times luck favours his enterprises and ideas. However, his impetuous and imperious ways can be checked or curbed by strong but devoted associates.

The theatrical Tiger type may be a joy to be with or a holy terror. Charming, captivating and passionate, he will never want to be accused of being lukewarm about anything. Like a lightning rod, he reaches out and grabs whatever currents are flying about. Telling him to shut up would be like putting a lid on a pressure cooker. He will only blow up with a greater force. Most of the time, he will insist on being actively involved in projects and on being part of all discussions.

If he is throwing a tantrum, do not shut him out or be drawn into an unproductive argument with him. In his negative state, he considers any criticism or opposition as a power struggle and will react with belligerence. In such cases, simply hold your ground, interrupt by saying his name repeatedly and then calmly state his main points and yours in a quiet, non-threatening way. You may have to do this over and over again before it can penetrate but it will be worth the effort. This will establish enough control (however temporary) for you to help him see reason or focus his attention on something else. Since he is not very persistent or objective when he is aroused, he is easy to mollify if one does not take his outbursts too seriously. In a confrontation, however, it is always advisable to work things out face to face and not delegate the Tiger-taming task to others. He cannot tolerate secondhand information and this can often lead to major misinterpretation on his part. This is because people of the Third Earth Branch tend to be suspicious and irrational when they are not reassured or advised on what is happening every step of the way. Like a wayward child, one has to hold the Tiger's hand and lead him slowly towards the right path. Once he sees the way and the reason for your assistance, he will be able to continue happily in the correct direction with his own speed and initiative. Punishment and threats do not work well on this personality and will only bring forth his rebellious spirit. He is also not good at working through channels and would rather get things straight from the horse's mouth, so to speak.

A person of this type is generous with his time, money, advice and support. He finds no difficulty making commitments, although they may not all be long-term. Easily distracted, it is hard to hold his attention for long. He will insist on learning things first hand—no matter how painful or futile. The experience will always be valuable to him. It will be quite useless to expect him to listen to the voice of experience, and often he prefers to take things right to the precipice, just to get a view from the edge. The attributes that usually save him are his lively sense of humour, quick reflexes and optimism. His idealism is rarely quenched and somehow he will always be able to rally himself and his friends for one more go. Perhaps this is why he never runs out of luck or supporters.

In business relations with this type of person, it is preferable to act decisively and confidently. Always err on the side of being conservative while he is raving on about the sky being the limit. It would not hurt to emphasise all the pros and cons, although when he is excited and inspired he will not listen to any of the cons, much less remember them. It is imperative to put things down in writing, repeat the rules to him a thousand times and have ample witnesses. The chances are you may not need all these precautions because he is basically a tireless and innovative worker. He will not even consider the possibility of failure when he is totally committed to his objectives. But later on, when the wind's direction changes, when his interest wanes or he feels too restricted by your insistence that he abide by the rules, you may have need of the proof. This person's unconventional attitude is as predictable as his unpredictability. But in life his function seems to be like some magic glue that holds relationships together. He tends to be there when you need him and then again goes off to play when things are not interesting. When things are most dismal, his innate curiosity and lovable kindness will surface and he may find solutions in the most unlikely places and with the strangest allies.

In his personal and business life this type of person will look for all kinds of challenges to keep himself busy. Not one to mind his own business, he will investigate everything and volunteer to help others (sometimes even when they don't need or want his help). His colourful personality and magnetism will never fail to impress. At heart, he could be a hopeless romantic. True, he tends to fly off the handle when circumstances go against him and he does not take bad news graciously, but as soon as he cools down he can be the nicest, most contrite person. He will be more than happy to make amends and get things back on track once he realises he was wrong. His most difficult shortcoming is his tendency to act on impulse without carefully thinking things through. But, then again, it's just his style. He'd rather pounce now and look later. Thank goodness for his very superior reflexes that he is able to extricate himself from some of the messes he manages to get involved in.

The Yin personality excels in communication and is able to relate to people quite easily. He loves being among people, children and animals—not necessarily in that order, although with his affectionate nature he may be devoted to all three. This is a male or Yang sign and aggressiveness is his strong trait whether or not he actively displays it.

Above all, Tiger personalities are dramatic and intense in all they do. They have enormous beliefs in their own convictions and are rarely indifferent to anything. Beethoven, Charles de Gaulle, Emily Brontë, Isadora Duncan, Diana Rigg and Marilyn Monroe are some good examples of this personality type. Most people of this branch have electric vitality and infectious enthusiasm in all they do. He or she will take on leadership roles and rally others towards a common cause without a second thought.

One moment this person could be on top of the world, reigning in brilliance and wowing all with his superb performances, and the next moment he could be down in the dumps, needing you to cheer him up. He has no patience with mediocre and timid attitudes that lead to nowhere. Instead, he is usually loud and clear about what he wants. Forever testing his boundaries, he will seek success and justice with boundless energy. It would be hard for anyone not to relate to his dreams and aspirations. His road to triumph will be lined with many supporters and admirers. In spite of his often temperamental ways, this person's generosity, passion for justice and unsinkable optimism and humour enable him always to bounce back into our good graces. The Tiger personality is one who is unmaterialistic and will readily share his good fortune and bounty with his friends and loved ones. Hence, his enormous popularity is richly deserved.

The key words in the life of the Yin type are: 'I feel'.

TRIANGLE OF AFFINITY

The Tiger or Yin personality of the third branch is the first member of the Third Triangle of Affinity which produces active, likeable and compassionate people indispensable to society. The trio in this triangle are composed of the Tiger (third branch), the Horse (seventh branch) and the Dog (eleventh branch). This group of 'Protectors' advocates fairness and opportunity for everyone, especially those who are most disadvantaged. Guided by their unselfish and extroverted natures, they seek to serve others by promoting understanding and peace whenever they can. Unorthodox, energetic and often acting with missionary zeal, they are aggressive in their idealism and democratic principles. Although they may display short tempers and impatience, generally they are kind, sociable and genuinely helpful. Loyal and selfless, members of this triangle are staunch and fearless fighters, reputed for their courage and aggressiveness. While they may be rebellious and stubborn at times, their negative qualities are balanced by their innate charm and generosity. Confident, outspoken and never afraid of controversy, this band of Protectors will charge to the rescue of anyone they feel is in need of their assistance.

To work well with residents of the Third Triangle of Affinity, one must appeal not only to their sense of honour and fair play, but tug at their emotional heartstrings, too. Honest and open in all their dealings, they will gladly make sacrifices for the good of all. They relish personal contact and will go out of their way to bond with others. Not calculating, small-hearted or vindictive, they can assess

situations relatively quickly and accurately and make fast, accurate judgements. Gifted with magnetic and captivating personalities, they have no problems persuading others to see things their way. These types know how to project themselves to the public and will often have careers or opportunities in communications, sales, promotions, on-stage or movie performances and in the sports, political or military arena where sharp reflexes and genuine combative passion are required. They believe in themselves with unshakable confidence and will show unerring loyalty to their team, family, friends and country.

The three branches of the Third Triangle of Affinity will be able to get along well in love and business. Working as a team is second nature to them. Capable of intuitively anticipating each other's desires, they have a common way of thinking and reacting. As marriage or business partners, they will have no difficulty supporting one another or identifying their common goals.

CIRCLE OF CONFLICT

The Yin personality of the Tiger branch will find his strongest antagonist on the branch directly opposite him in the Circle of Conflict, which is the Monkey of the ninth branch. The Tiger has an entirely different outlook from the Monkey-type person and the differences in their perspectives often cause them to be unreceptive to each other's ideas. The Monkey type is known for his wit and ingenuity and can be merciless in taunting the easily provoked Tiger person into some sort of competition or struggle. The Tiger is at his worst

**3rd - Yin
Tiger**

**9th - Shen
Monkey**

when he is baited by an elusive and mischievous foe and will react by falling into the trap. With each one insisting on having his way, there are bound to be major personality clashes.

On top of their uncompromising traits, both these types tend to be suspicious, argumentative and contentious when angered. Their competitive natures require them to prove to themselves and the world their superior prowess. In fact, the best advice for these two protagonists will be to steer clear of each other and deal through intermediaries or mediators. Somehow, the message will always sound better and be more acceptable when delivered by a neutral party. Direct dealings between these personalities have a high degree of bruised egos and unproductive competitiveness.

RELATIONSHIPS WITH THE THIRD EARTH BRANCH—THE TIGER

Within the Family

Usually the family charmer, the Tiger sparkles with vivacity and is always involved in a myriad activities that could keep everyone around him busy or in some way committed to some cause. This personality type is close to his loved ones and very affectionate and giving. He will tend to spoil the children, dote on his spouse and yet be equally demanding of attention, expecting home life to revolve around him. As a parent, he can be overly protective but not too domineering towards his offspring. He takes great pride in their achievements and will openly trumpet all their achievements to anyone who shows the slightest interest. Blind and deaf to the faults and shortcomings of his loved ones, he can be unreasonably defensive, so it would be best not to criticise his family within hearing distance.

Never one to keep a tight rein on his emotions or his words, this person does not hesitate to inform his family exactly what he is thinking or feeling. He is poor at keeping secrets or telling lies because his fiery emotions tend to get the better of his good sense, such as controlling his tongue. Do not tell him too much of anything in confidence unless you want to have it broadcast about. Indecisive yet impatient at times, he needs the unconditional support of those close to him. It won't be difficult to support him as he repays kindness tenfold with his generosity and warmth.

Children of this branch will love to bask in the light of their parents' adoring eyes. They need loads of sympathy, encouragement, attention and even cuddling to bring out the best in them. Bright, outgoing and confident, they are unusually curious and precocious. They make friends easily but could get into fights or find conflict just as easily. It is their nature either to love or loathe someone or something passionately. Like the adults of this branch, they are likely to be fun-loving little people who really know how to enjoy life, sports and comradeship. Their company is sought after by family and friends alike and they always perform much better with an audience than without one.

As a Teacher
The idealistic and democratic person of the third branch is bound to be an exciting and capable teacher. One can almost visualise him teaching by example and not only by rote. He will organise unplanned field trips for his students when it happens to be a sunny day and he will do unconventional things to make them remember their lessons well. His unpredictable yet exhilarating leadership will either endear his students to him forever or frighten and alienate them by his unorthodox methods. As a teacher, he will take it upon himself to awaken his pupils' curiosity, open new worlds for them and question their beliefs and commitments to the maximum. One must learn to interact with such a personality as he is anything but passive and unimaginative. Life to him is one great entertaining performance and everyone has a part to play. Of course, he assigns himself the biggest part and will play his dramatic role magnificently. If he is your teacher, be content to play second fiddle, and do not upstage him.

If one knows how to relate to him, one could get away with anything. This type is not unduly strict as he himself has difficulty with self-discipline or authority figures. However, he does expect teamwork and unfailing loyalty when it comes to what he considers important.

As a Lover and Spouse
Ardent, demonstrative and at times overwhelming in his affection, this personality type is decidedly passionate. A true believer in *l'amour*, he will woo and win the object of his heart's desire with unprecedented flair and extravagance. With him, the attraction will

always have to be instant and magnetic. Although he tends to be a flirt, he will know how to follow the dictates of his heart when it comes to someone he considers important. His love life will have ups and downs, but at least one can trust him not to lie or cheat in any relationship. It takes too much effort for him to pretend. Besides, he is no good at it and you'll probably know it when his attraction for you is waning. In the Tiger type's peculiar way of thinking, it is wiser for him to follow his heart than his head. Perhaps this is because he likes to change his mind frequently and if he waited for his brain to figure out all the whys and wherefores of that magic 'affliction' called love, he would never be able to act out his unerring intuitions. He will always be able to identify the people he loves and likes to be with, but don't expect him to explain that special attraction to you. For him, it is either present or not. He does not question his heart and will share whatever he has with the one he loves.

As a Business Partner

The native of the Third Earth Branch is easy to work with if one knows how he thinks. First, he is not likely to be caught up in details because he is usually fired up by ideas and challenges. Second, he can establish rapport quickly with the right people and will make a good business partner, especially where his connections and affiliations are invaluable. This type knows how to use and persuade people who can support his business or endeavour. Feisty and confident, he is an extroverted soul who could infect everyone he meets with his wonderful enthusiasm. The ultimate front man, he will be out advertising, promoting and unabashedly singing the praises of his joint venture.

However, in spite of his enormous energy and commitment, he must be able to sustain his optimism and drive or he could dissipate his efforts. He needs others to hold the purse strings, budget for the unforeseen and direct him to do what he is best at. The most important ingredient in a partnership with this type is always to be focused on an objective. Do not depend on him to make difficult or big decisions as he tends to procrastinate and may let good opportunities slip by while he makes up his mind.

His most compatible business partners will be the self-assured Horse types of the seventh branch and the reliable Dog types of the eleventh branch. Persons born under the other nine branches will also be favourable but in varying degrees. It would be ill-advised for the Tiger type to go into any partnership or enterprise with persons of the Monkey branch; there could be too many internal struggles for power and both might end up undoing what the other one had accomplished. Dragon, Rat and Ox personalities may also have reservations about the Tiger partner as they tend to worry about profits and security and may feel that the Tiger can be extravagant and foolishly bold in his undiluted optimism.

As a Boss

Unpredictable and unsinkable will be the two best ways to describe a Tiger type boss. He will no doubt enjoy being boss and view himself as the super coach behind a winning team. Although he is restless by nature, his drive and positive energy will liven up the office and he will constantly be one step ahead of the game. He will be able to mix well with everyone and his popularity is matched only by the sincere caring attitude he has for the people he works with. However, he will tend to favour certain people who sing the same tune he does, and he does not know how to hide his feelings and behave in an impartial and discreet manner. Generous with praise, he can be equally loud with criticism and he could make last-minute changes without even blinking. Be prepared for surprises in his reign. Often, he cannot understand what the fuss is about as he changes the schedule and the agenda for the thirteenth time. He just had another wonderful idea, that's all. One has to be flexible when working with the Tiger type and always rely on one's sense of humour to defuse combustible situations which the Tiger loves to create when he is bored, suspicious or trying to meet his own impossible deadlines.

As a Friend and Colleague

The Tiger of the Yin earth branch is wonderful to have as a friend and ally. As a colleague, he or she will certainly liven up the work environment. Considerate and generous, he will be solicitous of the welfare of those he values as friends. However, a Tiger type does not make a good confidant because he could blurt out your secret unintentionally when he is excited or angry. Adventurous and daring, he will often drag his friends and colleagues off to exotic restaurants, quaint gift shops, fortune-tellers (during the lunch break) and on similar little adventures or escapades to satisfy his curiosity. With his little band of conspirators, the colourful Tiger could be the maker of embarrassing situations when he is rejected or ignored. But whatever happens, he is not one who will ever turn his back on his friends when they are in need.

As an Opponent

This personality type never shrinks from a good fight—indeed, he is often accused of adding fuel to the fire. Most of the time he will probably start it; just to make a point or gain some attention or recognition. Whether he is on the offensive or defensive side, the Tiger relishes matching strength and wits with the most seasoned of foes. A tough and demanding opponent, he fiercely compels respect and surrender from his enemies. But he can also be strangely unpredictable, and just when he is about to win he may lose interest in the chase. Often, inconsequential things irritate and enrage him more than big issues which should really concern him. Half the time he is not as ferocious as he might lead others to believe. He can be benevolent and forgiving and may choose not to destroy the opponent when he enjoys the upper hand. However, do not expect him to be too consistent as he could employ many different tactics to confuse you. Yet once he is victorious and gets the recognition he wants, he is most likely to show mercy to the vanquished.

When this personality gets tangled up in lawsuits, things could be complicated as he tends to blow issues out of proportion. His judgement is often clouded by anger and suspicion. It is advisable to try and resolve issues early in the game by face-to-face mediation. Having his friends around will also put him in a good mood if he wants to impress on them that he is the 'good guy'.

As the Mediator

The native of this Third Earth Branch can only mediate for certain types of people, particularly those who admire and are impressed by his communication skills. Otherwise he could turn into a meddler instead of a true mediator. The Tiger type likes to control the situation and sometimes is not the good listener that every impartial mediator should be. He tends to jump to conclusions, prematurely take sides and make his own personal observations. His intentions are always honourable, but his efforts may be directed like a double-edged sword, cutting both sides when he sees things only through his idealism. If he could learn patience and practise discretion, he would be able to negotiate with more skill because of his ability to talk and relate to people. His popularity and openness also encourage others to trust him and depend on him to work hard for their interests. Although the Tiger type rarely has hidden motives, his sympathy for the underdog is legendary and he will always champion difficult or unpopular causes to help those he considers less privileged. He will not hesitate to lend his strength wherever and whenever it is needed, but to excel as a mediator, this person must continually maintain his objectivity in order to remain fair to all.

RELATIONS WITH OTHER BRANCHES

With a Rat—First Branch
The Tiger will find the Rat charming but parsimonious. On the other hand, the Rat may be impressed by the vibrant personality of the Tiger but not by his impulsiveness. Good communications can only result if they share similar interests and have the same priorities, which could be doubtful. The Rat must always do what is good for himself and his family before considering outsiders. The Tiger is generous and not as practical as the Rat would wish. Often, the Tiger will make a noble but foolishly extravagant gesture, much to his own detriment, and the enterprising Rat will find it unforgivable. Both types here are outgoing and energetic, but they have different outlooks and motivations.

With an Ox—Second Branch
The Tiger loves change and excitement which the Ox seeks to avoid as he prefers his life to be predictable and orderly, even if it may seem rather dull to the Tiger. Personality clashes in this combination may come from each side insisting on having his or her way. Mutual cooperation is hard to establish unless the Tiger has an Ox ascendant or the Ox has a strong Tiger ascendant. The Tiger gets over his temperamental outbursts quite easily, but the Ox may not change his opinion once he is angered and will be harsh in his dealings with the Tiger person. A good go-between could serve as a buffer between these two strong personalities and help create a workable relationship and better communications.

With another Tiger—Third Branch

The only rule to remember in such a combination is that these two equally captivating personalities must never get angry at the same time, although sometimes they may enjoy a good fight just for the pleasure of making up later. They are compatible to a certain degree as they know not to take each other too seriously and are able to start all over again once they have vented their emotions. Tiger types can be generous, forgiving and have a marvellous sense of humour which can defuse the most dismal situation. They love and work with passion and are never half-hearted in any commitment. The only problem two tigers may have will be fighting for the limelight. They will be competitive in outperforming each other and neither will agree to take a back seat.

With a Rabbit—Fourth Branch

The diplomatic Rabbit may allow the Tiger to believe that he is calling the shots, just to keep the peace, but in reality the tactful Rabbit personality can outmanoeuvre the Tiger any time he wishes. If the Tiger does not underestimate the intelligence and capabilities of the suave and prudent Rabbit, he will learn much and find himself an invaluable ally. If he tries to bully or dominate the Rabbit person, he may be surprised by swift and unexpected retaliation from such a docile and discreet fellow. The Rabbit will only respect and appreciate someone who can share his intellectual interests and love of art and music. If these two decide to bond, they must have the same interests and find common ground.

With a Dragon—Fifth Branch

Both personalities here love action and are highly motivated. If they share similar interests and goals they will have no problem getting along. Neither will be too intimidated by the strong will of the other if they can define their areas of responsibility. The Dragon could be a positive influence on the Tiger if the Tiger allows the Dragon to shine. However, the Tiger has superior instincts when it comes to business as well as romance and the Dragon would be wise to defer to the judgement of the dynamic Tiger person in some areas. Both have more than enough talents, ideas and opinions to go round and they will never lack excitement in their mercurial relationship.

With a Snake—Sixth Branch
The Tiger is often suspicious of introverted and secretive people and the Snake fits that description perfectly. The Snake person will not comprehend the Tiger's outspokenness and fault him for being overly dramatic. Each is intimidated by the other's view of him and the Tiger could become claustrophobic in the presence of the mesmerising Snake person, who rarely reveals anything about himself or his intentions. Conflicts could arise from silly misunderstandings, with both sides jumping to their own conclusions without checking the facts. Unless these two share a common ascendant and have similar likes and dislikes, any close relationship will be hampered by miscommunication and their different ways of expressing themselves.

With a Horse—Seventh Branch
The Tiger and the Horse march to the same drummer and will make good music together. They are both quick and lively on their feet and will spring to action at a moment's notice. Sharing the same impulsive and courageous attitude towards any challenges that life may throw their way, these two personalities bond readily and will fight and play side by side. The Tiger is the more aggressive of the two while the Horse person is well tuned to his environment at all times. Both will benefit immensely from their association and find it easy to overlook mutual shortcomings because they have a deep understanding of each other's nature.

With a Sheep—Eighth Branch
The Sheep does not enjoy confrontation and therefore will rarely challenge a Tiger person. His main tactic may be evading the temperamental Tiger instead of standing his ground. The Tiger can be protective and sympathetic if the Sheep type knows how to appeal to his better instincts and his oversized ego. These two may have good need of each other as they have much to contribute to a workable relationship. The Sheep can find friends and supporters where the Tiger fails and the Tiger will be bold and demanding where the Sheep lacks the audacity to be belligerent. The gracious Sheep may find it easier to cooperate if the high-powered Tiger can be less intimidating and more considerate.

With a Monkey—Ninth Branch

The Monkey delights in matching wits with formidable opponents and the Tiger falls right into the Monkey's trap when he should just ignore the clever Monkey and refuse to be baited. But the Tiger thinks it cowardly to run from a challenge and will confront the Monkey. Often these two are irresistibly drawn to each other and enjoy a love-hate relationship that could have many ups and downs. Both are aggressive and determined to have their own way. If they cannot deal through a mediator, it may be best for them to get smartly out of the arena, for there can be no winner in their conflicts. Operating in an antagonistic atmosphere will only make them more destructive than constructive. Ironically, the Monkey may be the first to realise the futility of trying to control the Tiger person. Sadly, both are bad losers who will itch for a rematch and refuse to accept failure or defeat in any way.

With a Rooster—Tenth Branch

These two colourful and captivating personalities often find much in common, until the Rooster shows his perfectionist side and demands that the Tiger follow his way—no arguments allowed. The independent Tiger will not find the Rooster so amusing when he is forced to work under the latter's supervision. Unless these two share a common sign as their ascendant they are bound to be critical and opinionated in each other's company, spending more time proving each other wrong than working towards a common goal. There may be painful lessons to be learned, and if the Rooster is the teacher he will be an uncompromising taskmaster, which could bring out the rebel in the Tiger personality.

With a Dog—Eleventh Branch

The sensible and likeable Dog person knows how to handle the impetuous but lovable Tiger type. The Dog will let the Tiger go his own way until he runs out of steam and will then rein him in gently, without recriminations or a good scolding. The Tiger appreciates the Dog's kind understanding and will find it easy to work with the rational and altruistic Dog who is modest and reliable. The Dog is also more defensive and hostile to anything that appears unfamiliar and will alert the curious Tiger to the dangers of stepping out of bounds. Both have volatile tempers but do not bear grudges for very long and can easily put aside their differences for the common good. The Tiger also respects the Dog who knows how to stand his ground with the Tiger and will not allow himself to be overly dominated in any relationship.

With a Boar—Twelfth Branch

Tiger and Boar types make good rowdy friends who will party with great zest. Both won't worry too much about the morrow and are outgoing and generous by nature. They can cooperate and support each other if they develop good communications and not merely superficial relations. However, they tend to overdo things and have difficulty controlling their emotions and appetites. Happiness and success could be short-lived unless each takes the responsibility required of him and perseveres through the bad times as well as the good. The Boar will discover that the Tiger can be a powerful ally, and the Tiger will learn to appreciate the intrinsic worth of the honest and unselfish Boar type. They will have a successful relationship if they do not take each other for granted.

4

THE MAO BRANCH
FOURTH LUNAR SIGN

The Conformist's Song

I am in tune with the
pulse of the universe.
In my quiet and solitude,
I hear the melodies important
to the soul.
I float above commonplace
dissent and decay.
I subdue by my ability to conform.
My world is coloured
in soft, tranquil hues.
I symbolise harmony
and inner peace.

I am Mao, the Conformist

Theodora Lau

THE FOURTH EARTH BRANCH: MAO
THE SIGN OF THE RABBIT

THE ASSIGNED LUNAR YEARS OF THE RABBIT

January 29, 1903	to	February 15, 1904
February 14, 1915	to	February 2, 1916
February 2, 1927	to	January 22, 1928
February 19, 1939	to	February 7, 1940
February 6, 1951	to	January 26, 1952
January 25, 1963	to	February 12, 1964
February 11, 1975	to	January 30, 1976
January 29, 1987	to	February 16, 1988
February 16, 1999	to	February 5, 2000

If you were born on the day before the lunar year of the Rabbit, e.g. February 18, 1939, you belong to the previous earth branch or animal sign which is the third branch (the Tiger).

If you were born on the day after a lunar year ends, e.g. February 8, 1940, you belong to the next earth branch or animal sign, which is the fifth branch (the Dragon).

THE FOURTH EARTH BRANCH
THE SIGN OF THE RABBIT

The fourth character profile of the twelve earth branches is that of the Rabbit whose branch is named *Mao* and symbolises diplomacy. This quiet, efficient person sees his world as a chess game. The object is to win, but when he cannot hope to win, the Rabbit type will make sure that it will at least be a draw because he is simply too good a player to lose. When things are not in his favour, he will manoeuvre matters so that he will come out even, or will withdraw from the game. Refined, congenial and even-tempered, he is the ultimate observer who rarely says anything out of turn or unpleasant. However, it will be difficult to get him to become involved or committed to some cause without a lot of arm-twisting and trade-offs. He can also become deliberately detached; refusing to open up to others and using an invisible wall to protect him from getting drawn into any conflict. The more you seek to tie him down, the more he will struggle to get free.

On the surface, this person is self-assured, collected and sophisticated; gifted with gracious manners, sensitivity and considerate ways—he is always easy to get along with. Just make sure you do not ask too much of him or cross the line from familiarity to contempt, when he would consider the relationship to have become an imposition. Then, he may make a quick, gracious exit. Smooth and impeccable in his handling of people, the Rabbit type is the perfect diplomat and may be found observing protocol to a fault. His seemingly docile nature is often deceiving as he keeps his thoughts to himself and never lets that mask of inscrutability drop. As a result, this person is not one to volunteer his opinion or give unsolicited advice. He does not pry; he detests gossip; he prides himself on keeping confidences well. However, he is also extremely shrewd and careful in protecting his own interests, so it will be wise never to underestimate him.

Of all the twelve earth branches, the Mao type has the best coping skills. One does not hear him openly complain. He is compliant in obeying rules and keeping the peace. But remember that winning an argument with him does not mean you have succeeded in changing his mind. Ingenious when it comes to getting his own way, the Rabbit type is a master of swift *coups de grace* and has his own brand of cunning that is sometimes hard to imagine coming from such an amiable character.

This personality type is a natural when it comes to forming useful alliances as his outer conformity is a key that allows him to be accepted anywhere he fancies going. A wonderful entertainer, a flawless organiser and a thoughtful friend, this type will always compose his inner self before he makes a decision. He weighs all the pros and cons before acting and will seek to please the majority to ally himself safely with the winning side. He will look to establish common bonds with those people he needs to work with and cope with whatever he cannot influence or change; the Rabbit type's purpose in life is to maintain his own harmony and prosperity.

The philosophy of the Fourth Earth Branch personality is to take the middle of the road and get on with everyone. He is therefore not one who will relish making enemies, having arguments or being drawn into conflicts. Studious, devoted to the arts or his hobbies, he enjoys his own company in a meditative sort of way. His private world is one place where he does exercise total control and he allows very few people into this sacred sanctum. Blessed with an inborn sense of discretion and caution which serve him well, the Mao type will choose to lead an uncomplicated life. You may often wonder how this person is able to remain serene under the most distracting or oppressive environment. Perhaps he can be so calm because he is secretly planning his vengeance which no doubt he will eventually exact with ruthless thoroughness when the opportune time arrives. Meanwhile he will be cordial and bide his time.

Never in a hurry or impatient, he can work diligently and with good concentration. In most cases, he will be an excellent bridge or poker player. Always observing others in a very discreet manner, he takes in more information than you can ever guess. By now, you must be aware that this personality plays his cards right. Astute in business and skilful in social-climbing, the Rabbit type is difficult to outsmart. To deal successfully with this personality one must above all be practical and respectful. Observe and learn from him. He will be happy to do his share provided he is well rewarded, but if things go wrong through no fault of his, he will quickly distance himself and try to cut his losses. He detests getting into tricky situations because he considers it evidence of poor planning and a lack of foresight. Rest assured, this person will not be suffering along with you through the hard, lean times. Yet, he is often a good business partner to have as he does his homework thoroughly and will not venture into anything too risky. He will also be able to give you solid advice on what to do to protect yourself or defeat your competitors. He will anticipate all contingencies and is unlikely to be caught unprepared. The Rabbit type is not impressed by the wealth or intelligence of others, so one can be sure he will quietly and quickly check out all the references he has been given and run a credit report on every customer, regardless of appearances. Don't ever discount his prediction, for he is able to be spot on about people and can see through any veneer of artificiality.

One can also rely on his superb sense of prudence and intuition. He won't be throwing away money to impress others or buy admiration, he has too much class for that. Instead, he could be the discriminating art collector; the self-appointed judge of what the public could consider aesthetic and elegant. Gifted with a keen eye for artistic bargains, the Rabbit can snap up priceless antiques before anyone else gets wind of his find. He will always keep his sources a secret. Aloof and calculating when he is in business, others may criticise him as self-serving and superficial in personal relationships.

But his strength lies not in his ability to debate his own merits, argue with detractors or deny the charges made against him. He sees his victory in his uncanny ability to assimilate, conform and accommodate the viewpoints of others, all the while formulating his own superb strategy and waiting for an opportunity to implement his plan. Needless to say, he will have very few enemies, at least very few who will dare to identify themselves outright. Because, no matter how self-centred this person may be, he will be careful never to show it. The Rabbit type knows how to cover his tracks well and for good reason. Why alert anyone to what he is really like or what he is thinking? He sees no useful purpose in letting anyone know him too well until he is ready. Besides, he feels more comfortable when he keeps some distance between himself and the public in general.

More materialistic than most other signs, this person can be avaricious, although he will not be obvious about it. Remember, he is a master at concealing his feelings and objectives. In spite of his pleasing demeanour, his feelings are easily hurt and, being extremely thin-skinned, he can often be offended by the insensitivity and thoughtlessness of others. However, he also tends to read hidden meanings into offhand remarks or jokes. Nursing his grievances in private, the Rabbit type may suddenly take extreme measures without warning to even the score. It is hard to predict with any accuracy what the demure Mao personality is planning to do. He can be tight-lipped and uncommunicative as his world tends to be centred around certain priorities that he has judged to be important. He will make time for himself, his interests and hobbies and then, and only then, will he look outside for amusement or involvement. The natives of this earth branch take their vacations and personal schedule very seriously. If the Rabbit washes his car every Saturday and goes to the museum every Sunday, you can be sure he will not like to reschedule. He can be flexible but only to a certain point and only if it does not conflict with his activities. A little self-centred in outlook, he will not drop everything to go and rescue a friend if it proves too inconvenient. Don't count on him to risk life or limb to save you if there is not much to gain. Naturally, with his ability to plan and think clearly, he will know all the right people for you to contact. He could probably give you better advice than your lawyer and he will check your insurance policy to see if you are covered in case of an accident; he will also have the presence of mind to phone your closest relatives to inform them of your predicament, even bring you a fresh change of clothing. But forget the idea that he will be putting up that bail money if you have been arrested, or standing as your guarantor. And you absolutely cannot hide out in his home either, as he prefers to stay out of trouble or other people's lives.

In love and romance the Rabbit type is the epitome of good taste and decorum. His discriminating tastes will cover flowers, perfume and the best wine. Here is a meticulous person who will attend to all the details and provide the most romantic setting. He loves to set the mood for the perfect dinner by candlelight and will provide for everything down to the violin serenade outside on the balcony. For him, ambience is everything. Not at all stingy in enjoying and pursuing the finer things in life, the Rabbit knows how to lavish attention on those he cares about.

Although he will not be fighting for the spotlight, he does expect others to recognise his abilities and pay him his just dues. Discreet, unobtrusive and always polite, one could never fault him for lack of manners. Yet he does enjoy being fêted for his accomplishments and being entertained regally. Failure to give him the recognition he craves could result in long stony silences and bouts of sulking.

However, the Rabbit type is also one to end relationships once the novelty wears off or if he meets someone else he would rather keep company with. Far from being so crude as to cut things off abruptly, he will know how to cool matters a few degrees at a time until he is able to distance himself to where he feels comfortable. Still, this is the most likely person one could still keep as a friend after breaking up, as he can be so unbelievably civilised and skilful in terminating relationships with as little offence as possible.

One of his special skills is his ability to keep people at ease and listen attentively to their troubles. There is of course no guarantee that he could do anything about their particular situation or sort out their problems, but he can be a good sounding board and he is genuinely sympathetic. The sensible person of the fourth branch is much sought after for his astute assessment of situations and his is the last word on the aesthetic nature of things. Do you need someone to advise you on whether or not to buy that strange-looking painting? What about the latest colours in which to do up your new flat? How can you get the best bargain on that cashmere coat that you have been saving for, and in what particular style? The suave Rabbit will have the ultimate word and answers down pat. Shopping with such a personality type is a joy. It does not matter if this person is a male or female: he or she can identify what works and what doesn't with an unerring sixth sense that is uncanny. Never unreasonable or impatient, he is a pleasure to work with, as planning and practical application are his forte. He is able to pace himself well and allows ample time to do whatever needs to be done without being rushed. But, he does not work well in stressful situations and neither will he be forced to work with difficult, demanding or unreasonable people. Tactfully, he will find a way to extricate himself from such quandaries. Life's too short for him to put up with such pointless struggles.

Before one can deal successfully with the Rabbit type, one must fully appreciate his way of thinking and his outlook on life. He is one who willingly reciprocates when treated well and likes to pursue things that are of importance to his life. Good music, fine wine, the theatre, antiques or fine furniture all appeal to his need for a beautiful, healthy environment and a pampered lifestyle. He makes few demands on others and will understand that we all get what we pay for. If something is too good to be true or too cheap to be real— then it probably isn't. It will be hard for anyone to pull the wool over his eyes.

The Rabbit personality approaches everything he does with caution and sagacity. Who do you think coined that phrase 'politically correct'? It must have been this person as he is valued because he knows the art of 'saving face'. He will never intentionally wound someone's pride in a moment of anger to the point of gaining an enemy. A person of the Mao branch does not like to jump to conclusions. He is never loud or accusing. Slowly but surely he does his homework and will be able to uncover the facts one way or another. He bases his worth on his ability to cope and to influence. Like a good puppet master, control is invisible; yet his mastery will be evident in the way his puppets move and take on a life of their own. We all know who pulls the strings behind the scenes, but we are just as enthralled. His marvellous contributions are always testaments to his unique ability to rule from behind the curtains or cameras. In the end, we unconsciously do his bidding because it would seem foolish to do otherwise.

In life, this personality does not struggle with self-recrimination or many regrets. He is able to set goals and rank values with little hesitation. One who continually betters himself throughout life, he seeks constant cultural and artistic stimulation. Unhampered by scruples, the Rabbit type will not hesitate to manipulate a situation to his advantage. Yet the ironic fact may be that things turn out even better because of his remarkable intervention.

In human relationships the Rabbit or Mao type prefers oblique manoeuvring and dislikes frontal attacks. Likewise, using heavy-handed methods on this person will only result in his devising new ways of escape. Skilfully using his mask of conformity, he will use devious compliance to get things done his way in the end. Self-denial is something he abhors, so don't expect a lot of sacrifices on his part. Overdoing or following orders to the detriment of others is called malicious obedience and the Rabbit type may employ this drastic method to prove to you that you are on the wrong track.

In love, business dealings and partnerships, this person is usually open to negotiation. He will never be blamed as the one who shut the door or cut the final link. Yet he seldom makes promises—only gentle reassurances. Given to sagelike introspection and deliberation, you will find he is a master at using retreat as a form of advancement. He understands legal manoeuvres and probably invented some of his own. Soft-spoken, low-keyed and docile-looking, the Mao type is not as harmless as he looks. Just when you think you can take him for granted, he will prove with amazing speed how wrong you are.

Nonetheless, no one is better qualified or more deserving of finding harmony and tranquillity in his life than the person of the Fourth Earth Branch. He is never overambitious, overoptimistic or overenthusiastic about anything; underneath his soft-looking armour of old-fashioned sensibility, he will be able to handle his affairs with great aplomb and realism.

The key words in the mind of the Mao personality as the fourth earth branch in the lunar cycle are: 'I comply'.

TRIANGLE OF AFFINITY

The Mao or Rabbit type is the first player in the Fourth Triangle of Affinity which produces a group of three Catalysts within the Twelve Earth Branches. There are four Triangles of Affinity under which all the personality types are grouped. There is one Circle of Conflict in which all opposite branches are determined as incompatible. In the Fourth Triangle we have the Rabbit, the Sheep and the Boar, respectively the fourth, eighth and twelfth branches.

This trio of the Fourth Triangle of Affinity are Catalysts who

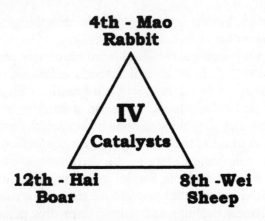

serve as useful agents in relationships. This group is composed of the intuitive, sympathetic and cooperative personality types who bring about changes in others without changing themselves. Supportive, generous and good listeners, the persons who occupy the Fourth Triangle of Affinity are keen observers, well-skilled in communications. Artistic, creative and impressionable, they are the guardians of the arts, theatre, publishing, computers and the world of music. Powerful movers and shakers behind the scenes, these types have their fingers on the pulse of society and know how to make things happen unobtrusively but in significant ways. Consciously or unconsciously they tend to dominate the arena they are involved in and their influence is often accepted and enduring.

Often a personality of this particular triangle tends to be sensitive, insecure and self-serving because he can sense negative vibrations as well as send them when he is unhappy or suspicious. In dealing with anyone belonging to this triangle, one must not expect unconditional support or unwavering loyalty. It is enough that he or she is able to bring parties together in a spirit of cooperation and open-mindedness. A Catalyst does not mind helping others find the right contacts and connections, but please do not expect him to stay and hold your hand through thick and thin. This personality type is not renowned for his undying constancy and will seek to watch over his own interests when given the choice or opportunity. True to his nature, he makes a good arbitrater and mediator as he finds it easy to understand and identify with others and is not competitive or aggressive in his approach. Hence, he is most likely to get everyone to join forces with him. With his innate diplomatic, obliging and approachable demeanour, he knows how to make friends and neutralise his enemies.

Anyone who wants to impress a native of this triangle should emphasise the virtues of compromise instead of confrontation and stress the benefits of negotiation instead of conflict. If anyone appreciates calm logic, the Mao person does—he is the indispensable expert of 'give and take' and will be successful in patching up failed relationships in his own special way, of being the peaceful catalyst.

The Rabbit, Sheep and Boar types will naturally be drawn to each other and share the same views. In love, partnerships and business, these three will understand and support each other with great tolerance and understanding. Undefeatable as a team, they will function harmoniously together.

CIRCLE OF CONFLICT

The Fourth Earth Branch will encounter opposition and personality clashes with persons belonging to the tenth branch or a native of the Rooster type. Anyone born with his ascendant during the hours of the Rooster (5 p.m. to 7 p.m.) will also find conflict with the Mao or Rabbit person. They will not share much in common and find their differences hard to understand or bear. The Rabbit type is polite, private and peaceful while the Rooster of the tenth branch can be too authoritative, dominant and competitive for the gracious Mao type. Even if both have the same interests or goals they may

4th - Mao
Rabbit

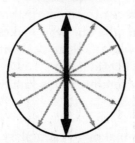

10th - You
Rooster

prefer to approach things from different angles, use different methods or travel by different routes.

This is not to say that one is right or the other is wrong. Incompatibility stems from incongruous viewpoints and the refusal of one or both parties to walk over to the opposition and take a look at the situation from a new or different angle.

RELATIONSHIPS WITH THE FOURTH EARTH BRANCH— THE RABBIT

Within the Family
The Rabbit type as a parent is security-conscious and congenial. His influence is encompassing like water and his children will learn by osmosis in his aura of sensitivity and intuitiveness. Practical and prudent, this type makes a good role model, especially as a parent. He teaches that patience and tolerance pay large dividends and can persuade those close to him to see the wisdom of his astute way of doing things. His may not be a particularly close-knit family, but peace and an atmosphere of learning usually reign.

As a child, the Mao person will be held up as a shining example of good behaviour and deportment. He realises early in life that people aren't all good or all bad and will not seek to make others change. Pleasant and easy to get along with, he can be cooperative and caring, so much so that other family members will rely greatly on his powers of deduction and tact. Certainly not one to sow discord or pick fights, this personality will be able shrewdly to guess the thoughts and feelings of others and act accordingly. Placing a high value on good grooming and refined manners; he is always well turned out and will take pains to display his social graces.

In his family, a person of the fourth branch is considered the mature and sensible one, the one who makes good judgements and intelligent suggestions, who is able to deal with problems calmly and acts with foresight and consideration. Always an asset wherever he goes, he will be a great comfort to his family.

As a Teacher
A native of this branch makes an exemplary teacher who is patient and organised. Known for his caring and polite disposition, he will explain things quietly and carefully over and over again. However,

he cannot tolerate disruption and rebelliousness and can be unforgiving to those who challenge him. This type of teacher tends to be conservative and would like to stick to proven ideas instead of experimenting on new approaches. In this way he is predictable as well as reliable. The Rabbit type prefers to be persuasive instead of dictatorial; he rules by consensus and will always cut some slack for his students. He does not believe in having everyone on a tight leash and will be able to make allowance for the shortcomings of his students. Yet, it would be unwise to push him too far as he probably has an iron fist inside that velvet glove.

As a Lover and Spouse

The Mao type is loving and caring but often is not so generous with his time in affairs of the heart. When he does the planning, he is happy calling the shots and will expect his beloved automatically to be on the same wavelength. Yet he can tire of too much togetherness and will suddenly want his privacy. Reserved and individualistic, he tends to hide his anger or show it in covert ways. Because he shuns arguments, open displays of anger or confrontation, he may always give the appearance that 'all is well'. Actually, he could just be in love with the idea of being treasured and courted. His outward charm and irresistible need for attention and fresh romance are always well honed.

In spite of his devotion to his loved one, it must be understood that he wants to have a secret side to his life, too. At times he can demand solitude and becomes detached in order to get in touch with his inner self. Such moodiness is typical of the introspective Rabbit type. He will show deep affinity with the sympathetic Sheep of the eighth branch and the fun-loving Boar of the twelfth branch. Together, they could pursue the pleasures of life; the arts and antiques and share the same preference for certain music. Although he will be creative and cosmopolitan, he will always have that need for stability and security in his love life.

As a Business Partner

This personality is able and intelligent, and makes an excellent business partner because he possesses few illusions about life. He is a conservative at heart but is not easily intimidated and can bluff and bargain with the pros. He possesses a good nose for bargains and his patience and defensive planning usually pay off. Careful with the finances, he dislikes taking high risks. Quick and agile in mental as well as physical pursuits, he will be skilful in business management and can steer the business to the right direction. At times he is a bit of a plotter and tends to be conservative, but he is gifted with a positive yet practical outlook that few can fault. He especially knows how to avoid trouble and identify opportunity. On the minus side, he can be too flexible in avoiding anything that displeases him; he shuns responsibility and hates futile struggles. He'll bail out if you ask for too much sacrifice and commitment, and if the business is sinking he will not volunteer to go down with the ship.

As a Boss

In this position he will want to be a little spoiled as he expects you to anticipate his wishes and be a self-starter once he has put you on a course. This personality type admires collective effort and team spirit, so you must show camaraderie and good will if you want him to promote you fast. As he hates bickering and back-biting; it is important to maintain the semblance of harmony and a congenial atmosphere at all times in his domain. On the other hand, he is a model of efficiency as he ably plans and organises without too much trouble.

A person of the Mao branch does not have trouble delegating and will give others ample praise and motivation to get the job done. Usually he has the good sense to find the right person for the job. He also hates bad news and interference; these occurrences will undermine his confidence and he could brood for days. Rank-conscious and respectful of his superiors, he expects the same deference from those who work for him. In general he is pleasant and easy to get along with as he normally does not create scenes; he is one person who knows the value of discretion and does not step on anyone's toes if he can help it.

As a Friend and Colleague

This person is most likely to be a kind and thoughtful friend who finds it easy to show sincere concern and consideration. Easily welcomed into any social circles, he will know how to get on the good side of everyone. Of course, he still has that selfish, even narcissistic, streak, but he knows how never to make it look as if he is imposing, so it will be unfair ever to criticise him as insensitive. However, should you dare cross that invisible line and make unreasonable demands on him or his time, he could suddenly clam up and shut you out. A popular party person, great travel bug and shopping companion, he could also be that well-informed man about town who baulks at intrusions and too much dependency. Don't crowd him. However, he does enjoy being consulted on dress, décor, travel, arts and restaurants. He gravitates towards refinement and the better things in life. Naturally, he is likely to maintain the same high standards for the people he mixes with and expect them to be of the same calibre as himself. Sometimes, he can be a bit of a snob.

As an Opponent

A person of the fourth earth branch can be a tough and resilient opponent who might pretend to appear uninterested just to throw you off track. An inscrutable foe, he keeps his aggression well concealed and will employ seemingly harmless manoeuvres to outwit the enemy. Only after one falls into his well-set trap can one appreciate his resourcefulness and that ruthless streak. The best strategy is not to underestimate him or believe his calm reassurances. He may be playing for time (which he usually does), so it is also unwise to cut off communications or discount his intelligence. He always has his ears tuned to new developments and suggestions, or he drops helpful hints on how to resolve things to his satisfaction. Negotiate. Make counteroffers. Send emissaries. As you know, he is a great bridge, chess or poker player, and he won't surrender easily. Rematches are also a certainty, whether he wins or loses.

As the Mediator

The Mao personality is an arbitrator par excellence. His main attraction is that he takes care not to criticise or rub anyone the wrong way. Intuitive and observant, he can sense hidden motives and bad vibrations from any direction. A difficult person to deceive or impress, the Rabbit is able to understand the finer points of each side of the quandary and he may turn out to be the best listener and mediator of all twelve earth branches. What's more he is able patiently to draw out differences between feuding factions and gently force them to face harsh truths and realities. With his true impartiality, he also makes an excellent judge.

The Rabbit or Mao type realises that good relationships are not based or built on having the same views, but rather on accepting the fact that others will have varying opinions, and he is one who allows other people the liberty of having conflicting opinions without condemning them in any way.

RELATIONS WITH OTHER BRANCHES

With a Rat—First Branch

The Rabbit type needs plenty of assurances before making a commitment and, unfortunately, the Rat may be the same. Too much calculating and weighing of pros and cons could undermine a normally congenial, workable relationship. Both parties in this combination may have high expectations and are shrewd when it comes to negotiations. If they share similar interests or a common ascendant in their make-up, they will have much to contribute to their relationship; otherwise, the affectionate and demonstrative Rat may find the Rabbit distant and aloof at times, while the Rabbit, who needs breathing space and his solitude, may feel that the Rat is often critical and too close for comfort. Both need to establish their roles early and allow the other to be himself. One good point here is that while the Rabbit is able to view the entire picture, the Rat will diligently attend to the minute details.

With an Ox—Second Branch

The refined Rabbit has expensive tastes and elegant manners and could find the Ox too tough or regimental for comfort. If these two have similar intellectual as well as artistic pursuits, they may be able to work together, but if the Ox proves demanding and inflexible the Rabbit may run for greener pastures. The Ox, however, may have need of the Rabbit's superior instincts and quick reflexes. If they are able to join forces there should be no strong clashes of personality, as the Rabbit type is not by nature confrontational and will come up with suitable alternatives to work things out amicably if the able Ox contributes his share to the relationship. The Ox will be the hard worker in this combination while the Rabbit goes hunting for good opportunities.

With a Tiger—Third Branch

The tactful but intelligent Rabbit personality could easily outwit and outmanoeuvre the temperamental Tiger whenever he wishes, with no effort at all. In this combination the Tiger will be in need of the Rabbit type's diplomatic capabilities, but the Rabbit may also be enchanted by the magnetic and colourful Tiger assets and promote their mutual interests. The good aspect of this team is that the Rabbit's calm demeanour and level-headedness could help to keep the volatile Tiger person in everyone's good graces. The fearless Tiger has the tendency to broadcast his feelings openly, while the discreet Rabbit will keep a poker face, only divulging what he chooses and nothing else.

With another Rabbit—Fourth Branch

Two people of the fourth branch will work together politely and diligently. In this combination, there will be a good deal of cooperation as both understand the rules of the game. Personalities of the Rabbit type are congenial and helpful by nature and know how to reciprocate. But in a conflict, these two peas from the same pod may isolate themselves and break off communications as they can become indifferent and unresponsive when things do not turn out their way. Not given to violent outbursts, they may calmly assess the situation and decide they have had enough. Although the Rabbit type is quiet and intellectual, he can also nurse grievances and be vindictive when opposed, albeit in a subversive manner. On the whole, two persons of the Rabbit type will work hard at keeping the peace and never openly declare war, no matter how provocative the circumstances.

With a Dragon—Fifth Branch

One hopes that the Dragon will recognise the great connoisseur in a Rabbit ally, for he needs someone to tone down his excesses and bring him the credibility he may need. The Rabbit is a *doyen* of society and will transform the Dragon into a real star, if the Dragon allows him to. A Dragon is domineering by nature and may be overbearing, often alienating the very people who could help him get ahead. The Rabbit will help him find acceptance in an unobtrusive manner. A good working relationship could result if these two realise that teamwork produces synergy. The Rabbit does not strive for recognition as much as the Dragon does. While the Dragon is driven by idealism, the practical Rabbit only worries about receiving just compensation for his efforts, plus a bonus on the side.

With a Snake—Sixth Branch

A Rabbit person could share a love of the finer things in life with the Snake type; together they could pursue knowledge, art or music. However, if they are to have fruitful and lasting bonds, both must give unselfishly to the relationship without counting the costs too carefully. These two could become calculating and difficult when it comes to making sacrifices and may opt to go their separate ways if the going gets tough. They may choose to go sailing together only in a calm sea. However, as both parties here are stable and practical, they do not lose sight of their goals. If they have a mutual objective, no doubt they will do everything in their power to get the job done before settling individual differences.

With a Horse—Seventh Branch

There may be a few hurdles for both parties in this combination before they can live or work together peacefully. First, the Rabbit does not appreciate the Horse's quick temper and impulsiveness, while the Horse finds the Rabbit type passive and too inhibited to be a fun-loving companion. Second, the fiery Horse personality loves adventure and action, while the Rabbit prefers to stick to his home territory instead of running around courting danger. These differences in outlook and attitude could rub both sides up the wrong way. Lastly, the Rabbit will always rely on his own assessment of things and make up his own mind. He will find it hard to understand the Horse type's penchant for frequently changing his mind and moods. These two can only work well together if they share a common ascendant.

With a Sheep—Eighth Branch

The Sheep person shares the Rabbit type's love of harmony and beauty and together they will be able to find much in common. These two types bond easily and are understanding and considerate by nature. The Sheep type is the more generous of the two, while his close ally the Rabbit is more astute and will safeguard their mutual interests at all times. Their close-knit interdependency will certainly nurture an excellent relationship and be beneficial to both sides. The Sheep person may depend on the Rabbit to set their priorities and make sure that they both adhere to a schedule. Both sides are aware of their own strengths and weaknesses in this relationship and each will be happy to know that he can count on the other to come to his aid.

With a Monkey—Ninth Branch
The Rabbit may share the same intellectual as well as artistic pursuits as the Monkey but may find the Monkey too quick and elusive for his liking. Unless these two have a common ascendant or a very strong goal to bind them together, they will develop petty differences that could mar a good relationship. The problem is that they are both selfish and shrewd and will hesitate to enter a deal unless it is to their advantage. If they cannot negotiate the best terms to keep both sides happy, they will keep rewriting the contract. With such able protagonists there is no telling who will be worn out first. However, these two civilised characters will be careful to control their tempers and will strive to keep their options open, just in case they can work things out amicably.

With a Rooster—Tenth Branch
The many differences between these two types stem from misinterpretation of signals. The Rooster carries his expertise like a flag, unfurled and flapping in the wind. He wants the whole world to know how bright and shiny he is. The Rabbit is just as clever and astute, but finds it distasteful to make a spectacle of himself or stoop to arguing and correcting others. The Rabbit considers the Rooster person smug and arrogant, even when he is trying to be genuinely helpful and informative. The Rooster, on the other hand, cannot understand the Rabbit's 'holier than thou' attitude at times, and could feel hurt and rejected by the Rabbit type's indifference. Neither side cares to explain how he thinks and feels because he doubts whether the other will comprehend. Unless they are able to find a good go-between or share a common ascendant, they are going to be far apart in their thinking.

With a Dog—Eleventh Branch
The Rabbit and Dog types will find common ground where they can work. They have compatible temperaments and between them can establish a good level of understanding and trust. In this combination, both are able to share what they have and come out happier and richer for the bargain. Neither of them is unreasonably demanding, although the Rabbit is more even-tempered and has a better hold on his tongue than the Dog does. However, neither will go out of his way to create trouble or upset the apple cart, especially if it will be detrimental to their mutual interests. Dog and Rabbit persons tend to like teamwork and will not let small differences get in their way.

With a Boar—Twelfth Branch
The Boar is known for his strength and stamina while the Rabbit is valued for his intelligence and wise use of strategy. Together they are a winning team as they will present a united front. Each understands the contributions of the other and appreciates whatever talents they possess. These two will establish good lines of communications and have the right chemistry to bond together in a long-term relationship. The Rabbit is the master of behind-the-scenes coups while the Boar is a great promoter and public relations man. No effort is duplicated as each excels in his own area of expertise. They will also take trouble to get to know each other well and will make allowances for each other's likes and dislikes. The Boar is more open and adaptable than the Rabbit; however, the Rabbit has a keen sense of how to bring out the best in the Boar person.

5

THE CHEN BRANCH
FIFTH LUNAR SIGN

The Visionary's Song

I am an unquenchable fire,
the centre of all energy,
the stout heroic heart.
I am truth and light,
I hold power and glory in my sway.
My presence
disperses dark clouds,
I have been chosen
to tame the Fates.

I am Chen, the Visionary

Theodora Lau

THE FIFTH EARTH BRANCH: CHEN
THE SIGN OF THE DRAGON

THE ASSIGNED LUNAR YEARS OF THE DRAGON

February 16, 1904	to February 3, 1905
February 3, 1916	to January 22, 1917
January 23, 1928	to January 9, 1929
February 8, 1940	to January 26, 1941
January 27, 1952	to February 13, 1953
February 13, 1964	to February 1, 1965
January 31, 1976	to February 17, 1977
February 17, 1988	to February 5, 1989
February 5, 2000	to January 23, 2001

If you were born on the day before the lunar year of the Dragon, e.g. February 7, 1940, you belong to the previous earth branch or animal sign which is the fourth branch (the Rabbit).

If you were born on the day after a lunar year ends, e.g. January 27, 1941, you belong to the next earth branch or animal sign, which is the sixth branch (the Snake).

THE FIFTH EARTH BRANCH
THE SIGN OF THE DRAGON

The fifth character profile of the twelve earth branches is that of the Dragon, whose branch is called *Chen* in Chinese and symbolises vitality, leadership and action. The regal Dragon personality views the world as his kingdom where he must work and rule with absolute power. Consequently he always feels obligated to do his very best for the good of all, for if he fails, he expects to be held accountable. On the one hand, he bemoans the heavy burdens imposed upon him; on the other, he demands obedience and loyalty from those he 'claims' to carry on his illustrious back. Actually, it does not matter whether or not you invited him to be at the helm: this person will just assume you need his leadership and guidance but were afraid to ask. Never fear—he, the mighty Dragon, is here. Being one who rarely relinquishes authority or responsibility, he will not enjoy taking a back seat, whatever the situation. Drawn irresistibly to challenges and hard work, he has no doubt of his own sterling ability to vercome opposition and triumph over adversity.

With his enthusiasm and positive attitude the Chen personality often appears larger than life, and although he may fight viciously for the leading position, he often still turns out to be a benevolent leader. In spite of being compassionate as well as highly strung, he may blow hot and cold in one breath and wreak havoc by biting off more than he can chew. But even as he is demanding, dogmatic and overconfident, he is also genuinely helpful and full of good will. A difficult person either to dismiss or ignore, one must both admire and fear the zeal of the Chen-type person.

Adept at expressing his views openly, a person of the fifth branch is never reticent about what he thinks or feels. Rather, he will make a point of broadcasting his opinions and will even ram them down your throat if you dare to question his authority. Upright, strong and decisive, he will never stoop to underhand or covert ways to conquer. With him, every fight will be a duel right out in the open. One cannot help but respect his forthright character and honesty; he may be completely wrong but at least he is never in doubt.

The native of the Chen branch takes his responsibilities very seriously and will try with all his might to live up to the faith placed in him, because to him there must always be some idealistic mission or special purpose in his life. Don't be concerned, he will find his role models and superheroes early in life, as the Dragon type has an overabundant energy and will always be on the look-out for causes to champion. With him you will not have to worry whether or not he does the job, but, rather whether he knows when enough is enough and has the good sense to stop when he should. He tends to outperform and overdo things if you do not limit his powers.

Strong and high-spirited, the Dragon is drawn to power and influence, and consequently has a great affinity with success. Bold and dynamic by nature, he possesses a strong temper and sharp tongue when angered, but he quickly gets over his outburst and does not have a vindictive heart or a long memory. Rather, he would prefer to get on with the task in hand and draw everyone together with his strength and encouragement to accomplish common goals. The Dragon type's aggression may be overpowering or it may be subtle like a dormant fire, but it is always there, ready to leap to the fore if he is challenged. However, whatever he chooses to do and whatever ventures he undertakes, this personality always has honourable intentions at heart.

A native of the fifth branch will insist on being socially active and involved in everything that crosses his path—the kind of person you could never tell to mind his own business, because he simply won't. Usually part of a powerful network (which he himself probably established), he will relish being in the thick of things or, better still, at the helm. Skilful at putting his ideas across, he may have trouble listening or being on the receiving end. He suffers from narrow vision because he is usually so confident that his way is the one and only way to succeed. Consequently, he may drown others out by not giving them a chance to speak and later regret his egotistic behaviour. If the Dragon type could try to be less domineering and opinionated he would benefit immensely.

When the Chen or Dragon type believes in something or decides to support someone, you can be sure his dedication will be total. Deeply religious, almost fanatical in his convictions, he will abandon everything to follow the object of his devotion and never look back in regret. He is gifted with the unquestioning faith of a child, and the innocence, too. As a tireless, selfless leader or ardent follower according to circumstances, he will opt for total commitment without complaints or recriminations.

Most of the time, this personality is not aware of his controlling or aggressive ways. He just feels the need to emphasise his strong beliefs and convictions or perhaps reinforce his views as strongly as possible. He is the type who can focus so intensely on a subject that he may set it on fire, like concentrating a magnifying glass on one spot to create a spark. Intolerant of opposition and non-believers, his main fault is his oversized ego which may be wilful and pompous. Yet, in spite of his cavalier attitude and strong prejudices, he is able to inspire others effortlessly with his outgoing and extremely dazzling powers of persuasion. Whatever else he may be, his emotions come straight from his heart, for he strives hard to keep his promises and hold true to his words. Like a gallant captain, he will lead the troops at the head of the charge and never ask anyone to do anything that he is not capable of doing. He could never forgive himself if he was derelict in his duties or failed in his responsibilities.

However, the self-centred personality of the fifth branch can also be belligerent and intimidating when he is crossed or defeated. He does not accept failure graciously and will be unreasonable and loud in his demands, so it may be difficult to convince him that his team lost or that he has followed the wrong path. Eventually, when he finds another cause to champion, he will gradually lose that fanatical grip on the former object of his devotion. By nature, he cares little about his finances and is not materialistic. Whatever resources he has are used to further his ambitions and support his many causes.

An invaluable fund-raiser, he will give generously of his time to charity.

Like the first earth branch, the Rat, and the ninth earth branch, the Monkey type, the Dragon person is a Doer. His bases his total worth on what he can offer others and will constantly measure his own progress and performance, rather like diligently monitoring his own pulse rate or blood pressure. He does not need others to assess, motivate or chastise him; scrupulously honest and selfrighteous, he will strive to measure up to his own high standards. So although he tends to bully others into submission, he is just as hard and unforgiving with himself. He likes to rate himself as a superperformer and prefers to do or to view things on a grand scale. Often, rather than run a pilot project or make a simple scale model, he prefers to go full steam ahead and create either an unbelievable success or a disaster. Of course, it will then have to be a disaster on a grand scale, too. Thankfully, this person will always find people who will come to his rescue and give him wholehearted support.

The native of the fifth earth branch must always believe in his own invincibility; as a result he unconsciously draws those who believe in him to abandon whatever they are doing and blindly follow him like lemmings. The pure Dragon personality will be an extremist who may at times act like a fanatic with an overinflated self-image that makes him difficult to relate to. However, in his positive state he radiates clout and power and his presence injects magnetism and enthusiasm into whatever he is promoting.

As a self-starter, the Dragon type needs no permission, and will ask for none, to get going. Grabbing the bull by the horns, he likes to tackle whatever needs to be done and will take the straight, no-nonsense approach instead of the long winding path of diplomacy. It may not even occur to him that there are several ways to solve his problem. Obstacles in his path may simply be bulldozed out of his way. It's his way or nothing. Yet, despite his intimidating personality, this person cannot function without the company of his loyal supporters and believers. Like a general without an army, he is quite lost by himself. Therefore, he does not relish being isolated or being uninformed about what is going on. He can turn into quite an ogre if he discovers that people are keeping secrets from him or keeping him out of the picture altogether. And you were worried about him causing a little fuss?

Fortunately for everyone, this personality knows the value of good relationships and comradeship. Fiercely loyal and protective of those he loves or supports, he will fight courageously to the bitter end without any regard for himself. This is a strong ally to have on one's side in times of trouble because the formidable Dragon person often accomplishes the impossible just by getting others to believe that he is capable of performing miracles. If anyone can show the merits of positive thinking and the untapped powers of the mind, the Chen personality can.

The best time to get the Dragon to act is when he is all charged up. He tends to be driven by his idealism and selfrighteousness and can make up his mind easily about what action he will take. Not likely to switch sides, he will use all his power to boost his team and unhesitatingly carry them high above his shoulders. As long as he has a cheering squad, there is nothing he cannot or will not do.

An extrovert, avid sportsman, military type, public speaker, religious leader, announcer, media person, lawyer, teacher and politician, a person of the Chen branch is a visionary and his visions are grand. This type of person needs associates who are down-to-earth, perceptive and realistic—people who will capitalise on his many talents yet give him good direction and counselling. Otherwise, he may overextend himself and leap from crisis to crisis; his triumphs as magnified as his failures. This is also the person who may most likely be stressed out because of overcommitment, yet he will never admit it to lesser mortals (that includes all of us). The more one tries to steer him away from controversy, the more headstrong and determined he becomes. At times, he is his own worst enemy.

The Chen branch's amazing buoyancy of spirit and secure faith in himself ensures that he will never pretend or try to be something he is not. He will live up to his reputation and hang on tenaciously, even when matters are most unpleasant. Vocal and militant in defence of his beliefs, he will also display deep religious convictions. A pillar of strength and encouragement in times of trouble, he has a circle of friends and influence that will grow throughout life if he takes care to tone down that direct, often brusque, attitude that could antagonise well-meaning people, especially those of the quiet Sheep and Rabbit types and definitely the Dog (eleventh branch) personality.

The Dragon's immense optimism could work against him, making him prone to rash judgements erring on the side of impulsiveness.

Excitable and impressionable, he hears what he wants to hear and ignores danger signs. He may also conceive instant animosity against those who oppose him or belong to different camps. Scornful of taking the middle of the road, he will love to try the untried and break old records. Tell him something has never been done or cannot be done and he will immediately rush out to do it. When he weaves that magic charm around you, just remember that he sees life in bright, magnificent hues and could overestimate and exaggerate things, making them appear better than they actually are. His visions are potent and very believable, but sometimes illusory as most visions are.

He likes to stimulate those around him to throw caution aside (as he does) and is not above inciting rebellion and revolution when he is disillusioned or stirred up. Always ready to enhance his importance, he will certainly dress for success and will know how to make the best of his appearance. Confident, he exudes a bright aura of personal magnetism that radiates success and strength. However, he does not take advice easily or readily and those who know and love him are aware that the very time when he most adamantly refuses advice may be when he needs it most. The proud person of this earth branch often needs shock treatment to wake him up to the realities around him, and this must be delivered by assertive friends who will not be afraid of him or back down in the fierce backlash of his anger. Although he may refuse to be bothered by minutiae, he needs to have associates who insist that he pays attention to pertinent details, no matter how tiresome he finds them and no matter how much he scoffs and scolds. His downfall may come from leaving details to others after he has made the initial contact, formulated a brilliant strategy, finalised terms and signed the contract. Sometimes, the small day-to-day decisions are what make or break an important company or a good relationship.

Lover of the great outdoors, avid sportsman or sports fan, and an active participant in every sort of movement or new trend, this personality may have the biggest heart of all the twelve earth branches. He unselfishly gives of himself to whatever cause he champions. His best partners are the other members of his Triangle of Affinity: the Rat or first branch and the Monkey or ninth branch. The Rat type, being the Initiator, will most likely come up with bright ideas for the Dragon to visualise and will support him energetically. These two will gravitate towards success and the fruition of their plans, often for different reasons but with the same attitude of mind. The Monkey, the Innovator of the ninth branch, will also realise the Dragon's immense potential and know how to enhance his powers and popularity—pure synergy. Together, these two will make the impossible happen as they combine ingenuity and power. This first triangle of the Doers is the most ambitious and pioneering of all the four Triangles of Affinity.

The Ox of the second branch, the Snake of the sixth branch and the Rooster of the tenth branch are all able to work fairly well with the Dragon type as they are not easily intimidated and are too practical to be swayed by the Dragon's arguments once they have made up their own minds. The Rabbit personality of the fourth branch, the Sheep type of the eighth branch and the Boar person of the twelfth branch are less compatible as they are sensitive to criticism and do not like challenging the often pompous, highly strung Dragon. The Triangle of the Tiger (third branch), the Horse (seventh branch) and the Dog (eleventh branch) is the area where the Dragon personality will encounter the most resistance. These outspoken personalities will not be afraid to question his motives, investigate his sources and scrutinise his moves. The Dragon will be shocked and offended that they should dare, but he must realise that these three aggressive extroverts are just as idealistic, passionate and forthright as he is.

Remember, the Chen type of the fifth branch is the Visionary of the cycle and his key phrase is: 'I see'.

TRIANGLE OF AFFINITY

The Dragon type is the second player in the First Triangle of Affinity which consists of a group of three positive Doers of the Twelve Earth Branches. There are four Triangles of Affinity in which all the personality types are grouped. There is one Circle of Conflict in which all opposite branches are incompatible. In the First Triangle we have the Rat, Dragon and Monkey, respectively the first, fifth and ninth branches.

The trio who make up the First Triangle of Affinity are a group of positive people who are identified as Doers. They enjoy hands-on activity and are performance and progress orientated, adept at handling matters with initiative and innovation. These three players prefer

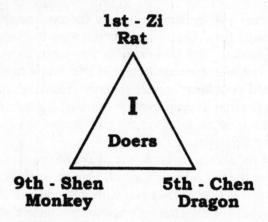

1st - Zi
Rat

I

Doers

9th - Shen   **5th - Chen**
Monkey   **Dragon**

to initiate action, clear their paths of obstacles and will not hesitate to forge ahead. Restless or short-tempered when hindered or unoccupied, they are fuelled by dynamic energy and ambition. The occupants of the First Triangle are the ones who produce revolutionary ideas and who strive to make great things happen. They can team up beautifully as they have a common way of understanding or doing things and will certainly appreciate each other's way of thinking.

CIRCLE OF CONFLICT

The Fifth Earth Branch will encounter his strongest opposition and personality clashes from persons belonging to the eleventh branch, or natives of the Dog sign. Those whose birth time or ascendant is

5th - Chen
Dragon

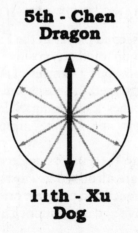

11th - Xu
Dog

during the hours of the Dog (between 7 p.m. and 9 p.m.) will also come into conflict with the Chen personality type; they tend to have opposing points of view. The tough and rational Dog type can be too guarded and hostile to be enchanted by the Dragon personality. With his tendency to be pragmatic and cynical, the Dog person will question the Dragon too closely for comfort. The Dragon type is not able to work well with someone who will challenge or investigate him when he finds things not to his liking and he may discover that people of the eleventh branch are too realistic and independent to follow him blindly. These two cannot see eye to eye, nor will they keep quiet about their misgivings. To avoid senseless and unproductive confrontations, it would be best for them to work through intermediaries and mutual friends who could bridge their differences.

RELATIONSHIPS WITH THE FIFTH EARTH BRANCH—THE DRAGON

Within the Family

Within the heart of his immediate family the Dragon type will want top billing, and he will work hard to earn his position. He would like to be seen, heard and deferred to. Of course, he is ever mindful of his duties and responsibilities and he fulfils his obligations well. The family with a person of the fifth earth branch in it will always rally to a common theme. Somehow, the Chen personality will always volunteer his services to help others and will expect his family members to do the same. They will be most united in times of crisis.

As a parent, he or she will have a goal to unify everyone and it will be them against the world or the forces of evil. He will always find something to conquer, a deadline to meet, someone to rescue or a special project to complete. Idleness is quite foreign to him and his pioneering spirit. Often, his strong willpower galvanises his family to maintain a high profile and take strong stands on dominant issues. It doesn't matter if it's just a small function in his neighbourhood, church, football team or local school—he is always motivated to get involved and show his leadership abilities.

As a child, he will take the initiative, insisting that his parents trust him implicitly and give him responsibilities and important tasks to perform. One can imagine the little embryonic Dragon running about giving orders and taking charge of his playmates. If he feels neglected, suppressed or ignored, he may misdirect his energies and turn into a real troublemaker.

This personality is always ready to make great sacrifices for his loved ones and carry burdens for them. He willingly holds the torch for the family name and honour and will place great emphasis on his reputation and accomplishments. Above all, he needs to be needed and respected more than loved.

As a Teacher
Helpful and awe-inspiring, the Chen personality of the fifth branch revels in his role as an educator. He considers himself the ultimate, larger than life example to emulate, so one can be sure that he will relate his lessons to his own life experiences and successes. One way or another, this type of teacher loves referring to history, war campaigns and conquests, triumph over adversities or obstacles and, of course, his own heroes and mentors in life. He demands respect from his students and erases any self-doubts that he may find in his charges. Above all, he feels that as a teacher and role model, he must instil confidence as much as knowledge.

He makes a marvellous teacher as he is always positive and enthusiastic. His dedication is admirable and he will go out of his way to make his students relate to him and what he is trying to teach them. It should be easy for them to draw from his strength and forgive him his eccentricities. Somehow, all who come in contact with his magnetic personality leave benefiting from the genuine helpfulness and sincerity of his strong character. Unlike someone who likes to preach but not perform, the Dragon or Chen type has the aptitude to do both.

As a Lover and Spouse
Passionate, giving and totally partial when in love; this type is blind to the faults of his loved ones and will shield the object of his affection against anyone or anything that could hurt or threaten his love. More than happy to give his all in a relationship and to prove himself worthy (you must always allow him to prove his worth), he will be gallant, demonstrative and forceful in courtship and marriage. The person of the Chen branch is most likely to place the object of his admiration on a pedestal (along with his other heroes) and pay homage with his heart in his hand. However, if he discovers that the one

he adores is unworthy of him or has betrayed his trust, he can be jut as vilifying. More valuable to him than love is mutual respect and a sharing of ideals and common beliefs. If possible he will seal his bond of love with shared victories in which his love participates in the battle against the opposition.

He will bare his soul to his loved one and have no secrets whatsoever. But in spite of his trusting nature, beware of his demanding ways and love of being in control. This is a very difficult person to change and, in most cases, it may be futile to make the attempt.

His best partners in love are persons from the first and ninth earth branches who know how to read him well and understand his way of thinking. Together they form the elite inner circle and express their passions and dedication without reserve. In love and romance he may move very fast or be totally unaware of his strong feelings until they hit him hard, right between the eyes. However, once he realises his true emotions, he will never deny what he is feeling. Honest and sometimes naive to the point of being credulous, he could be quite easily hurt in tender affairs of the heart because of his lack of inhibitions or defences against the intricacies of love.

As a Business Partner

A person of the fifth earth branch will be able to raise money for any venture and sound the trumpets far and wide. Drawing upon his enormous circle of friends, he will energetically work for the success of the business. However, he does not like to share equal billing with others in the team and could be hard to supervise or control when it comes to decision-making. His aggression and normal competitiveness may lead the company into dangerous waters, so more conservative people need to hold the purse strings, tone down his expectations and unrestrained promotion as well as watch the legal aspects and exposure of the firm.

Responsible and responsive to the right kind of partners, he will work well with the first branch (Rat) and ninth branch (Monkey) people who know exactly how to talk to him and steer him to where he is most needed. Often, it is best only to let him know what is absolutely necessary so that he will not over-predict profits or underestimate losses. He tends to concentrate on the bright side and will be most surprised when you inform him that there is a downside to things, too.

People with Dragon ascendants, born between 7 a.m. and 9 a.m. but belonging to more pragmatic earth branches such as the Ox and the Rooster, will also be excellent partners who could safeguard the welfare of everyone in a partnership. In business, the Dragon type needs able partners to trim his sails occasionally in a storm and help him wait out a difficult period without losing his enthusiasm or confidence.

As a Boss
A natural-born leader, this personality's self-esteem can be overwhelming at times. He definitely enjoys 'bossdom'. Outspoken and ambitious, he does not shrink from duty but rather pursues his objective and assumes everyone will go along wholeheartedly with him once he leads the way. Not above cracking the whip, he cannot tolerate a break in the ranks or any whiff of disloyalty. Yet he favours self-starters and bright, spunky persons who will work on their own initiative and who will not allow him to bully them or shut them up without a fair hearing. He could even find it amusing if his subordinates refuse to be intimidated and fight back sometimes to show they have some mettle.

I once had a Dragon-type boss who managed a large hotel chain. He paid the highest wages and gave the most benefits, but now and then he would get so incensed about someone's failure to follow one of his imperious directives that he would fire everyone within hearing range in an angry fit, calling all those around him jellyfish (because he was the only one with the spine). The following day the staff would all return to work and act as if nothing had happened. It seemed he needed such displays to vent his frustrations, and after a while we took them in our stride. Of course, there were always timid souls who were frightened out of their wits and who could not or would not tolerate the fireworks that came with this personality, or felt most threatened by his domineering presence.

As a Friend and Colleague
The native of the fifth branch makes a loyal and genuine friend although as a colleague he may have a degree of superiority complex and make you feel that he is just one tiny notch above you, but since he is ready to take the lead and initiative, he will usually pave the way for others to have better working conditions, and that can't be

all bad. He also tends to be overzealous and condescending as a friend, and if you are not assertive he will run your life and the office domain, too, as he prefers to take charge. Unknowingly, he may be critical or domineering even when at heart he is truly concerned for your interests. In reality, he often allows himself to be carried away by his need to show everyone the way and neglects to solicit opinions and ideas from others.

Yet one could not find a more devoted, open-hearted friend or stalwart ally than this personality type. His vibrant, positive attitude is wonderful to have around and one can always count on him to support his friends unequivocally in times of need.

As an Opponent

Unrelenting, fierce and about as subtle as a runaway goods train that has gone off its tracks, the Chen-Dragon type will definitely come after his rivals and make the first explosive move. One can expect this person to seek out his opponent and issue a direct challenge; he does not like to mince words. Unafraid of retaliation, this type is usually brilliant at the outset but may not keep any reserves or ammunition for future battles. Perhaps he assumes others will be bowled over by his fierce charge and will surrender. Consequently, he may not be equipped for long-term or drawn-out struggles and litigation; his patience and determination could wear thin after several bouts.

Often, he will not allow others to get a word in edgeways and may then suffer from a lack of vital information, since he has effectively cut off the communication links. Although he often has the outward confidence of a sure winner, it would be wise for him never to assume that the other side is as weak or as unprepared as he may wish to believe.

His strength lies in his ability to impress upon his opponent his love of justice and fair play and his willingness to forgive or negotiate in order to reach agreement. Contrary to his beliefs, the mere flexing of his legal and rhetorical muscles may not always scare the opposition off, so he must look for ways to allow others to save face and give assurances that he can and will behave reasonably when given the upper hand. It is always much better when the Dragon decides to behave nicely than having others resort to extreme measures to force him to swallow his pride.

As the Mediator

This personality type of the fifth earth branch could be an untiring and truly dedicated mediator. You may not even have to solicit his help: he may simply volunteer for the job. His main assets are his clout and popularity. He does not allow details or minor differences to get in his way when he knows the objective is to get both sides to the table and open the lines of communications. A person of this branch will strong-arm his way around and drag obstinate and unwilling parties to the negotiations with missionary zeal. Chairing the discussions, he will use his influence wisely and appeal to the higher instincts and values of those involved.

Like a wise but impartial judge, he has the charisma to preside royally over the warring factions and will not tolerate any underhand or dirty tricks from either side. This offends his integrity. However, if he fails to work out an amicable settlement after all his valiant efforts, don't be surprised if he takes matters into his own hands and issues his own judgement anyway, dictating the best terms of any resolution by himself. Sometimes, his unconventional and dictatorial ways could persuade others that his determination to resolve matters is immeasurably greater than their petty quarrel. And, fearing that his cure may be worse than their affliction, they would rather settle with his blessing than his curse.

He will not feel he has done his duty as a mediator or act as a good arbitrator unless he shepherds everyone diligently to a workable solution. He takes it as a personal failure if both sides do not manage to work out their differences, despite his vigorous intervention.

RELATIONS WITH OTHER BRANCHES

With a Rat—First Branch

Being members of the same Triangle of Affinity, the Rat and Dragon types have a natural sympathy for one another. The Dragon is enchanted by the Rat person's intelligence and innovation while the Rat is drawn to the Dragon's vitality and idealism. This dynamic pair will love, work and play well together, each encouraging the other to do his or her best. The Dragon provides the energy and power while the Rat shows great support and resourcefulness for the Dragon's dreams. A lasting and strong relationship is in store for both parties as their potential is doubled when they join forces.

Both types here are self-assured and dependable in performing their duties and will find their association beneficial and gratifying. The Dragon personality will chart the course and forge fearlessly ahead with his foremost cheer-leader, the Rat, loyally at his side.

With an Ox—Second Branch

The Dragon type is the ambitious idealist in this combination while the Ox is the calm and collected realist. Both have strong convictions and take responsibilities seriously. The Dragon values the integrity he sees in the Ox personality and the Ox recognises the Dragon's qualities of leadership. If there are any battles between these two, they must be resolved fairly quickly or they could escalate into major wars. However, both are work-orientated and view their accomplishments highly rather than dwelling on their individual opinions. They can both stay focused on their goals and will not allow their personal or subjective wishes to get in their way. The Ox is the more reliable of the two but the Dragon gives impetus and life to their joint ventures should they decide to cooperate.

With a Tiger—Third Branch

Both personalities here are easily motivated and ready for action. The Dragon will be able to share his lofty ideals with the courageous Tiger person and their similar interests and goals could create a good relationship. Neither will be intimidated by the other once they have defined their areas of expertise. The Dragon could be a positive influence on the Tiger and direct him when he tries to dissipate energy by doing too much, while the Tiger's innate charm and ability to influence people on a large scale will prove beneficial for the Dragon's purposes. There won't be a dull moment in this exciting partnership provided each can accept the other as an equal, because neither is comfortable playing second fiddle for too long.

With a Rabbit—Fourth Branch

If the Dragon recognises the Rabbit personality as a mitigating force that could be useful in his life, these two will get along well. Otherwise, the Dragon may unwittingly oppress the unassuming Rabbit and gain an enemy instead of an ally. The Rabbit may also be intimidated by the imposing ways of the Dragon and find his domineering attitude hard to swallow. Yet the magnanimous Dragon has much to offer the Rabbit in return and will reward the Rabbit generously for his services or assistance. Unlike the Dragon, the Rabbit may not crave the limelight but would still like to be recognised for his contributions. If the Dragon is wise and wants to have a long-term association with the Rabbit type, he must always remember to solicit the Rabbit's advice and never neglect or take him for granted.

With another Dragon—Fifth Branch
In such a combination the forces are equally matched. These two like personalities may find each other enormously appealing and become inseparable because they share the same philosophy and fight for the same causes. Conversely, they may fight for leadership and refuse to recognise each other's rights. Everything depends on how they choose to direct their power and energies. However, since Dragon people usually know what they want and do make up their minds fairly quickly, these two should be able to sort out their differences or move on to another team. They are not likely to change their strong convictions or reverse their stance, so the decision to work together will, in most cases, be sincere and not forced. On the whole Dragon types respect authority and integrity and, hopefully, they will see these mutual qualities in each other.

With a Snake—Sixth Branch
The Dragon and Snake are both drawn to ambition and success and will therefore join forces if there is much to gain. The Snake is the introverted Thinker while the Dragon is the positive Doer. Together, they will seek to address all the issues and conquer any odds that may be in their path. The Dragon will be the more outgoing and aggressive partner while the Snake could match him with his constancy and secretive nature. Each partner here is his own man or woman and will not accept an inferior position if he or she can help it. The Snake will be more of a pragmatist in this combination and is always anticipating trouble and preparing for unforeseen contingencies. On the other hand, the Dragon is the high-powered optimist, who often needs the voice of wisdom and caution that the Snake type will provide.

With a Horse—Seventh Branch

The Dragon personality has an affinity with power while the Horse is known for his agility and speed. When they team up, both will realise that each has something the other needs. It would be foolish to assume that there will be no struggles or flared tempers in this combination, as both sides are competitive by nature and have strong wills. However, both the Dragon and the Horse are skilled in communication and will readily affirm or object when things are not to their liking. Because they do not hesitate to air their views, it is easy for them to clear the air quickly in any disagreement or misunderstanding. Both parties here do not carry grudges and will allow bygones to be bygones once they forgive and forget.

With a Sheep—Eighth Branch

The Sheep is drawn to the vibrant Dragon personality yet intimidated by his domineering nature. The confident Dragon could do wonders for the creative Sheep if the Sheep type can accept the Dragon's leadership, which he most likely will find useful. However, the Dragon can overpower the Sheep with his demanding ways and the Sheep may not be able to get away with much when he is under the control of a dynamic Dragon. The Dragon hates doing things halfway or with little conviction and will no doubt grab the Sheep by the horns and shepherd him all the way to the finishing line, whether the Sheep likes it or not.

With a Monkey—Ninth Branch

This partnership will have two very energetic characters who represent both sides of the coin. The Monkey is a problem-solver and will invent new solutions where none exist. The Dragon is hypnotised by the Monkey's clever and shrewd tactics and believes that the Monkey type has all the answers for which he searches. Together they make a formidable team of wits and strength. Each is able skilfully to handle the other without too much trouble. The Monkey knows how to stroke the Dragon's ego to his advantage and the Dragon will more than give the Monkey just recognition for his ingenuity. If they bond well, these two will find each other indispensable in a relationship.

With a Rooster—Tenth Branch

The Dragon appreciates the Rooster's administrative qualities and organisational talents. He does not mind the Rooster type's critical eye and need for perfection. Both are able to stand their own ground and hold their own in any confrontation. The Rooster is an optimist like the zealous Dragon and will aggressively seek to pursue their objectives. The Dragon may plan things on a grand scale and woo the public with his brilliant enthusiasm while the Rooster attends to everyday details and balances the books. The Rooster is also a strong enough personality not to let the Dragon step out of line or put up with his pompous or unreasonable demands.

With a Dog—Eleventh Branch

The Dragon and Dog personalities have serious problems with communications and cannot have a dialogue because each tends to misread the intentions of the other. The Dog is a realist who finds the high-spirited Dragon too extreme for his taste, while the Dragon does not like to have his dreams and ambitions questioned or ridiculed by the cynical Dog who would rather be conservative than overoptimistic. In retaliation, the Dragon may refuse to associate with someone who is as outspoken and unsupportive as the Dog personality. Unless these two share a common ascendant, it would be advisable for them to deal through intermediaries or mutual friends. Otherwise the underlying friction that exists between the two could ignite personality clashes in which both sides lose.

With a Boar—Twelfth Branch

The honest and outgoing Boar personality will be honoured to be one of the Dragon's friends and will find his enthusiasm contagious. They will find no great barriers in their path if they decide to have a close relationship. The Boar is easygoing and not averse to the Dragon taking the lead so long as he can join the party. The Dragon finds the sociable Boar congenial and popular with all the right people. Both are passionate and sincere when it comes to pursuing their desires and objectives, although the Dragon is more egotistic while the Boar may carry things to excess and have trouble knowing when to stop. Neither party in this combination is sensitive by nature or easily offended by criticism and, due to their positive attitudes, they can both recover quickly from setbacks without too much difficulty.

6

THE SI BRANCH
SIXTH LUNAR SIGN

The Strategist's Song

Mine is the wisdom of the ages,
I hold the key to the mysteries of life.
Casting my seeds on fertile ground
I nurture them with constancy and purpose.
My sights are fixed.
My gaze unchanging.
Unyielding, inexorable and deep
I advance with steady, unslackened gait,
The solid earth beneath me.

I am Si, the Strategist

Theodora Lau

THE SIXTH EARTH BRANCH: SI
THE SIGN OF THE SNAKE

THE ASSIGNED LUNAR YEARS OF THE SNAKE

February 4, 1905	to	January 24, 1906
January 23, 1917	to	February 10, 1918
February 10, 1929	to	January 29, 1930
January 27, 1941	to	February 14, 1942
February 14, 1953	to	February 2, 1954
February 2, 1965	to	January 20, 1966
February 18, 1977	to	February 6, 1978
February 6, 1989	to	January 26, 1990
January 24, 2001	to	February 11, 2002

If you were born on the day before the lunar year of the Snake, e.g. February 1, 1965, you belong to the previous earth branch or animal sign which is the fifth branch (the Dragon).

If you were born on the day after a lunar year ends, e.g. January 21, 1966, you belong to the next earth branch or animal sign, which is the seventh branch (the Horse).

THE SIXTH EARTH BRANCH
THE SIGN OF THE SNAKE

The sixth character profile of the twelve earth branches is that of the Snake, whose branch is called *Si* in Chinese and symbolises ambition and wisdom. The Snake personality is coiled around his environment and draws strength from it as well as nurturing it. Cool and collected, he is never in a hurry—for there is no need to be. His influence is encompassing and enduring. Patient yet simmering with pent-up ambition, he is quietly aggressive in his own dignified way. The Si or Snake type delights in biding his time, gathering his forces and striking with speed and accuracy at the exact moment. Zap! In the blink of an eye, he has taken control. And, once he has assumed control there is no way he will give up what he has acquired. One may have to pry him off and then may even be caught in the Si's vicelike grip if one is not careful. Rarely one to give any warning, this person asks for no quarter and won't be giving any either. The shortest distance between him and the object of his attention is a straight line and one can be sure he will take that route. The problem is trying to guess when and how he will strike out.

This personality is the second of the Thinkers in his Triangle of Affinity. He is most difficult to fathom and does not like to reveal how he works things out or how he arrives at his decision. Like the other two signs in his triangle, the Ox (the Enforcer) and the Rooster (the Administrator), this type thrives on careful planning. He is called the Strategist of the Twelve Earth branches and he carries an army of tactics in his superb brain. Gifted with an intelligent and sharply analytical mind, he knows how to separate and weigh facts by their own merits. Like a harmless-looking sponge, he will soak up information quickly and efficiently but release little, even when he is saturated. It is not his nature to be open and candid—even in the most relaxing situations.

The Snake person prefers to be an enigma and does not like others to know too much about him; perhaps it would lessen the mystery in which he has enveloped himself. Tension is usually hidden in this personality like a coiled spring, and the tighter it becomes, the more nervous he is internally. However, one rarely sees any visible clues to his inner disposition. Self-contained and intensely competitive, he can be vindictive in his slow-burning anger. However, the Si or Snake type never plays any game without carefully understanding or laying down the ground rules. He masterfully projects a carefully crafted image of himself as an expert in whatever game is afoot. In reality, he may be slothful and taken to enjoy long periods of dormancy and idleness. Then, when he awakens and is stimulated by something that captures his imagination, he will use the element of surprise in his attacks and strategies. The Snake person likes intrigue and draws upon his own sixth sense to make predictions that usually hold true.

Unlike the Dragon or Tiger personalities who go in search of adventure and may stalk their prey, the Snake type sees no necessity for stalking anything or anyone. Patiently, he waits for them to come to him. And we all know that 'all things come to him who waits'. Because of his seeming lack of interest in making unnecessary efforts, this person may give the appearance of being superficial or a dilettante. He could be a late riser or a languid person who enjoys the comforts of a soft, pampered life. But his keen powers of observation are always switched on, and if something piques his interest he will come alive with amazing speed. A reclusive intellectual, he can concentrate on one thing at a time until he masters it. By nature he may be sentimental and susceptible to mood changes.

There is a sceptical streak in this personality and he must investigate everything closely before giving it his personal stamp of approval. He does not warm easily to new acquaintances, inventions or revolutionary methods of doing things, nor does he adjust well to changes in his environment or even changes in the weather or the temperature around him. Because of his introspective nature and suspicious mind, he may suffer bouts of depression or loneliness unless he learns to confide in others and develop close ties with loved ones. Companionship and friendship are essential to keep him in balance with the world around him and bring out the best in him.

The Snake type will often withdraw into himself and meditate. He will ponder long and deeply before deciding what action to take or while plotting a new course. This type is careful, even paranoid and fastidious in his habits, and as a rule he cannot and does not take rejection easily. Possessive, jealous and self-centred (although he may never openly admit it), he has difficulty letting go and could become obsessed with a person or thing. Yet socially he can be witty, humorous and very charming. Some outstanding Snake personalities have been John F. Kennedy, Mao Zedong, Mahatma Gandhi, Abraham Lincoln, Pablo Picasso, Greta Garbo and Jacqueline Onassis.

A lover of beauty and the finer things in life, this reflective personality gravitates towards cultural pursuits and could have many artistic talents. He is also a skilful judge of character and can identify potential, which makes him an excellent talent scout, agent, publicity manager and discoverer of tomorrow's stars and headlines. The Si branch is a feminine sign and belongs to the Yin side of balance. Likewise, as a sign of the Yin side, the Snake will have a duality in his nature and his passiveness is a weapon in itself; his motives are usually hidden, and for good reason. It is his ability to endure and cope that will help him attain those high goals he seeks.

In life, his shortcoming may be his inability to communicate well with others and his tendency to withdraw inwards at times when it is essential for him to reach out and ask for help or information. Too sparing with his words, it will be hard to extract information from him and help him. He also tends to isolate himself and make his own judgements. And although he may be superior in his ability to assess and deduce, he must realise that no one is infallible. However, because he is fearful of failure, rejection or ridicule, he will hold everything inside and put up a brave front.

In business relations with the Snake type it would be wise to rely on his shrewd planning and ability to link up with the right or important people. This personality knows where and who to go to when he needs vital information or approval. However, it is also difficult to work closely with him as he always holds something back to bargain with later on; this could cause problems as others may accuse him of not being entirely forthright. His reserved and secretive nature makes him conceal little things that may be inconsequential, but the truth is that he does not relish opening his heart and mind. Forcing him to change may merely result in his being more reclusive than ever. He is usually successful in business because as a strategist he is always planning and scheming the next move and likes to stay a few steps ahead of the opposition. He also makes a point of knowing the competition and keeping tabs on exactly where they are and what they are doing. Espionage and the buying or selling of valuable information could be employed by this person to his advantage. As far as he is concerned, business is war and he will employ the best tactics to win whatever battle he is fighting.

A native of this earth branch will have distinctive public and private faces. He does not give out information about himself readily— only on a 'need to know' basis. And if he thinks you don't have to know a certain thing about him, he will never divulge it to you. No, he won't offer explanations, nor will he make up excuses. He will guard his privacy with a vengeance and coldly tell you to mind your own business.

Consequently, people may have different opinions of the Snake type. A colleague he works with may know him as studious, quiet and thorough, while a friend with whom he shares a love for a certain sport may know him as an avid fan and devoted enthusiast. No two persons will get the same reaction from him. In private, he may allow those close to him or his family to call him by his pet names and tease him, but in public he will not tolerate even the slightest disrespect. In times of extreme stress and conflict he will go to extremes and erect high walls around himself, or set up iron defences.

In affairs of the heart he can suffer romantic entanglements which could cause his perspective to become distorted by passion and possessiveness. He may find himself at the centre of a dilemma, and the more he tries to extricate himself the more complicated matters become. The best strategy for the Snake person in such situations is to come clean and apologise, confess or do whatever is necessary to defuse the problem before it gets worse. Prolonging the agony or delaying the inevitable will only make him more bitter and self-destructive. However, the Snake personality does not have the inborn ability to compromise with ease, so he will need a lot of outside help in this respect. With him, it may be a tug of war between his public and private sides.

One of the quirks of the Si personality is his need to draw associates closer when he feels they are moving away, and then to put distance between himself and those who try to get too close to him. He seems to have two comfort zones and he moves back and forth to suit his moods. However, he is never as complacent as he may let you believe and most of the time he is worrying about something while pretending all is well. He loves to plot and create scenarios and may be manipulative and status-conscious when he is insecure in a relationship. His mind is always at work and he is hard to predict or control. To work effectively with this personality type, it is necessary to gain his confidence and address his insecurities and worries right up front. Speak frankly and agree on what rules to play by. Once he respects you and feels you have much to contribute, he will be attentive and cooperative. But be forewarned that he does not like to relinquish his authority and cannot endure too much interference. He can be merciless to meddlers who intrude on his privacy. A pursuer of power and clout, the Snake person is often subdued and observant, carefully taking mental notes. Not one to make the first move or give any promises without doing his homework or getting the proper reassurances, he likes to hedge his bets and eliminate risks whenever possible.

His remarkable tenacity and resoluteness enable him to stay on track and remain focused on his objective. He will set his priorities and does not like to budge from his position. Actually, he is one of the people most likely to become entrenched in a position once he has made up his mind to stay on that course. Unafraid to make the necessary sacrifices to fulfil his dreams, he is not an easy person to sway or induce to change his mind.

In his habits, especially in personal hygiene, diet and dress, he can be particular and even paranoid. Obstinate and unyielding on personal issues and tastes, he may have ears only for certain music, eyes for certain kinds of arts and a nose for his favourite perfumes or cuisine. His tastes will definitely be classical and refined. His possessions seem to increase in value as the years go by because of his foresight and uncanny flair for accurately recognising value. Well turned out, with elegant manners, he may be a distinguished speaker who can sway the crowds with his eloquence. On the other hand, he may also make the most frightful threats without ever raising the tone of that soft-spoken, cultured voice. It would be unwise for anyone to take his threats lightly as he will not issue the same warning twice.

On the whole, the Si personality is more evasive than aggressive. He retaliates only when he has to, and if he is ruthless in crushing the enemy it is only when he reasons that it would be better to annihilate his foe to prevent future attacks. After all, a wounded foe is more dangerous than one who is still uninjured. In this area, the native of the sixth branch has the Killer instinct. Furthermore, he has a good memory and will keep lists and files on everyone. He feels secure knowing where everything is and how everyone is doing. You can be sure he will take care never to turn his back on his opponent.

Aloof and uncommunicative when he is under siege, he has an extreme fear of failure and dreads ever being rejected. He tends to overanalyse the motives of those around him and when he feels threatened may magnify his problems by suspecting everyone. Remember, he keeps his problems close to his bosom and likes to worry and prod a puzzle from every angle. With calm resolution and tenacity he will turn a puzzle over and over in his head until he finds the missing piece.

On the surface, he personifies charm and elegance. He will cater to the wishes of those he needs to cultivate and know how to get the influence or assistance of those in a position to help him achieve his ends. Suave, smooth and debonair, he can be the life of the party and a steadfast supporter of important issues. Cerebral, he can solve complicated problems with ease, especially when he is not personally involved or has a stake in the outcome. This type has the knack for seeing past obstacles and smoke screens and getting to the crux of the matter. Difficult to deceive and hard to deter, he has much to contribute. He gives sage advice; is able to impart calm and accurate analysis and often comes up with novel ways of resolving issues. Of course, sometimes his brutal practicality could earn him the reputation of being ruthless and self-serving, but in times of trouble he possesses clarity of mind and is not afraid of acting decisively.

The Snake personality works best with members of his Triangle of Affinity and will have close relationships with people of the Ox (second branch) and the Rooster (tenth branch). All three being thinkers and worriers, they will enjoy discussing, plotting, scheming and planning all the details before acting upon anything. Not likely to be blamed for shoddy investigation or poor strategy and research, this trio will support each other and reinforce their particular way of thinking and doing things. They dislike leaving anything to chance and will definitely want to influence or control the outcome of their endeavours. As a result, they have the highest probability of successful relationships.

The least compatible allies of the Snake or Si branch will be people of the twelfth earth branch or the Boar personality. The Boar type is too trusting and will rely on the good will and generosity of others to further his cause, which the Snake person may find foolish, naive and even objectionable. These two see life from different ends of the spectrum and will not find it easy to work together or combine their resources for the common good. The honest Boar is too open and forthright for the introverted Snake, who will insist upon a self-discipline and discretion that the Boar does not possess.

Generally, the Snake personality prides himself on being organised, knowing what he wants and being well-informed. He usually keeps his opinions to himself and does not give counsel unless requested to do so. However, he does weigh himself on different scales and rationalises his need for security and power. His wisdom and ambitiousness could act like a double-edged sword, cutting both ways. A solitary fighter; his inner struggle is constant but invisible. The secret of his success is his vision, combined with constancy and tenacity. With these traits he is able to rise to great heights and achieve his lofty ambitions.

As the Strategist of the cycle, the Si type's key phrase in life is: 'I plan'.

TRIANGLE OF AFFINITY

The Snake or Si personality is the second member of the Second Triangle of Affinity which produces a group of three introspective Thinkers of the Twelve Earth Branches. There are four Triangles of Affinity in which the personality types are grouped and one Circle of Conflict in which all opposite branches are incompatible. In the second triangle we have the Ox, Snake and Rooster, respectively the second, sixth and tenth branches.

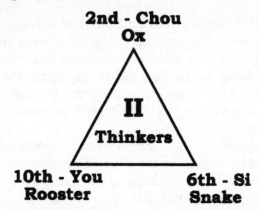

2nd - Chou
Ox

II
Thinkers

10th - You   6th - Si
Rooster   Snake

The members of this trio occupying the Second Triangle of Affinity are a group of purposeful thinkers who like quietly to compose their thoughts and strategy before taking any action. They are the planners, the schemers and the meticulous decision-makers who base things on statistics and information. Unlikely to need the approval of others once they have made up their minds, these personalities only need their own validation that they are doing the right thing and following the correct course. They prefer to observe, ponder and investigate before making any judgement. They check out facts, look into details and generally like to have all available contingencies thoroughly explained before they will make any move.

The three Thinkers tend to have introspective and egotistic characters. Secretive, reserved and often stoical, they are also consistent, tenacious and gifted with foresight and fortitude. They will be recognised for their dedication to duty, patience and ability to inspire others by their example. Able to wait out and out-think the competition, the Ox, Snake and Rooster personalities can reach their goals through calm resolution and determination.

In order to work well with these personalities, one needs to have the facts and figures ready and to address their analytical capabilities. Explain how they will benefit both in the long and short term; how to plough back the profits and how things will pay off in stages as they profit slowly but surely. They tend to avoid taking risks and dislike gambling or speculative ventures. They can be ruthless in their quest for power and will not hesitate to eliminate those who block their path. This is because power translates into control. Intelligent, practical and calculating, they are as systematic in dealing with their problems as with their enemies. Cautious, deliberate and industrious, they will follow their intellect instead of their emotions. Always careful to address all issues before making a decision, they are hard on themselves and their partners when an enterprise or business venture stumbles or fails. These are very business-minded personalities who will always be out to turn a profit or reap some reward for their efforts, and being great believers in their own capabilities, they will work tirelessly until their efforts bear fruit. Others tend to rely on them to be the visionaries of the future and will hitch a ride with this stalwart trio to new heights of success.

The three performers of the Second Triangle of Affinity will be able to get along fabulously in love and business. Working as a team is easy and beneficial for them as they appreciate each other's way of thinking. As marriage and business partners, they will find understanding and work productively towards common goals. They value stability and long-term relationships and will have the endurance and confidence needed to support one another in their endeavours.

People with their ascendant signs belonging to this Second Triangle of Affinity will also be able to establish close ties with the natives of this group and find much in common.

CIRCLE OF CONFLICT

The Snake personality of the Si earth branch will encounter his biggest clashes and opposition from persons belonging to the twelfth branch or a native of the Boar sign. The kindly Boar personality will

6th - Si
Snake

12th - Hai
Boar

find the Snake much too complicated and intense for his tastes. He feels that the Snake is introspective, analytical and unsympathetic to his views. He is probably right because the Snake is the emotionally detached fact-finder while the Boar likes to be guided by his feelings and friends.

From the Snake's perspective the Boar may seem short-sighted, overly giving and dependent upon others. In the eyes of the self-reliant Snake personality, people of the twelfth branch never seem to be worried about anything in life and are the first to spend and satisfy their own urges without regard to or fear of repercussions. Consequently, their separate ideas and definitions of 'fun' are entirely different and they may not move in the same circles unless they share a common ascendant or were born during the same two-hour segment—for example, if the Snake were born during the hours of the Boar or vice versa.

RELATIONSHIPS WITH THE SIXTH EARTH BRANCH—THE SNAKE

Within the Family

This person is usually respected and relied upon in his family and accorded special treatment because *he* is special. Presiding with a quiet aura of confidence and dignity, he usually knows how to get his way unobtrusively if possible. As a parent he is religious and ambitious for himself as well as his offsprings. Farsighted in his vision, he will make the right connections and get the maximum mileage from them. He moves towards the cream of society, so one will not find him settling for second best. He'll go first class if he can afford it—or even if he can't but wants to meet the right people and get into the right circles.

As a child he will cultivate his own charismatic image and impress teachers and peers with his maturity, presence of mind and ability to act with intelligence and diplomacy. Cool and cautious, he knows how to steer clear of controversy and prefers to assess each situation on its merit before making a move. A person of the sixth earth branch has his priorities identified and ranked, so needs no one to push him forward or remind him of his objectives. He is more than able to provide his own initiative and will take the appropriate action when he is good and ready.

As a Teacher

The native of the sixth branch is a dedicated, kind and patient teacher who is able to be inspiring as well as organised in his soft-spoken and intelligent approach. He will do things in stages and never push his students through hurriedly, nor expect them to learn quickly and without question. One who is able to recognise talent as well as shortcomings; he can move at different speeds to accommodate the needs of everyone. Because he is a good listener, he can be a positive and forceful influence in the lives of his charges. The Snake type is not averse to being the mentor of those who show promise in his eyes as he sees everything from a long-term perspective.

He can and will work well where he is given a free hand and his astute guidance can bring out the creativity and special talents of those he teaches. Skilled in developing abilities, he can provide encouragement and inspiration for young minds. The Snake personality is in his element when he is allowed to use his influence in the ways he sees fit. His intricate mind and his deep love of knowledge will make him probe deep within himself to find ways to challenge and benefit his students. This type will also be noted for giving difficult tests and even problems that are hard to solve, in order to find out if his students are using their full potential. Resourceful and resilient learners who are able to do independent research and projects will be given the highest marks.

A progressive and far-sighted teacher, he will always be ready to open new doors and introduce fresh ideas to anyone in his charge.

As a Lover and Spouse

Witty, passionate and amusing, this type can be a very intense and exciting lover. The Snake turns into an extrovert when he or she is in love. He is a natural flirt and likes to test his sex appeal on the opposite sex whenever he has the chance. Wrapping himself around his conquest, he can be hypnotic in his attentiveness and sometimes tends to smother or mesmerise the object of his devotion. Although his passion could be all-consuming at the start, it could eventually turn into warm affection and lasting friendship if there is much in common to bond him with a certain person.

Energetic in his pursuit of romance, his ardour may cool quickly if his feelings are not reciprocated. Hence, he has a reputation for having many affairs and casual flings. In truth, only he knows for sure where his heart is concerned. The more elusive the object of his desire, the more intrigued he is. Disarmingly seductive, he enjoys romantic liaisons but may not work hard on a relationship after the initial 'conquering' stage is over. One must always keep him guessing and maintain that bit of mystery. The Snake personality is an enigma in itself and you must never allow him to take you for granted or the relationship could go stale.

Unlike the hard-working Ox, the Snake likes to be pampered and spoiled. He will insist on being Number One in your life and in your schedule. His generosity often has strings attached, so never delude yourself that he has lost his calculating traits. He will also be providing his own air of mystery and intrigue to keep you on your toes. However, once you have established mutual respect and a solid degree of trust, he will reveal that he values friendship more than fiery passions. To him, sharing the same love of music, art, good food and wine or books are the important things that bind souls together.

As a Business Partner
A native of the sixth branch does not form partnerships without a lot of soul-searching and investigation, but when he does, one can be sure he has prepared for all contingencies. Your business plan will have to be carefully written and projections will have to be made conservatively. He may be slow to warm up, but it is just his natural trait to be suspicious and cautious. However, once things start going well he will plan on a large scale and you may be surprised to realise how tremendous his ambition and will-power are. Constant in his resolve, he will not allow anything or anyone to deter him from his goals and he can be quite ruthless in eliminating competitors or would-be challengers. On the surface he may appear calm, benevolent and gentlemanly, but cross him and you will see the other side. He cannot tolerate failure and lack of commitment from those he works with so everyone in the partnership must concentrate fully to make the business prosper, or risk dire consequences. On the whole he makes a reliable and patient business partner who will know how to strike out and take advantage of lucrative situations when the time is ripe. His wisdom, tenacity and sense of timing are great assets to have.

His most compatible partners will be the hard-working Ox type and the exacting administrative Rooster native of the tenth branch. These steadfast characters will be able to communicate well with the Snake type and do their best to make the business relationship go smoothly. People born during the hours of the sixth branch (between 9 a.m. and 11 a.m.) should also be able to form strong business ties with the Snake personality.

It would be advisable for a person of the sixth earth branch to avoid long-term associations or commercial ventures with those born under the Boar sign of the twelfth branch. This is because Boar people lack the consistency and intense focus of the Snake and will frustrate the Snake's effort to direct operations with efficiency and discipline. Both are charming and have great business acumen, but unfortunately they do not care to operate with the same style. The gregarious Boar is outgoing, generous and counts on the good will of others to get ahead, while the serious Snake will place his trust in his own judgement and ability and leave nothing to chance.

As a Boss
This person will quickly establish his way of doing things and how he expects everyone to behave in his presence. Decorum and dress are important to him, so the office atmosphere will be pleasant, tasteful and conducive to work. He does not expect too much flattery, although one may laugh at his jokes—it can't hurt. But he will demand performance and knowledge of the job. Unable to tolerate shoddy work and inefficiency, this type will retaliate swiftly when he or she is displeased. He has the good sense not to make criticism public and will encourage discretion and respect from those who work with him. Usually, he will keep employees for many years once he has trained them or if they have become accustomed to his ways. He does not like too many changes of personnel and will probably depend on a few key people whom he can trust to free him from mundane tasks, so that he can pursue new, more exciting opportunities. Being goal-orientated, he will always make sure everyone understands the company's direction and vital interests.

As a Friend and Colleague
Considerate and never intrusive, this person will be a cooperative friend and workmate. Not one to court trouble or behave scandalously or rebelliously, he is known for his wise counsel and sensible

approach. Nonetheless, he will cultivate his own polished image and identity to form his own little clique or close-knit circle. The purpose may be to exchange important information and pursue similar interests. Secretive and private, he readily gives advice and workable suggestions, but does not solicit any help if he can avoid it. His ears will be open to gossip from all sides but he will give out little information in exchange. Always ready to spot an opportunity, you can expect him to jump at a promotion and get himself noticed by all those in power. Conscientious and understanding, he can genuinely extend a lot of help to his friends and will direct them on the best possible way to achieve their goals, and he does make lifelong friends in whom he will confide. To his enemies he gives nothing, not even a single warning.

As an Opponent

A person of the sixth branch is a dangerous and merciless opponent who is silent and intense in his resolve but has great staying power in battle. Unlikely to be gracious or forgiving when he loses, he will harbour lifelong grudges and will never show any weakness to his foes or be indecisive in getting the upper hand. To deal with the Snake type, one must play one's cards defensively and maintain a poker face at all costs. If he sees even the tiniest crack in your armour, you could be done for. He will go to great lengths to learn all he can about the opposition—after all, half the battle is won by studying the competition and correctly anticipating the moves of the other side. This the Si branch does with aplomb. But beware of his unconventional methods and even daring attacks; remember, he fights to win and he may not really care what means he uses in order to triumph. The fainthearted will not last long in a struggle with the Snake personality.

As the Mediator

The native of the sixth earth branch makes an excellent mediator because of his ability to be a good listener and understand how each side feels. He will ask pertinent questions and uncover facts that amaze both parties. As a go-between he does not force his opinions on others, nor does he pass judgement lightly. He maintains his impartiality and keeps his own feelings hidden until the time is opportune for him to make a statement. As an arbitrator, he can talk sense into the protagonists and make valuable suggestions on how they could resolve their differences. His clarity of view and wise presentation of facts will certainly impress upon the warring factions their strong and weak points. He will not forcibly impose sanctions on others if they do not agree with his judgement but he is not above making veiled and vile threats that could shock resisters into compliance. On the whole, this person strives for harmony and will execute his duties faithfully and fairly if called upon to mediate. He will do his best to restore order and work out a reasonable settlement. With his superior negotiating skills and keen insight into human nature, one cannot expect anything but a favourable outcome.

RELATIONS WITH OTHER BRANCHES

With a Rat—First Branch

In this combination the Snake may find the Rat charming and clever while the Rat type admires the Snake's intelligence and elegant demeanour. However, both parties here are possessive by nature and do not like to relinquish control. The tenacious Snake is a Thinker and a loner while the aggressive Rat person is a Doer who thrives on open discussions and mutual exchange of ideas. Should the Snake resist the Rat's advances, the Rat may be conniving and inquisitive to no end, which could irritate the very private Snake person. But if both make the right adjustments, they could team up into a very resourceful duo who will be quite unmatched in their shrewdness and use of strategy.

With an Ox—Second Branch

These two partners will have an enduring relationship as they could develop a deep understanding of each other's nature. Both value their privacy and know how to respect the wishes of others. The devoted Ox will give the Snake type his wholehearted support and together they will present a united front that is impenetrable. Both are realistic, although the Snake may have a stronger influence on the Ox. But the Ox loves being needed and will gladly lend the Snake his strength and stamina so long as he is made to feel worthy and a part of the Snake's master plan. These two will have no problem identifying their goals and following through, as they will always lay a strong foundation before starting any endeavour.

With a Tiger–Third Branch

Although the colourful Tiger has a vivacious personality and can be quite captivating, the Snake may feel uneasy in the company of one who is so volatile. The Tiger type is ruled by his heart while the Snake will listen to his head. The Snake may feel that the Tiger is too emotional to rely upon and prefer to make his own cool-headed decisions alone. On the other hand, the Tiger is uncomfortable with the introverted and secretive Snake who keeps his opinions to himself. Both may be unable to make an impartial judgement of the other and only agree to work together in an emergency or at arm's length. They have different styles in expressing themselves and may be prevented from establishing good communications because of preconceived prejudices.

With a Rabbit—Fourth Branch

The elegant Snake has a great deal in common with the discriminating Rabbit personality, and together they will share a love of music, art and literature. Both are sensitive, discreet and influenced by a love of material things. However, they may have difficulty putting aside their own selfish desires when it comes to making a long-term relationship as they could become calculating and overprotective of their own interests. Unless they have a strong affinity, a common goal or share the same ascendant, these two tend to be fair-weather friends who may not volunteer to help the other if it means making sacrifices. They know what they want out of life and will set out a direct course to attain their goals. If they are travelling on the same road they will be great company, but if not, neither will interrupt his journey to assist the other.

With a Dragon—Fifth Branch

Ambition and success will unite these two into a forceful team. The high-spirited Dragon has great drive, but the long-lasting Snake type will persevere with his unshakable tenacity. In this combination, the Snake is the introverted Thinker who has great faith in himself, while the Dragon leads as the confident Doer. Both like to win and have a natural affinity with success and power. The Dragon likes to maintain a high profile and outward control, while the Snake prefers to establish long-term connections in a quiet but effective way. Neither will surrender power once he or she attains it, although the Snake is always anticipating unforeseen contingencies and planning ahead. Both parties must work hard to bond in a relationship, although the Dragon makes commitments more readily than the Snake type.

With another Snake—Sixth Branch
Two Snake people have no difficulty in communicating their wishes to each other and will co-exist peacefully, even if they have different interests. Since they both belong to the same patient, enduring but tenacious sixth branch, they will not go out of their way to be unnecessarily aggressive. Rather, they will wait for things to come their way. These two will have no problems staying on a task or focusing on their goals. Because they both have fixed ideas of what their goals are and will be very definite about their likes and dislikes, they may be able to confide in and influence each other. The one thing that could get in the way of their love or friendship may be that jealous streak that usually surfaces when one is able to get something or someone the other covets.

With a Horse—Seventh Branch
The Snake is a passive, cautious intellectual while the vibrant Horse personality is active and very involved. The Horse needs to gratify his senses immediately and energetically, while the Snake's passion runs deep and is not always evident. Both can be intuitive and opportunistic, although the Horse is the more outgoing of the pair. They will try to work together and may be successful if they can determine from the start their fixed areas of responsibility. However, the Snake rarely changes his mind or takes an alternative route once he has made a decision and plotted his course. The Horse is just the opposite. The Snake may find it very unsettling if the Horse makes too many changes with little or no notice and may dissolve this partnership.

With a Sheep—Eighth Branch
The Snake is a Thinker who must carefully evaluate things before he can give his approval. The Sheep is compassionate and creative but ruled by his heart. While the Snake digests the real facts, the Sheep may be concerned only with the implications of his actions on the feelings of others. Both may share the same interests and objectives, but their individual approaches are as different as day and

night. The Snake is usually unshakable in his beliefs and likes to stay focused, finding the Sheep personality too sentimental. In a relationship, the Snake will take command and may not allow the Sheep to indulge in his whims or procrastinations. The Sheep could benefit from the Snake's foresight and direction if he allows the Snake to plan their mutual strategy.

With a Monkey—Ninth Branch

The Snake can be resolute where the Monkey can be calculating. Both are ambitious and independent personalities who know what they are after and will not hesitate to exploit whatever opportunities are available. Unless the Monkey has a Snake ascendant or the Snake has a strong Monkey ascendant, they will have difficulty communicating as they are plagued by a mutual distrust of each other's motives. After they have both finished sizing each other up, they may feel threatened or fearful of each other. Actually, they do share a keen appreciation of good strategy and networking, and if they can relax in each other's company and not assume the worst of each other's intentions, they might find a workable partnership.

With a Rooster—Tenth Branch

The Rooster complements the Snake's cool and collected nature. Both parties here like to be sharp and focused and will have a natural affinity with each other's way of thinking. The Snake may be the plotter in this team while the Rooster will execute their plans with efficiency and precision. These two work well as they anticipate the wishes of one another without reservations. The Snake is a contemplative intellectual who will admire the Rooster's decisiveness and industry. Both like to work hard, but will avoid duplication in their endeavours. Instinctively, they are both drawn to accomplish much through their own merits and efforts. The Snake is the more intuitive and practical personality while the Rooster is authoritative and meticulous.

With a Dog—Eleventh Branch

The Dog has a healthy regard for the talents of the wise Snake and these two will be compatible to a high degree. The amiable Dog is trustworthy and the ambitious Snake could find in the Dog a loyal and steadfast companion. Both tend to be idealistic, although the

Snake is more intense and possessive while the protective Dog works hard for mutual understanding and cooperation. If they have similar goals and interests, the Dog will recognise the Snake's intelligence and work unselfishly to achieve their joint objectives. The Dog is not jealous or too demanding by nature and will allow the Snake his need for privacy, introspection and secrecy.

With a Boar—Twelfth Branch

The sensual Boar could come on too strong for the contemplative Snake personality. One prefers quantity while the other opts for quality. The Boar may be charitable and obliging, but he is given to excesses and can be naive and wilful where he should be concerned about his own welfare instead. The complex Snake is the opposite of the spontaneous Boar personality and must consider every angle of the problem before devising his strategy. The Snake cannot and will not act without a plan while the Boar will dive head-on into a relationship or business venture without suspicion or much preparation. It is easy to see why their philosophies preclude these two from having mutual interests or a lasting relationship. They favour different ends of the spectrum and may not appreciate what the other has to offer.

7

THE WU BRANCH
SEVENTH LUNAR SIGN

The Adventurer's Song

I am the kaleidoscope of the mind,
I impart light, colour and perpetual motion.
I think, I see, I am moved by electric fluidity.
Constant only in my inconstancy
I am unshackled by mundane holds,
unchecked by sturdy, binding goals.
I run unimpeded through unexplored paths,
my spirit unconquered—
my soul forever free.

I am Wu, the Adventurer

Theodora Lau

THE SEVENTH EARTH BRANCH: WU
THE SIGN OF THE HORSE

THE ASSIGNED LUNAR YEARS OF THE HORSE

January 25, 1906	to	February 12, 1907
February 11, 1918	to	January 31, 1919
January 30, 1930	to	February 16, 1931
February 15, 1942	to	February 4, 1943
February 3, 1954	to	January 23, 1955
January 21, 1966	to	February 8, 1967
February 7, 1978	to	January 27, 1979
January 27, 1990	to	February 14, 1991
February 12, 2002	to	January 31, 2003

If you were born on the day before the lunar year of the Horse, e.g. January 20, 1966, you belong to the previous earth branch or animal sign which is the sixth branch (the Snake).

If you were born on the day after a lunar year ends, e.g. February 9, 1967, you belong to the next earth branch or animal sign, which is the eighth branch (the Sheep).

THE SEVENTH EARTH BRANCH
THE SIGN OF THE HORSE

The seventh character profile of the twelve earth branches is that of the Horse whose branch is named *Wu* in Chinese, symbolising perception and speed. A person of this personality type is cheerful, lively and high-spirited. Goaded by a happy-go-lucky attitude and an independent spirit, he will enjoy striking out on his own. As a person who follows his heart and his intuitions, he does not like a lot of planning and soul-searching. Going by his gut feelings and instincts, this personality is not one who procrastinates too long— rather, he is often too hurried and impulsive. Yet thankfully, his innate self-confidence and perceptive skills are above par, and even when he makes a mistake or travels the wrong path he can easily adjust or correct his errors in mid-stream. At his best, he is the kind of man who is able to change the tyres while the car is still running. Brave, bold and self-reliant, he views the world as his playground and has full run of it. Moving at a quick pace, he intends to cover as much ground as possible and of course, still manage to enjoy himself thoroughly while racing about. Vivacious and energetic, he is the most adventurous of the twelve branches. Although he may be impetuous and inconsiderate at times, he does have a practical side to his nature and will take the short cut if he can without worrying too much about what others think of him or whether he has trampled on anyone's feelings. Some may see this as a selfish streak, but one must not expect this person to modify his ways drastically to fit any mould. On the surface he is very personable and likeable, but he can also be obstinate and rash when his all-important freedom is at stake. Obviously, he will not trade his independence and love of adventure for anything in the world.

The Horse of the Wu branch is definitely self-centred and gifted with the power of persuasion. Consequently, he can appraise both personal and business situations quickly and accurately and is able to manipulate people and events to his advantage. Aggressive in an honest and rather disarming kind of way, he is quite liberal-minded and a dare-devil. He will enjoy both mental as well as physical exercise and will be easily bored by repetitive or detailed tasks. Here is someone who prides himself on quick decision-making and positive action as he needs constant challenges to display his competence. A restless soul, he tends to search out excitement; yet although he is able to hold his own playing several games at the same time, he may tire of the chase and abandon projects when his interest wanes. He is also known to be capricious and fickle-minded because he pursues the pleasure of the moment and may not worry too much about tomorrow or what the long-term repercussions may be. However, his fearlessness and presence of mind in times of crisis more than make up for his other shortcomings. Agile of mind and body, he will be a good sportsperson as well as a good sport. With a shrug of his shoulders, he can dismiss defeat and bounce right back to give it another try. Unlikely to be vindictive, underhanded or unforgiving, the Wu person can and will recoup quickly on his own. However, he does not like to bottle up his emotions and may be known to erupt in order to vent his pent-up feelings, and sometimes he could blow his stack altogether. No real damage comes from his outburst, if one takes it with a pinch of salt and learns not to add fuel to the fire by violent opposition or by rejecting him completely. The person of this earth branch is not likely to bear grudges and can easily forgive and forget once the incident is over. He will not nurse petty hurts or dwell on past injuries, neither will he harp on inconsequential matters or bargain over details. He considers these things beneath him and will expect you to forgive him just as fast as he would do if he had done anything to hurt you without meaning to. Frequently, he can be demanding and outspoken in an impatient sort of way which some people may find offensive and intimidating. The trouble is usually that he is in a rush and does not take time to explain his ideas or why he must do certain things. His impatience, combined with his assumption that others are on the same wavelength, may come across as arrogance or intolerance and no one is more surprised than the Horse personality when others accuse him of insensitivity and lack of consideration. He was just too busy to notice. After all, shouldn't we all applaud the outcome—that he did the job so splendidly and in record-breaking time?

A native of the Wu branch finds it hard to restrain himself and his spontaneous desires. He likes to express himself, is usually talkative and animated and may call attention to himself by dressing in bright colours or loud geometric patterns. He can also be vain about his appearance, as all these qualities are but part of his multifaceted personality, which do not go unnoticed. The Horse openly solicits attention and will bask naturally in his supporters' admiration. This candid lack of guile will make him come across as an outgoing, boisterous yet truly honest person, who can be taken at face value.

Even as he behaves with carefree abandon and does not seem to worry excessively, this personality has a keen sense of judgement and could be a perceptive problem-solver when called upon to do so. He can get to the heart of the matter without much ado and one will get his undiluted opinion or diagnosis. If he has stepped on your toes and bruised your ego, so be it. He may or may not apologise. Then again, he may not even see the need to. He will expect you to recover from the bad news or defeat as quickly as he does. You'll live. He'll philosophically tell you that worry never changed the course of destiny and encourage you to climb back in the saddle and give it another go.

The Horse person may be irreverent, even controversial, when it comes to getting his own way. He needs but one sanction—his own. Among his shortcomings may be his short attention span and lack of staying power, which cause him to become easily frustrated and temperamental. Often, he could pick fights or throw a tantrum just to clear the air. Then, after he has got whatever grievance he may possess off his chest, he will be able to start again from square one, none the worse for wear. He does not do well in a carefully controlled bureaucracy or if he has to jump through many hoops to get something accomplished.

As he is not one to be hemmed in by long-term commitments, the temperamental person of the Horse branch is quick to warm up and reach peak performance; then he could be just as quick to get out of the same relationship. Suspense, intrigue and other intricacies do not appeal to him. He prefers to be curt, direct and proceed quickly to his destination with no detours. No uphill, downhill, zigzag and round-in-circles manoeuvres, if you please. If he is put through too much rigmarole he can be rebellious, jump to his own hasty conclusion—and bolt!

This personality type has very good comprehension of how things and people work but often does not bother to find out why. For instance, he'll know immediately if he can get along with someone or not. But not being a person who questions the whys and the wherefores, he will simply accept the fact that he either likes you or dislikes you. He makes up his mind rather quickly and with him first impressions usually stick. His brilliance is quick and flashy but it may not be very deep, as he leaves himself no time to reflect thoroughly on important matters. He is guided mostly by his intuitions which are like antennae sweeping the atmosphere around him for positive or negative vibrations. Often, he may favour the quick fix versus the long-term repair or replacement of the basic foundation, which could take up a lot of time and effort. Naturally, the patched-up repairs will not last long and could be more expensive to fix in the long run. In the same way, relationships are easily made and just as easily broken or bent by him. If the person of the Wu branch could develop more sympathy and empathy for those around him, and understand that not everyone thinks as fast as he does or moves at his pace, he would eliminate the majority of his problem.

As he matures, he will no doubt see the advantages of keeping his temper and of not expecting conflicts to be resolved as he wishes. Dealing with others through calm, methodical and impartial mediators will do wonders to tone down his abrasiveness or urgent need to have the answer immediately. Sometimes, he needs patient associates who will have the perseverance to show him the middle of the road and rein him in before he jumps over the cliff.

The Horse of the seventh branch is the second member of the Protectors in the third Triangle of Affinity. He, like the other two residents of this triangle, the Tiger (third branch) and the Dog (eleventh branch), are guided by instinct and emotions. Armed with noble intentions, they will be the self-appointed defenders of justice and idealism. Protectors of the disadvantaged; they may be opinionated, unorthodox and aggressive in the face of oppression. They simply do not back down under pressure and could react by being rebellious and confrontational. In general, natives of this group are true to their conscience and react swiftly, motivated by gut feelings. They are recognised for their courage and their ability to act on their convictions.

The seventh earth branch will encounter the strongest personality clashes and opposition from people of the first branch or natives of the Rat sign. The Horse branch loves adventure. He will rush out to explore new horizons, try the untried or set new records. In contrast, members of the first branch are security-conscious, sentimental, thrifty and crafty. The Horse personality may resent the Rat type's nagging and constant need for reassurance. In the end, the Horse may simply avoid dealing with the Rat's demanding and critical nature. All that togetherness is not something the person of the seventh branch will relish. He must run free and set his own boundaries, while the clannish Rat will enjoy being close to home and devoted to his friends and loved ones.

To get on with the Horse personality, one must understand that he does not do things with the specific aim of displeasing or irritating others. Such premeditated efforts would take too much time and energy. To him, the expedient way is the right way and he cannot understand why one must travel the long, winding path instead of racing full speed ahead to the destination, as he does. Although he is definitely open and honest in his relationships, he is overconfident in his own abilities and may tend to take it for granted that everyone is following his lead. One must be absolutely sure of getting his undivided attention and agreement before assuming that one has his cooperation. However, once he is with you, there will be no holding him back. Progressive and proactive, he will take on a high-profile role and announce with fervour his full support and dedication to the cause. A forceful and commanding performer, he will know how to assume power when called upon to do so and will not hesitate to act swiftly with courage and conviction.

Captivating and enthusiastic, the person of the Wu branch works from inspiration and self-motivation. As you know, he cannot tolerate rigid schedules, intensive details, record-keeping or a restrictive environment with too many rules. So give him a free rein and he will respond by surprising you with his creativity and self-reliance. Keep him penned up and he will be unproductive and even self-destructive. Identify clearly what you want him to accomplish and then leave him alone to do the job. He may astound you with his speed and ingenuity. Hovering over him, criticising and interfering, will bring out the worst in this personality. Then he may lose whatever little objectivity he has.

The Wu branch of the Horse is considered a Yang or masculine sign. Passionate but also mercurial, he can be affectionate and demonstrative when not off chasing his rainbows. His restless and inquisitive spirit needs constant stimulation and challenges. He will be creative and intellectual in his own fashion but he is also ruled by a practical and realistic outlook—sometimes too practical, so that he abandons things quickly if they do not yield results right from the start. Patience and perseverance are not his greatest virtues. Yet in life, he learns fastest from actual experience and osmosis. Catching on and improvising independently are his specialities and he is able to fend for himself if left on his own.

In business relations with a person of this branch, it is best to be as decisive and confident as he is. Don't bait or string him along: he may not stay around long enough to play silly games and guess what is on your mind. However, he does like to honour his promises and contribute his fair share. Just make sure he reads the fine print and understands all the pros and cons; otherwise, this is the kind of partner who may be quickly disillusioned if things get off to a bad start. Don't ask for his permission but have ample reserves and back-up plans ready for any emergencies. For his part, he will be bringing his superior reflexes and keen insight into any partnership. Able to recognise opportunity before others and daring enough to strike and strike hard while the iron is hot will be the Horse person's trademark. He may be able to wrap up the deal before anyone is even aware of what is going on. He loves working in an exciting atmosphere and will opt for the great outdoors and frequent changes of scenery. This way, he can recharge his enthusiasm and push himself intensely without ever watching the time.

Although the Horse type is not a gambler at heart, he loves to take calculated risks to prove that he can surmount considerable odds—in other words, do the undoable, break the record and plant his flag on top of the highest mountain. Forever looking for ways to prove his ability and sharpen his already acute skills, this personality is at his happiest when he has achieved something extremely challenging, over which people doubted he could have triumphed.

Mobility and outdoor activities seem to bring out the best in this type and he is most relaxed when he is exerting himself in his favourite sport or hobby. Competitive and unpredictable, he acts out what is on his mind and does not like to keep secrets. He will give any challengers a good run for their money and he will quickly and expertly learn from his own mistakes. Yet should he fall flat on his face, do not fear, for he will pick himself up, dust himself down and dive back into the fray. This person may or may not be a team player, but in the end he knows he must still rely on himself and not be dependent on anyone else. This is his creed and he is unlikely ever to hand over the reins when he is in control.

In both his personal and business affairs, this person will have varied interests and find new challenges to keep himself involved. He is not calculating and won't mind helping others out, and will even go out on a limb for his friends and team-mates without expecting anything in return. He knows where to find the answers to his searches and can usually rely on his own sixth sense to steer him out of trouble. He lives every waking moment to the fullest. His zest for life is able to brighten up the most dismal predicament and give encouragement to all about him when spirits are at their lowest.

The Wu person loves to be in touch with all around him. A sensual soul, he lives by his senses. He will excel in communications and the visual arts and relate to most people in his affable and entertaining way. Children, animals and any underdog who needs his help will be welcomed with open arms. What's more, he does not scold or blame unnecessarily. This is the kind of person who will give you a loan or extend his immediate assistance without asking to hear the whole unfortunate story or pointing out where you went wrong.

Above all, this personality likes to be dramatic, daring and intense in his actions. Armed with great convictions and idealism, he rarely looks back in regret. To him, moving forward and meeting life head on are all that really count. Franklin D. Roosevelt, Igor Stravinsky, the Duke of Windsor (Edward VIII), Chris Evert and Barbra Streisand are good examples of this personality type.

With his strength and speed, the Horse type forms useful alliances and knows how to build bridges to where he wants to go. A go-getter, he is not shy about speaking up and making it clear what he wants. And he plans to get it too. Unhampered by a reserved or timid nature, he does not conform readily to authority, nor will he degrade himself by currying favours. Instead, he applies himself wholeheartedly to the mission in hand without allowing any doubt to cross his mind and make him stray from his course. His displays his dreams and vivid aspirations like colourful flags whipping in the wind. One finds it hard not to be infected by his buoyant and delightful love of life.

Commanding yet compassionate to those less fortunate, the native of the Wu branch is not small-minded or calculating. He will share his good fortune and wealth with his friends and family and ask little in return. All he may want is to come and go as he pleases, with few or no questions asked. It isn't that he cannot be trusted or that he is up to something questionable, it's simply that he needs to know he has his all-important freedom. He would like you to believe in him completely and always give him the benefit of the doubt. When he realises that he has your trust, he is not likely ever to stray. He values the security of good relationships and will always find his way home—late maybe, but he'll be there.

In life, his most important asset will be his unsinkable optimism and presence of mind. He knows priorities and sets values on his goals. He has the strength of character to rebound from losses and start all over again with no complaints. Lucid and liberal-minded, he is not judgemental or too critical. He lives and lets live. A high-profile character and capable leader who knows how to deal with urgent priorities and make astute decisions without too much handling, he can be relied upon to steer others out of difficulties.

The Wu personality is the Adventurer of the cycle and his key phrase is: 'I act'.

TRIANGLE OF AFFINITY

The Horse or Wu personality of the seventh branch is the second member of the Third Triangle of Affinity which produces active, likeable and compassionate people indispensable to social life. The trio in this triangle is composed of the Tiger (third branch), the Horse (seventh branch) and the Dog (eleventh branch), a group of

**3rd - Yin
Tiger**

**III
Protectors**

**11th - Xu
Dog**

**7th - Wu
Horse**

Protectors who advocate fairness and opportunity for everyone, especially those who are most disadvantaged. Guided by unselfish and extrovert natures, they seek to serve others by promoting understanding and peace. Unorthodox, energetic and often acting with missionary zeal, they are aggressive in their idealism and democratic principles. Although they may display short tempers and impatience, generally they are kind, sociable and very helpful. Loyal and selfless, persons of this triangle are staunch and fearless fighters, respected for their courage and aggressiveness. While they may be rebellious and stubborn at times, their negative qualities are balanced by their innate charm and generosity. Confident, outspoken and never afraid of controversy, they will charge to the rescue of anyone they feel is in need of assistance.

To work well with residents of this Triangle of Affinity, one must not only appeal to their sense of honour and fair play, but tug at their emotional heart strings, too. Honest and open in all their dealings, they will gladly make sacrifices for the good of all. They love personal contact and will go out of their way to bond with others. Not small-hearted or vindictive, they can assess situations relatively quickly and accurately and make fast and accurate judgements. Gifted with magnetic and captivating personalities, they have no problems persuading others to see things their way. These types know how to project themselves to the public and will often have careers or opportunities in communications, sales, promotion, on-stage or movie performances and in the sports, political or military arenas where sharp reflexes and genuine combative passion are required.

They believe in themselves with unshakable confidence and will show unerring loyalty to their team, family, friends and country.

The three branches of the Third Triangle of Affinity will be able to get along well in love and business. Working as a team is second nature to them. Capable of intuitively anticipating each other, they have a common way of thinking and reacting. As marriage or business partners, they will have no difficulty supporting each other or identifying with common goals.

CIRCLE OF CONFLICT

The Wu personality of the Horse branch will encounter his strongest opposition from the branch directly across from him in the Circle of Conflict, which is the Rat of the first branch. The Horse has an entirely different outlook from the Rat type of person and the difference in their perspectives often causes them to be unreceptive of each other's ideas. The Horse type is known for his speed and perception and can be intolerant and easily provoked by the Rat type who may be too critical for his tastes. The Horse is at his worst when he is baited and criticised and will react with anger and indiscretion.

**1st - Zi
Rat**

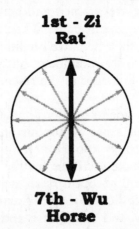

**7th - Wu
Horse**

On top of these incompatible traits, both these types tend to be argumentative and contentious when angered. Their competitive natures require them to prove their superior prowess to themselves and the world. In fact the best advice for these protagonists may be to stay clear of each other and deal through intermediaries or mediators.

Somehow, the message always comes across sounding better and more acceptable when delivered by a neutral party. Direct dealings between them bring a high degree of bruised egos and irrational competitiveness that are unproductive.

RELATIONSHIPS WITH THE SEVENTH EARTH BRANCH— THE HORSE

Within the Family

In his family, the Horse personality is willing to give as well as expecting a lot of liberty. Not conservative in his outlook, he imposes little or few restrictions on the freedom of other family members and will allow everyone to work at his or her own speed. However, one is expected to hold one's own and the Horse type may or may not pick up anyone who falters or falls. Naturally, he will want sufficient autonomy and lots of space to call his own, as horse persons are irritable when they do not have enough elbow room.

As a parent he will be efficient, practical and a little impatient or pushy at times. He loves to take trips with the family, go hiking and visit new places. A trail-blazer, he is inquisitive and knowledgeable about faraway places, exotic food and foreign cultures. He will develop his offsprings' open and restless minds and encourage them to explore every avenue of their imaginations. Vigour and confidence light up this outgoing personality. He has a giving nature and is not inclined to be calculating or critical, but his affable and easy-going character may also be unpredictable at times and, changeable as the weather, he may turn petulant and antagonistic if, for instance, his golf game is suddenly cancelled or spoiled.

As a child, the Horse-Wu personality will quickly learn to walk, talk and act. He will not be clinging or too dependent on his parents. Although he may always be tugging at the reins because he is easily bored or plagued with a very short attention span, he is a quick learner with an impressionable and intelligent mind. Because of his cheerful and self-reliant nature, he is much sought after, popular and easy to get on with. However, he may be irreverent towards authority and oldfashioned mores, as well as rebellious when placed in a very restrictive environment.

On the whole, this type will prefer to keep family life simple and uncomplicated. He may well distance himself from emotionally needy friends and family who are looking for pity or attention. This is because he lacks patience and, although not selfish with his money, may be less generous with his time. Also, this type is more than capable of fending for himself and may expect others to do likewise, unaware of their need for approval or reassurance.

As a Teacher

The Horse or Wu type is an unorthodox and practical teacher who is known for his candour and ability to relate to people directly. Colourful, friendly and self-assured, he may use visual aids, field trips and hands-on opportunities to teach. He draws students towards a common objective with his unconventional wisdom and realistic outlook.

He will love students who are self-starters, adventurous and gifted with exploring minds like his own. Realising the value of actual experience, he will encourage his charges to experiment and test new methods without fear or hesitation. He knows that not all answers can be found in books or through the experiences of others. Domineering, upfront, frank, impatient and scornful of weakness in others, he will still be honest and honourable and never ask anything of others that he cannot perform or achieve. He is a teacher who will clearly teach by example and integrity, but students must never be oversensitive to his 'right to the point' style because he does not deliberately want to hurt or humiliate anyone in his team. He just wants to get his message across quickly.

As a Lover and Spouse

A love affair with the Horse of the Wu branch will be full of exciting surprises and unpredictable twists and turns. He is never one to suppress his impulses or curb his enthusiasm. Spontaneous, ardent and uninhibited in love and romance, he is both demanding and demonstrative at the same time. He will insist on mutual breathing space and may not care for complex relationships. His philosophy of love is simple: boy meets girl, they fall in love, boy sweeps girl off her feet and they ride off into the sunset. Uncomplicated and not too deep by choice, this personality hates analysis and emotional sentimentality or dependency. Don't expect long heart-to-heart chats; he does not like baring his soul or confiding too much in others. Just learn to read between the lines, for his actions will no doubt speak louder than his words.

Although he is passionate, aggressive and given to grand spur-of-the-moment gestures to express his affection, he does not invest as much of himself in a relationship on a steady basis as others would desire of him. He likes to be the one to set the pace but may not always be around when the ones he loves feel they need him most. Hence, there will tend to be highs and lows and starts and lapses in his affairs of the heart. Since he may also be unable to hold his tongue and may divulge secrets and resentments when he is agitated, he could unintentionally offend and hurt others with careless and thoughtless remarks. Consequently, the Horse type must learn to step carefully where matters of the heart are concerned and will no doubt be much better at relationships once he has had a chance to mature and gain experience.

As a Business Partner

This type of person makes an unconventional and very active business partner. He wants hands-on participation and does not like to become entrenched in routine or boring desk work. He will prefer to work with people like himself, who make quick decisions. With his ability to grasp and appreciate logistics and statistics with ease, he will want to concentrate on workable ventures and be performance-orientated. Setting his own track records in progress and speed, he will appreciate people who can get a broken machine back into production with as little fuss and excuse as possible. As a partner, he will always take the positive road and can improvise with practical solutions.

The Horse of the Wu branch will excel in promotion and sales. He can direct any partnership with optimistic and progressive leadership. Gifted with keen business perception and the ability to interact with people at all levels, he is a naturally convincing talker but prefers to discuss and debate facts rather than emotional issues. At a meeting, he will want concrete facts, decisions and directions. Indulging in aimless discussions and hypothetical scenarios frustrates him as he hates to waste his time and energy.

He is comfortable taking calculated risks but can often make promises recklessly. So a good partner must show him the advantage of being more reserved, hedging bets and giving special care to details, contracts and business commitments. This person needs able people who will insist on a slower speed and a schedule that allows for time to check for errors. Spur of the moment deals do not always prosper and could have painful repercussions. One must teach the Horse to 'measure twice, cut once'.

As a Boss
This is not the type of boss who will be constantly supervising his staff or breathing down their necks. He allows people to work with a minimum of supervision. On the whole he is cheerful, tolerant and optimistic in dismal situations. But, while he is helpful and quick to react in emergencies, he may also be impatient and demanding when performance or progress is not up to par. He will insist that everyone knows his or her duties and performs well without being reminded.

On his positive side, he is not likely to be too critical or to blame others for mistakes. He would rather spend time and effort correcting the errors and seeing that they do not happen again. He is open-minded and accepting of new changes and improvisation. Workable suggestions and ingenuity from employees are always welcomed and rewarded. He likes to entertain, organise company events and teams, to provide encouragement and friendly competition. However, he is not particularly watchful about what he says and may often end up with his foot in mouth.

As a Friend and Colleague
Efficient and energetic, this personality will be liked for his open and optimistic ways. Sociable and outgoing by nature, he enjoys participating in many functions and is active in his community. Having him as a friend and colleague means one will always be kept well-informed and abreast of exciting coming events and newsworthy items. Quite disposed to sharing and cooperation with his friends and associates, the Horse type likes interaction and teamwork. Adventurous and outgoing, he is always game to try new things and explore new places. Of course, being high-powered and ambitious, he will refuse to tolerate mediocrity and will always gravitate towards the successful and competent. Helpful and fairminded to those who depend on or support him, he can also be capricious in other relationships or with acquaintances. This quirk should not be taken as abandonment but rather that he likes variety and may want to be in several circles or work with several groups at the same time, hoping he won't miss too much of the action. Evidently he feels that he is competent enough and will somehow be able to fulfil his promises

to all his friends and colleagues. At all events, he is certainly one who will try his best not to let anyone down.

As an Opponent
The Wu or Horse type is an aggressive and combative opponent who may enjoy matching his strength with anyone who dares challenge him. Daring and fierce, he can and will retaliate without hesitation. This is one foe who will not suffer silently; with his unpredictable temper, he may lash out unreasonably and he could also take drastic action and engage the elements of speed and surprise. Although he can grasp the dynamics of a situation well and appreciate why and how conflicts come about, he is not able to reflect properly on the motives of others in a logical, calm manner during a confrontation. When he is angry or provoked, his judgement could be clouded by rashness and intolerance. His emotional side is easily aroused in a struggle or competition and he views his opponent with arrogance and antipathy. Abiding strictly by the rules is not always important to him. He may want to play by his rules and then proceed to make them up as the game is in progress. Determined to vanquish the opponent, he will compete and conquer at all costs and launch attacks from several fronts.

As an opponent, the Horse personality may lose out when he allows his temper to get in the way. He could abandon diplomacy and be tactless and inconsiderate, thereby destroying good will in the event of an amicable settlement. To be most effective, he must retain a cool and practical outlook and deal only with pertinent facts. He should also employ emissaries and arbitrators to defuse explosive situations instead of dealing with matters or with opponents himself.

As the Mediator
The Horse personality has a deep-rooted need to make things work, and this applies to relationships. As a mediator, he is not emotionally involved and can apply himself well to the job of being impartial, lucid and practical. His openness and ability to relate to both sides will make it easy for others to confide in him and tell him what it would take to effect a resolution. His keen sense of fair play and his perceptiveness as a problem-solver will give him a special edge when he acts as the go-between for two feuding parties. He will do his best to draw everyone together on common ground, thereby bridging

differences with new or unconventional solutions. Unlikely to be put off by any unruly or contentious behaviour, the thick-skinned Horse may keep his optimistic spirits going until both sides are convinced and enlightened by his positive intervention.

RELATIONS WITH OTHER BRANCHES

With a Rat—First Branch
The Horse will not have the same values and priorities as the Rat personality. Major conflicts can therefore arise from the way these two types think and deal with their problems. The Horse loves action and values his independence. He won't appreciate the Rat poking his nose in where it is not welcomed and will not tolerate any meddling from the Rat. However, the Rat does like to keep everything in his perspective and will cajole, threaten and bargain until he gets his way. The Horse speaks his mind plainly and prefers the short, uncomplicated route to getting things done, rather than the critical Rat's longwinded and calculating approach. It will be difficult for these two to establish strong links in a relationship.

With an Ox—Second Branch
Relations between the Horse and the Ox will not always be smooth as the Ox tends to be heavy-handed and authoritarian when dealing with the intelligent Horse personality. The Horse has finer instincts and certainly more speed and agility than the slow but steady Ox type, but the Ox may not appreciate the Horse's talents if he breaks any of the rules or ignores the Ox's directives. The Horse is more than able to motivate himself and has a good sense of humour, but he will not give his cooperation if the Ox is inflexible and dictatorial. Both parties here need to be reasonable and open-minded to establish any kind of dialogue.

With a Tiger—Third Branch
The Horse and the Tiger make great partners as they both love the same things and are able to communicate their feelings without inhibitions. As a result, they will share the same intellectual as well as physical pursuits. Both are self-confident, passionate and proactive. The magnetic Tiger, who can be rebellious and headstrong like the Horse, understands his need for independence and self-

expression. Restless, witty and outspoken, this pair will bond without much hesitation. Of the two, the Tiger is more emotional while the Horse is level-headed but quick to react in times of trouble. These two liberal but unselfish spirits will love, play and work together with great zest.

With a Rabbit—Fourth Branch

The self-assured Horse personality may not be at his best when working with the Rabbit. Although they may have similar priorities and interests, the Horse may find the Rabbit too inhibited and passive to suit his taste. The Rabbit is analytical and deliberate, whereas the Horse type will rely on his gut feelings and quick reflexes. As a result the Horse, who is always ready to make a commitment if it serves his purpose, may find the Rabbit reticent and pessimistic. They could cooperate, but one has to speed up and the other to slow down in order to work or think on the same level. The Rabbit may find the Horse too impulsive and changeable while the Horse does not appreciate the prudent Rabbit's need for reassurances and investigation.

With a Dragon—Fifth Branch

The Horse likes people who move fast, think fast and talk fast. He hates being put on hold or having to wait for anyone or anything. The decisive Dragon has good communication skills and great confidence in himself, which definitely appeals to the Horse. There may be some struggle for dominance between these two but they will both actively seek to work out their differences and get on with their game. They do not like to waste their time on futile tasks or associations, so they will be honest, open and to the point. There will be no room for guesswork in their relationship as both are impatient and achievement-conscious.

With a Snake—Sixth Branch

At times the Snake can be too deliberate and uncommunicative to interact well with the Horse. The Horse is not as cultivated and cerebral as the Snake may wish, but he certainly knows how to get things done, and done quickly. As a result, the Snake could use the Horse's many talents to his advantage. Where the Horse will want to speak his mind openly and without prejudice, the Snake type may be reserved in his assessment or judgement. The Horse is certainly not as controlling or possessive as the Snake can be and will resist being tied down or dominated in any way. Consequently, although these two can work well together, they may not choose to have a close, meaningful association or a long-term relationship.

With another Horse—Seventh Branch
Relations between two horses are usually good as they seem to find common ground quickly and get into step with one another. Both believe in teamwork and communications and will not care to fuss over petty details if they are geared towards a common objective. Horses find it easy to rely on each other for the cooperation needed to accomplish a task, although horses of the opposite sex make better friends than those of the same sex where there could be competition and a struggle for dominance. In such instances, each will opt to go his own way rather than wage a drawn-out battle.

With a Sheep—Eighth Branch
The Horse will give the Sheep personality confidence and direction which he could lack as he is a procrastinator by nature. The creative Sheep will always need someone to promote and market his many special talents and will look to the quick-witted Horse to manage his affairs. Both tend to change their minds easily and work on many things at the same time. But where the Sheep is more tolerant than the Horse, the Horse is more adept at managing money and people. If they join forces, the Horse will certainly be able to protect the Sheep and guard their mutual interests. Both partners will be enriched in the process.

With a Monkey—Ninth Branch
The Horse and Monkey are both flexible, clever and cooperative to a high degree. They rarely make a fuss over unimportant issues and like to link forces to achieve common ends. Both are practical and will be able to assess situations quickly. If things do not look too promising or do not work out as they plan, these two will not hesitate to cut their losses and move on to better opportunities. Strong ties could develop if both parties learn how to give as well as take in this relationship. The Monkey is more shrewd than the Horse and will be able to control his temper or bide his time. However, the

Horse enjoys working with the innovative and resourceful Monkey type who will excel in teaching the Horse a few new tricks of his own.

With a Rooster—Tenth Branch
The Horse can be generous and popular in his likeable way and will not mind working with the Rooster if the latter is not too rigid and critical. The democratic Horse is quick to sense changes and will adapt himself willingly, whereas the Rooster thrives on regularity or permanence and can be inflexible and opinionated. If the Horse has to make all the adjustments, you can be sure he will rebel and lose his temper with the demanding Rooster. The Rooster finds it hard to comprehend how the restless Horse can attempt to do so many things at the same time and still claim to be having fun. The impatient Horse will likewise have no need of the Rooster's rhetoric and argumentative nature. And although he may respect the Rooster's expertise and ability, he may find the Rooster personality too controlling and particular to develop close ties.

With a Dog—Eleventh Branch
The Dog will not seek to control the Horse but would rather keep pace with him and go places together. The Horse finds the Dog a loyal partner in love as well as in business. The Dog is a good listener and will be able to communicate and cooperate easily with the independent but quick-witted Horse person. Their temperaments are equally matched and neither has a possessive or competitive nature, which allows them both to retain their individuality while establishing a close and useful relationship. The Horse may be the more positive and aggressive of the pair while the Dog tends to worry about their welfare and will be more guarded and vigilant in his outlook.

With a Boar—Twelfth Branch
The Boar loves action and may seek out the popular and ubiquitous Horse who likes high visibility. The Horse type does not mind the lack of discipline in the Boar because he himself hates to be restricted. The generous Boar will not mind sharing what he has with the passionate and commanding Horse type because in the end the Horse will be able to contribute more than originally expected. Both parties

here like to work with people and have good social skills. The Boar can be strong-tempered and thick-skinned when he is bent on gratifying his own wishes but will be able to deal with the inconstant and mercurial Horse personality. Their relationship should range from modest to good, depending on how much they need each other's skills.

8

THE WEI BRANCH
EIGHTH LUNAR SIGN

The Peacemaker's Song

I am nature's special child
I trust and am rewarded by trust.
Fortune smiles upon my countenance.
All things blossom
in the gentleness of my love.
I strive to nurture peace,
to find beauty in all I behold.
I am fair of heart
and compassionate of spirit.

I am Wei, the Peacemaker

Theodora Lau

THE EIGHTH EARTH BRANCH: WEI
THE SIGN OF THE SHEEP

THE ASSIGNED LUNAR YEARS OF THE SHEEP

February 13, 1907	to February 1, 1908
February 1, 1919	to February 19, 1920
February 17, 1931	to February 5, 1932
February 5, 1943	to January 24, 1944
January 24, 1955	to February 11, 1956
February 9, 1967	to January 29, 1968
January 28, 1979	to February 15, 1980
February 15, 1991	to February 3, 1992
February 1, 2003	to January 21, 2004

If you were born on the day before the lunar year of the Sheep, e.g. February 8, 1967, you belong to the previous earth branch or animal sign which is the seventh branch (the Horse).

If you were born on the day after the Sheep's lunar year ends, e.g. January 30, 1968, you belong to the next earth branch or animal sign, which is the ninth branch (the Monkey).

THE EIGHTH EARTH BRANCH
THE SIGN OF THE SHEEP

The eighth character profile of the twelve earth branches is that of the Sheep whose branch type is called *Wei* in Chinese, symbolising peace and harmony. This considerate and compassionate person sees his world as a bountiful orchard where there is tranquillity in the midst of plenty. There is no strenuous job for him to perform and time is of no great consequence, as all things come to fruition and the seasons are constantly renewed. In his world, he will always be well provided for and will have no large inner struggles or painful bouts with his conscience over things he did and did not do.

Generally, the Sheep of the Wei branch is sensitive to changes and will not be very adventurous. His inability to cope with extremes, and his definition of extremes, depend a lot on his upbringing. However, he may only be comfortable in a narrow range of likes and dislikes and reluctant to venture outside his comfort zone. He also dislikes upsetting the status quo, so don't ever ask him to give people bad news or fire employees. It could make him physically ill to upset others, and he will try at all costs to maintain peace and prevent discord. His love of propriety and his sensitivity to the feelings of others leave him with the joy of patching up broken relationships and sometimes offering his home or office as a neutral zone, so that feuding parties can come and work out their differences.

On the surface, this type will appear very well behaved. A picture of decorum, he is a good listener and sympathetic friend who will do all the right things to put you at ease and calm your fears. However, he may not provide any useful answers or force you to take unpleasant measures to correct the situation. Lending you a shoulder to cry on and giving you his sympathetic ear are about all you may get. This person prefers to let others take the lead but may be the first to complain when things go wrong or when there is any pain or inconvenience. Definitely not a candidate for long-suffering martyrdom, you must not expect great personal sacrifices from him. His job may be as the ego-booster and he could be an excellent sounding board to allow others to work out their own problems. This type has no affinity with pain or sacrifice, although he may hold your hand and cry with you. Although he is always careful in trying not to offend anyone, he is also supersensitive to criticism and takes things out of context. In his depressive moods, he often magnifies his suffering and may lay the blame for his problems on everyone but himself.

Belonging to the fourth and last Triangle of Affinity, that of the Catalysts, the Wei-type person does not have coping skills as well developed as the Rabbit (fourth branch), or the thick skin of the other member of his group, the Boar (twelfth branch). However, these three friends do get on remarkably well and understand each other. Of this trio, the Sheep or Wei type is most susceptible to stress. He tends to complicate his own life with too much involvement and too many emotional ties. He is vulnerable to surrounding conflict, even if problems do not stem from or relate to him. At times he can be masochistic or may blame himself unnecessarily for things not within his control. Depressed by bad news and rejection, he does not have the staying powers to fight or persevere for his convictions.

On the other hand, he is master of the roundabout route and even if he does not take the straight and righteous path of confrontation, he will eventually manage to get his way in a clever yet unobtrusive manner. Thus, persevering and stubborn in his own way, the Sheep personality could launch a quiet kind of protest or resistance which may be more effective than harsh words or ultimatums. He may wear you down with those doleful, sad looks that could wreak havoc with your conscience. Like the constancy of dripping water, his complaints and protests can erode holes in the solid rock of authority. The

Sheep person knows how to yield outwardly yet somehow triumph through subversive submission. Never openly critical; he insinuates, gives tactful hints or sulks dramatically if he cannot have his way. When he is too emotional he can be unstable and should not make important choices under pressure.

There is no doubt that he will be talented and artistic, but he may also be an argumentative procrastinater when he cannot make up his mind. Very much affected by his environment and by how others treat him, he hates being pushed or pressurised to do things or meet deadlines. This person could write the definitive book on how to give believable excuses for delays. His associates know that the best approach could be to take him by the hand and lead him on. Perhaps it might actually be beneficial to submit his work, even if he says it is not yet completed to his satisfaction. It may never be, as he has an elastic sense of time. Stretching deadlines past their limit, he seems to fuss over details endlessly and will never consider something good enough to present until you wrench it from his hands and get it to production. He is basically a worrier and may even imagine problems where there are none. The Wei type also takes sad stories and the misfortune of others to heart and may be found helping total strangers or working for charity.

This cosmopolitan personality can be beguiling and drawn to the finer things in life. Trendy and well informed, you will find him cultured and elegant in his tastes and manners. He loves to project a glamorous image and may be vain where his grooming and attire are concerned. Because he fears abandonment or disapproval, he will be successful in 'faking it until he makes it'. He knows how to buy time with his irresistible charm and powers of persuasion until, inevitably, he gets his way. Always acting with the best intentions at heart, he tends to promise more than he can deliver and is unrealistic in his goals. He may act this way because he secretly fears being excluded or isolated from the fold. Without even realising it, this type could stretch the truth to suit his perspective. Of course, his perspective is bound to be more subjective than objective.

Although he is blessed with an honourable and generous soul, he does have expensive tastes and enjoys being cosseted and spoiled. Enjoying now and paying later is his motto, for he finds it hard to deny himself the luxuries he craves. Socially he is active and can be found in a big circle of friends having loads of fun and entertaining themselves with the expensive toys that money can buy. The indulgent Sheep's approach is to live well and take it one day at a time. So if he earns extra money or comes into a windfall, he will spend it straight away—treat his friends and celebrate lavishly. It will not occur to him to hoard or save some for a rainy day. Perhaps he reasons that if he spends it fast enough, his lucky streak will continue and his purse will be replenished or reimbursed by some magical source.

Yet ironically the Sheep personality is most likely to end up inheriting some fortune from a long-lost relative or friend. He is somehow rewarded for his kind and giving heart and his ability to forgive others. You may also wonder how he is able to get into the good graces of even the most unlikeable people. This is because, as a do-gooder without selfish or ulterior motives, he will find love and acceptance in the most unlikely places. His nurturing traits will yield abundant fruit when he needs it most; his good deeds will not go unnoticed and he will find protection and love from the many people he has helped in the past or befriended along his path.

The Wei or Sheep type does not like to toil at menial tasks or slave away in manual labour. One way or another, he will find a clever way to get someone else to do the dirty work. Congenial and creative, he recognises talent and is able to coordinate difficult and intricate tasks by putting people in the right slots where their abilities will prove most useful. This is the person who knows how to ask a favour and from whom. Naturally, he is often successful in getting the right people to listen to him or see things his way. Although he loves being the centre of activity, he can be overimaginative and irresponsible when the going gets too rough. Anxious and dissatisfied when he is under siege, he can harp on about small errors, dig up past mistakes and dwell on things which cannot be undone or changed. Paralysis by overanalysis may also be one of his ailments, and the Sheep will have everything grinding to a halt while he wallows in indecision.

But in general it is easy to trust the warm and versatile Sheep personality, as his endearing qualities far outweigh his faults. His receptive and generous way makes him the ideal peacemaker. He will want to mother others and protect their interests even to the detriment of his own. As a friend or confidant, his sincerity is unquestionable. He will not mind sharing whatever he has with those he cares about and does not recriminate if others do not reciprocate in kind. For those the Sheep favours he will always manage to find excuses, and will rationalise their shortcomings, for he prefers not to face unpleasant truths until the very last moment. He will always hope and pray that others will redeem themselves or reform their ways—and he is always the first to forgive and extend his hand in friendship.

Health-conscious, he takes good care of himself and those around him. Rather particular about the food he eats and what he drinks, he will want to know who prepared it and what the ingredients are. He also has a thing about cleanliness and hygiene, and although his place may be in a shambles, or 'just a poorly organised mess' as he terms it, physically he will look well turned out in matching colours, with every hair in place. Not too drawn to competitive or team sports, the native of the eighth branch will like to excel on his own at his own speed. So when he does get involved in any sport, one can be sure he achieved it on his own merits and he will have his own unique style.

Never too proud to ask for help or advice, he knows how to make the best of a difficult situation in his own flexible way. Being conservative in outlook, he will seek to minimise risks in business and willingly pay for technical expertise instead of doing any experimenting on his own. In this way he is able to shorten his learning curve and will find professional people with the genuine expertise to benefit him.

Outwardly he may give the impression of being timid, docile and passive, but inwardly he can be intractable and traditional. At times he may put up a show by being theatrical and overly dramatic in order to get attention. Not adventurous or rebellious by nature, he is a keen observer and a cautious player. Taking notes on who is winning and how to take advantage of the situation, he can come up with remarkably ingenious solutions that may not have occurred to others. As a spectator *par excellence*, he will see and learn more than the actual protagonists and eventually benefit most from their mistakes or failures.

At heart, this type is the most compassionate of the twelve branches, but he may find it hard to separate his emotions from the dictates of his mind. He mixes sympathy with reason and always looks for the good in others. Consequently, his perspective is often clouded and his judgement not entirely objective, but somehow he is able to triumph because he acts in a spirit of reconciliation and cooperation with which it is easy to identify. Blessed with a strong sense of what is right, he does not like to break any rules or hurt others intentionally if he can help it. He is one who is able to live and let live. This type has an almost romantic love of fantasy and is a real believer in fairy tales. Perhaps that is why they come true for him. Debonair, cultured and respectable, he may look a picture of moderation and elegance, yet he has his pulse on corporate life and arts, making a point of knowing what is going on about him and nurturing all the right friends in the best circles. A great believer is having mentors and loyal supporters, you can be sure he will always manage to get good press reviews and articles written about himself. The film industry, visual arts, computer industry, communications, broadcasting, public relations and the fashion business would be lost without his influence. Somehow, out of the confusion and almost hysterical scenes he may create, the curtains will rise on opening night and, with all doubts and inhibitions cast aside, his play will commence flawlessly on stage to rave reviews from the press. How does he do it? Well, that's his secret.

Some people born in the eighth branch are: Catherine Deneuve, Andrew Carnegie, Lord Olivier, Bill Gates and Mikhail Gorbachev.

In the final assessment, the inimitable Sheep person has great faith in himself and knows the value of his talents. He makes his contributions unselfishly and without ulterior motives. Usually inspired to express and pursue beauty in all its forms, he listens to his own heart and follows his own intuitions. This person also has that secret place in his mind to which he can escape and find inner peace and tranquillity. In the end, his favourite hobby or leisure pursuit may turn out to be extremely successful and he will be able to reap untold benefits from doing what he enjoys most and being paid for it. Things flourish in the warmth of his touch. A Sheep lady was once asked for the secret of how she grew the most beautiful orchids in town. She refused to take credit and simply replied, 'I know when my orchids are happy and they blossom when given the amount of light they need, but the most important thing is to leave them alone. I suppose my contribution is simply benign neglect.' As a result, this personality's presence is more evident in the final result somehow things multiply under his watchful eye and ministrations.

In his life the Wei or Sheep person will need strong and reliable associates on whom he can lean, people who will guide him and take care of his interests without exploiting him, as a person of the eighth branch brings his own luck and good fortune wherever he goes. He will find success and happiness through trust and cooperation with those who value his creative talents.

As the compassionate Peacemaker of the cycle, the Wei personality of the eighth branch is ruled by his heart and the words: 'I love'.

TRIANGLE OF AFFINITY

The Wei or Sheep type is the second member in the Fourth Triangle of Affinity which produces a group of three Catalysts within the Twelve Earth Branches. There are four Triangles of Affinity in which the personality types are grouped and there is one Circle of Conflict in which all opposite branches are incompatible. In the Fourth Triangle, we have the Rabbit, the Sheep and the Boar, respectively, the fourth, eighth and twelfth branches.

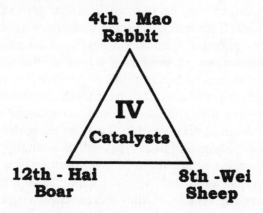

4th - Mao
Rabbit

IV
Catalysts

12th - Hai　　　**8th -Wei**
Boar　　　　　**Sheep**

The members of the Fourth Triangle of Affinity are Catalysts who serve as useful agents in making relationships work. This group is composed of the intuitive, sympathetic and cooperative personality types who bring about changes in others without changing themselves. Supportive, generous and good listeners, the people who occupy the Fourth Triangle of Affinity are keen observers, well-skilled in communication. Artistic, creative and impressionable, they are the guardians of the arts, theatre, publishing and the world of music. Powerful movers and shakers behind the scenes, these types have their fingers on the pulse of society and know how to make things happen in unobtrusive but significant ways. Consciously or unconsciously, they tend to dominate their arena and their influence is often well accepted and enduring.

The personality of this particular triangle tends to be sensitive, insecure and self-serving. He can sense negative vibrations as well as send them when he is unhappy or suspicious. In dealing with anyone belonging to this triangle, one must not expect unconditional support or unwavering loyalty. It is enough that he or she is able to bring parties together in a spirit of cooperation and open-mindedness. He does not mind helping others utilise the right contacts and connections, but do not expect him to stay and hold your hand through thick and thin, as this personality type is not renowned for his undying constancy and will invariably seek to watch over his own interest when given the choice or opportunity. True to his nature, he makes a good arbitrator and mediator as he finds it easy to understand and identify with others, nor is he competitive or aggressive in his approach. Hence, he is most likely to get everyone to join forces with him. Diplomatic, obliging and approachable, he knows how to make influential friends and neutralise his enemies.

Anyone who wants to impress a native of this triangle should emphasise the virtues of compromise rather than confrontation and show him the benefits of negotiation rather than conflict. As the indispensable expert of 'give and take', he will be successful in patching up failed relationships in his own special way by being the peaceful catalyst. The Rabbit, Sheep and Boar types will be naturally drawn to each other and share the same views. In love, partnerships and business, they tend to understand and support each other with great tolerance and understanding. As a team, they will function harmoniously.

CIRCLE OF CONFLICT

The eighth earth branch will encounter his strongest opposition and personality clashes from people belonging to the second branch, or natives of the Ox type. Anyone born with his ascendant in the hours of the Ox (from 1 a.m. to 3 a.m.) will also be in conflict with the Wei or Sheep person. They will not share much in common and will find their differences hard to understand or bear. The Sheep person

2nd - Chou
Ox

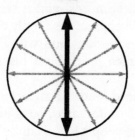

8th - Wei
Sheep

is docile, private and peaceful, while the Ox of the second branch may be too authoritative, dominant and unsympathetic to the kind-hearted Wei type. Even if both have a similar destination or goal, they may prefer to use different methods in their approach or travel via different routes. After all, the forgiving Sheep is decidedly lenient on offenders, while the Ox person, as the Enforcer of the Twelve Branches, will be strict in upholding discipline.

RELATIONSHIPS WITH THE EIGHTH EARTH BRANCH— THE SHEEP

Within the Family

The Sheep personality is secure in the nurturing bosom of his family. He is always solicitous and overly concerned about his loved ones as the thoughtful Wei personality cares deeply and can be blindly devoted to his family. He will indulge his children and spouse and probably spoil them by his lack of discipline. Yet although he may fume and threaten, he will rarely enforce the rules as they are supposed to be enforced. Rationalising and looking for plausible excuses to exempt those close to his heart will be the more characteristic thing for him to do. As a parent he will find it impossible to refuse to help his children or say no to their demands.

Artistic and fashionable, he enjoys entertaining and will maintain open house for freeloaders, overstaying guests and long-lost relatives. A gracious host, he does not forget friends or favours done and will be more than happy to reciprocate, even extending his hospitality and generosity to undeserving people or parasites who will take advantage of his kindness and congeniality. Luckily, the Sheep will always have more than he needs, and it seems the more he shares, the more he receives. He appreciates family closeness and tranquillity but he is also security-conscious and will always try to have a soft pillow of other resources to cushion his family from life's hard knocks.

As a child, he will need loads of attention, cuddling and reassurances. Moody and easily infatuated, he is impressionable and likely to follow more assertive people like a lamb. He is also easily affected by crass remarks, teasing and disapproval from his peers, and may want to hide in his room or refuse to go to school if someone is bullying him. He may also be inconsistent, easily swayed by the opinions of others and fickle, but on the whole he will be compassionate, warm and trusting. He is a great comfort to his parents.

As a Teacher

A careful, understanding and patient teacher, he works well with children and anyone who needs special attention. He does not like to go at too fast a pace for his students and will feed them bite-size information if he can. Not as organised or decisive as other types, he is flexible and tolerant of excuses and will make allowances for the personal handicaps and weaknesses of his students. Refined and kind-hearted, he may pretend to be stern, but he usually does not like to play the part of the authoritative, domineering disciplinarian. Once his students know how to get round him, they may be able to manage him instead. Yet this is not a person one wants to hurt or disappoint because the loss of his love or approval is more damaging than winning some silly game.

His main weapon could be his silent reproachful look and sad countenance of disappointment, which could cause extreme remorse in those he is teaching, more than harsh words or punishment could do. Failing that, he will withdraw into himself and make them feel like unwanted orphans.

Teaching comes naturally to this type as he has a nurturing streak in his nature. His problem is becoming too attached to his charges and learning when to let them go. One has to remove the water-wings from the swimmer eventually and let the learner try to stay afloat by himself. At times he could become too sensitive or emotional and veer off course by becoming involved in areas and issues that should not concern him. It is all right to take a personal interest in one's students occasionally, but the Sheep has difficulty remaining objective. For all his good intentions and sincere wish to help, he may not challenge his students enough unless he is willing to let them fail once in a while and bear the consequences.

As a Lover and Spouse

Subjective and emotional, he wants the world to revolve around him and his beloved. In affairs of the heart he is a willing victim, ready to change to win the approval of his loved one. He will force himself to take a serious interest in the hobbies or career of his love, and is a great motivater and supporter of anyone he is involved with romantically. But while he may be supportive, he also tends to be possessive, oversensitive and overprotective. He will love pursuing all the pleasures life has to offer with his loved one and will spare no expense when entertaining. Totally giving of himself, he can be overindulgent and permissive. Often, he may be hurt because he goes out on a limb to please someone and is rewarded by rejection or apathy. But because he is basically forgiving, he will be able to give the object of his affection a second chance. He will treasure close relationships and is not demanding so long as he feels reassured that he is 'the one and only'.

He compensates for his shortcomings by his loving disposition and willingness to listen and commiserate. The Sheep type will show affinity for the Rabbit personality of the fourth branch and the fun-loving Boar of the twelfth branch. Together they will pursue similar interests in the arts and music and share the same preferences for a stable and stress-free life.

As a Business Partner

Intelligent, artistic and creative, the Sheep personality is instinctive in his understanding of how things should go together. He just knows what will work and what won't. Don't ask him how he does it, just be glad that he is the great identifier of new trends and fashions. Gifted with a flair for colour and design, he can work miracles with unlikely raw materials and even incongruous subjects. He will definitely be a very dependent partner, expecting loads of support and encouragement from the other partners who had better have sufficient funds to carry him through all his creative modes. He can be unreasonable and emotional when he is out of sorts. Nervous and worrying, he also has the tendency to complain and blame others when things do not go his way.

While he is brave and daring in trying out his inspirational ideas, he tends to be passive when it comes to asserting his own opinion and may defer to less knowledgeable but more vocal people. This type needs an aggressive half of the equation to become a success— someone to watch the finances and remind him of the main issues; someone to pat him on the back and urge him on when he gets frustrated or depressed. Once he is focused and assured by a strong backer, the Wei personality can do wonders with his many talents.

As a Boss
The Sheep does not like being the top dog and having to enforce the rules, most of which he may not even be too sure of himself. He tends to rule with a lenient, easy-going style. Caring more about his popularity ratings, he does not like to make overt enemies or embarrass anyone. He may be demanding and petulant on his pet projects, but he can be casual about other things such as punctuality or long lunches. A person of this eighth branch tends to delay decisions to the last minute. He procrastinates and solicits the opinions of everyone and may insist on a consensus before he acts. Generous but not time-conscious, this person will be notorious for his postponements and constant changes.

As a Friend and Colleague
The Sheep type of the Wei branch is a genuine and very caring friend to have. Solicitous, non-judgemental and thoughtful, he is willing to share whatever he has with his friends. This includes secrets and sensitive information which sometimes it would be wiser not to divulge. This type always looks for a confidant, a special friend to entrust with his woes and ask for advice. Sympathy is very important to him and so is the approval of people he respects. However, he sometimes requires too much attention and imposes too much on those close to him. It would be hard ever to deny the Sheep person anything because he is so kind and considerate, yet at times he can truly test one's patience and endurance.

However, as a friend, he will always be at your side in times of need and be a willing listener. Above all, if he should come into any good fortune, one can be sure he will spend lavishly to entertain his friends.

As an Opponent

A person of the eighth branch finds it difficult to appreciate both sides of a problem when he is personally involved. Don't expect him to be calm, logical and reasonable. He won't. In his book rules are made to be changed, and of course they do not apply to him. He will want special treatment, dispensations or waivers, perhaps also a change of venue, of arbitrator, or of time, and possibly a long delay while he takes that long holiday to work out his problems. Finally, he may still want you to fade away quietly like a bad dream.

Failing all the above, he will use concealed tactics, lament long and hard and use his connections to the maximum; he may be very formidable as he calls in favours from his important friends and protectors. Coy and inconsistent; he may be adamant on trivial matters that are blown out of proportion because he becomes paranoid under attack. Also he does not relate well to authority and will cry harassment and discrimination of all kinds. In the end he may settle peacefully, but the process may be dragged out and there may have to be several referees and consultants to wrangle over all the concessions he demands. Now what you thought was a simple disagreement has turned into a landmark case and the Sheep person can easily lose sight of his objective. With too many advisers around, he will also go to unnecessary expense trying to buy advice and reassurance from all sources. The best approach in a dispute with the Sheep person is to talk it out, however long it takes. Let him tell you his entire life story, show you pictures of his children and pets and preferably have a nice meal in a place with a soothing ambience. Let him explain things from his point of view and, no matter how wrong his premise, talk himself out. When he is reassured that you have given him a chance to tell his side of the story, he may feel so relieved that you are not going to bully or take undue advantage of him that he will generously resolve the matter without recriminations.

As the Mediator

The Wei or Sheep personality is a capable mediator when he is not emotionally involved. He is easy to talk to, easy to trust and confide in. As a peacemaker, he can see things clearly and without prejudice. His inborn compassion enables him to identify with both sides in a true and sincere way. However, he must do his homework and check that all information is correct and relevant. He must not allow himself to be influenced or let one or other party take advantage of his trusting heart and vulnerability to hard luck stories.

If he can detach himself from sympathy and act with reason, he will be able to gain the proper perspective and make a wise judgement that will be acceptable to all concerned. The main task for the Sheep type acting as mediator is to distance himself to obtain objectivity and to divorce his emotional side from the issues before him so that his mental observations and genuine desire to bring reconciliation can find a suitable resolution.

It would be inadvisable for this personality to act as mediator for the Ox type (second branch), Dragon type (fifth branch) or Dog type (eleventh branch) in disputes. They may not care for his soft-hearted, indirect approach and he may not have the required toughness to deal with their aggressive and combative natures.

RELATIONS WITH OTHER BRANCHES

With a Rat—First Branch

The Sheep person is easily influenced by his environment and associates. Stress and strife will affect his performance drastically and he cannot concentrate in an atmosphere of dissent. The Rat is an aggressive self-starter and always anxious to succeed ahead of schedule, so he will be critical of the Sheep when things don't go as quickly as he wishes. The Sheep needs a great deal of encouragement and attention to bring out the best in him and the Rat will be affectionate and supportive up to a point. But the thrifty Rat will not agree to spend lavishly or foolishly to satisfy the extravagant tastes of the indulgent Sheep personality. There is likely to be no great attraction between these two unless the Sheep was born during the Rat's hours or the Rat has the Sheep branch as his ascendant.

With an Ox—Second Branch
The Sheep and the Ox personalities differ greatly in their ways of thinking and in their priorities. The regimented Ox is disciplined. He will set his priorities and stick to them rigidly, while the creative Sheep type cannot appreciate, much less tolerate, the Ox's strait-jacket approach. The Sheep cannot understand the Ox's frustration with his lack of punctuality and refusal to be hurried. As a member of the Catalyst group, he succeeds through negotiation, good communications and cooperation, while the Ox type is the rugged individual who does not like to depend on anyone, least of all the Sheep. He will carry his own load and accomplish much through his own merits and efforts. Their views are far apart and irreconcilable if both sides don't make major adjustments. To have a workable union, these two must work through intermediaries or share a common ascendant.

With a Tiger—Third Branch
The Sheep is peaceful by nature and will have good to moderate ties with the captivating Tiger. The Tiger may be protective and sympathetic towards the Sheep because he loves to help those who appear defenceless. Of course, the Sheep is far from helpless but he knows how to appeal to the Tiger's oversize ego and his noble instincts. These two will have need of one another and work and play well together. The Tiger is more likely to be combative, outspoken and unpredictable, but the Sheep excels in being understanding, patient and kind-hearted and will be able to understand and make allowances for the Tiger's many moods because he realises that the Tiger personality only feigns bravado to intimidate others into giving in to his demands.

With a Rabbit—Fourth Branch
The talented Sheep communicates by pouting, sulking and giving out other roundabout messages. He will never come right out and tell you what's wrong. His great potential may lie dormant because he suffers from a lack of tender, loving care or may not be getting the recognition required to bring out the best in him. The Rabbit is an expert at knowing how to read the Sheep and in anticipating his needs. Together, this materialistic team will exploit opportunities and emphasise their strengths. The Rabbit will not only identify the

many strong traits of the Sheep type but will be able to get maximum cooperation out of him—which is not all that easy. The inscrutable Rabbit is astute and diplomatic and he will attend to all the needs of this relationship and allow the imaginative Sheep to work on what he does best.

With a Dragon—Fifth Branch
The Sheep is basically sensitive and obliging and may flourish under the guidance of the Dragon if the latter can motivate the Sheep in a non-belligerent fashion. However, the Dragon is high-spirited and could be too demanding of the Sheep person. So, while the Sheep is drawn to the magnetic Dragon, he is also easily intimidated by his domineering nature. There is bound to be much accomplished if both sides work hard at establishing this relationship, as the optimism and drive of the Dragon and the many capabilities of the artistic Sheep will be enhanced. The agreeable Sheep will be more able to adjust to the Dragon type, while the Dragon will carry the capricious Sheep on his back if that is what it takes to succeed.

With a Snake—Sixth Branch
The loving but dependent Sheep could alienate the intellectual and aloof Snake person who does not like anyone clinging to him unless he initiates the embrace. The Snake views the many whims and inconsistencies in the Sheep as weaknesses and will not take the Sheep into his confidence or be too sympathetic towards the Sheep's frivolous complaints. However, both of them are discriminating lovers of beauty and the arts, and in this area the Snake will realise the excellent skills of the Sheep type. The Sheep may also have need of the Snake's ambition and wise direction if he is to capitalise on his talents. Both could influence each other in a positive way, so long as they focus less on their negative traits and concentrate on how to make this relationship pay off.

With a Horse—Seventh Branch
The Horse is an optimist by nature while the Sheep is the pessimist. The Sheep person will have need of the Horse's courage and speed to take advantage of opportunities he would otherwise miss due to his procrastination. The confident Horse will have no trouble promoting or marketing the Sheep's creations. Both tend to indulge in

caprices, the Sheep being the more extravagant of this pair. The quick-witted Horse is intelligent and entertaining, but the Sheep cannot count on him being around to pamper or console when the going gets rough. The Horse rarely has time to listen or have long heart-to-heart chats such as the Sheep desires, so the Sheep must accept the Horse for the person he is and not make too many demands on such a partner or the relationship could go sour.

With another Sheep—Eighth Branch

There won't be much rivalry when two Sheep personalities form a team, but there won't be much leadership or decision-making either. Both will tend to defer difficult decisions or avoid taking on too much responsibility. They may also waste time on frivolous pursuits instead of applying themselves diligently. Their talents could go a-begging if they cannot establish strong ties with those who can exploit their potential. These two also tend to be extravagant and possessive in a relationship, and their lack of direction may be detrimental to their partnership. In business and in love they will be good friends only if one of them has a very enterprising and strong-minded ascendant to create a deep bond and a long-lasting relationship.

With a Monkey—Ninth Branch

The Sheep is trusting and may be naive and dependent. The opportunistic Monkey may take advantage of the Sheep or he may offer his assistance—in return for a hefty piece of the action, of course. The Monkey is the invaluable problem-solver that the Sheep may need, and if the Monkey can put together a deal and the Sheep agrees to the Monkey being at the helm, this could be a workable partnership. However, the practical Monkey will stress productivity and punctuality and may not allow the Sheep to slack off. The good thing in this joint venture will be that the clever Monkey knows how to motivate the Sheep skilfully to perform. The honey-instead-of-vinegar approach of the Monkey may be the encouragement the Sheep needs in this relationship.

With a Rooster—Tenth Branch

The Rooster, like his best friends the Ox and the Snake, has no sense of humour when it comes to spending within the budget or their work principles. A taskmaster and rigid administrator, he could only bring out the negative traits of the otherwise amiable Sheep native. The Sheep expects special treatment for his many talents and creativity, but the Rooster always enforces the rules and never likes to make exceptions. Both will be frustrated by the differences in their natures and will not even try to communicate because they speak such different languages. Neither will agree to make adjustments or to conform to the wishes of the other. Unless these two have a common ascendant or helpful intermediaries to work with them, they will not care too much for each other's company.

With a Dog—Eleventh Branch
Even if these two do not have much in common, they do have an innate willingness to cooperate and a need to help others if they can. The Dog is sympathetic, loyal and protective, but the Sheep may test his patience with his demand for attention and his numerous complaints. Yet the reliable Dog is not one to neglect or abandon the Sheep, especially if he feels that the Sheep person is in need of his assistance. In this relationship, the Sheep may be in a position to take advantage of the Dog's noble ideals and his need to do his duty, no matter how unpleasant, such as baby-sitting the Sheep. However, the Sheep is the more generous and compassionate of this pair, will always reward the faithful Dog for his devotion and will show his appreciation in many other ways so that the Dog will be compelled to take care of him.

With a Boar—Twelfth Branch
If ever the Sheep person needs a broad shoulder to cry on, he can depend on the Boar. These two will find mutual understanding and be able to cooperate well as they are both unselfish and giving in a relationship. The Boar is tough and will not mind making sacrifices for the sensitive Sheep. Both are sociable and communicative catalysts who enjoy working with people. The Sheep is skilled in areas where the Boar may lack expertise and certainly more refined and discreet in his approach, while the earthy Boar has larger appetites but a more positive and confident outlook. Together they will make an excellent team if they are able to curb their spending and love of material things.

9

THE SHEN BRANCH
NINTH LUNAR SIGN

The Innovator's Song

I am the seasoned traveller
of the Labyrinth.
The genius of alacrity.
Wizard of the impossible.
My brilliance yet unmatched
in its profound originality.
My heart's full of potent magic
that could cast a thousand spells.
Seeking answers to my endless queries,
I overturn barriers and boundaries,
opening new paths and portals
for my own curiosity.

I am Shen, the Innovator

Theodora Lau

THE NINTH EARTH BRANCH: SHEN
THE SIGN OF THE MONKEY

THE ASSIGNED LUNAR YEARS OF THE MONKEY

February 2, 1908	to	January 21, 1909
February 20, 1920	to	February 7, 1921
February 6, 1932	to	January 25, 1933
January 25, 1944	to	February 12, 1945
February 12, 1956	to	January 30, 1957
January 30, 1968	to	February 16, 1969
February 16, 1980	to	February 4, 1981
February 4, 1992	to	January 22, 1993
January 22, 2004	to	February 8, 2005

If you were born on the day before the lunar year of the Monkey, e.g. January 29, 1968, you belong to the previous earth branch or animal sign which is the eighth branch (the Sheep).

If you were born on the day after the Monkey's lunar year ends, e.g. February 17, 1969, you belong to the next earth branch or animal sign, which is the tenth branch (the Rooster).

THE NINTH EARTH BRANCH
THE SIGN OF THE MONKEY

The ninth character profile of the twelve earth branches is that of the Monkey. His branch type is named *Shen* in Chinese and symbolises irrepressible curiosity and creative energy. His is the sign of the innovator as the Monkey or Shen type is extremely progress-minded, and his prowess is often displayed by his ingenuity and wit. Viewing himself at the centre of his universe, which is of course his playground, this person places himself where he is able to make all the rules. Occasionally he escapes into a labyrinth which could be a most intriguing and exciting place inside his intricate mind. Like a computer genius, he knows all the right commands and he can push all the right keys to open new worlds and create new options. Is he satisfied? Never. He'll probably devise harder games to play and invent new and previously inconceivable options to challenge himself. Scoffing at the faint-hearted and slow-witted, the shrewd and optimistic Monkey type tries his hand at anything and will never abandon his efforts to outsmart the competition.

This personality is very intelligent, hyperactive and strong-minded. He represents the unfettered mind freed from inhibitions and guilt. Relieving himself from the heavy burdens of a touchy conscience, the Monkey type will not hesitate to test his theories, experiment and think the unthinkable. In his domain, everything is possible.

What is difficult, he could do right away; what is impossible may take a little longer. Inquisitive and at times irritatingly smug, he will have his nose and fingers stuck into everything. Like the Rat (first branch) and the Dragon (fifth branch) who are his co-members in the first triangle of Doers, the confident Monkey type likes to call the shots and oversee the entire game plan which, by the way, he designed. Carefully prodding, redesigning and fine-tuning situations to his satisfaction, he is not beyond scrapping the entire project and starting from scratch if he suddenly has a better idea. He will amaze and confound people with his agile mind and infinite resourcefulness.

Inventive and versatile, he has a phenomenal memory and is a master of improvisation. Striving constantly to improve himself, he is not discouraged by his own failures as he knows setbacks are only temporary and serve to propel him forward. Objective, factual and ruthlessly logical, he needs but a single approval—his own. The Shen or Monkey learns quickly and his proficiency increases by leaps and bounds once he masters a task. He is also the only person who will intentionally render his own invention obsolete by coming up with something even more imaginative and useful. His capacity to solve problems and wriggle out of dilemmas is legendary and he tends to have many rational explanations to justify his actions. However, one must also realise that this personality will use whatever is at his command to extricate himself from a trap and must not blame him for being so practical. At least he does not depend on others to rescue him or toss him crumbs. He would much rather rely on his own intelligence and swiftness, and of course pay for his own mistakes. But that could be another matter and with this fellow's inventiveness he may not have to pay after all.

Spontaneous and unconventional, he is always alert for opportunities. Looking for that proverbial crack in the armour or the unprotected spot on the Achilles heel, he will pounce on such little windows of opportunity to get ahead in life. He sees no problem in camouflaging his intentions until the last minute because there is no need to warn the opposition of his strategy. He can behave like an instigator and conniver when he feels something he wants is deliberately withheld or hidden from him. Consequently, this person can be a formidable opponent or a wily detective.

Always open to new ideas, no matter how far-fetched an invention is he will find some useful application for it—the unsinkable person of the Shen branch is constantly tinkering with devices for a better, more efficient mousetrap. But he does not work for free—definitely not for love or compliments. Of course it is not fair to call him mercenary, but he wants to be recognised for his contributions and the best way to achieve that is to put a monetary value on his talents. This type is quick at calculating his gains and equally practical in cutting his losses. A realist, he is not going to extend credit or waste time on unfeasible ventures or futile causes. Love, friendship and even family relations do not have a large influence on him if the person concerned lacks merit to begin with. You must fully convince him of your ability to handle a job before he will grant you the opportunity to work for him or with him. It is difficult but always worthwhile to gain his respect and cooperation.

Resolute, bright and crafty, the Shen type tends to be self-assured and independent. He delights in checking out facts and sources just to satisfy his own curiosity and spends endless hours contrasting and comparing statistics and details that he collects. Smart and well informed, he does his homework before making any major purchases and will insist upon getting the best bargain in town. He may come up with special deals you never dreamed existed or make ludicrous bargains in which some merchant will pay him to take his goods. Perhaps that is why his critics always think he has something up his sleeve and never know what sleight of hand he will pull on them next.

The Monkey personality of the ninth earth branch is a wonderful conversationalist. He is a veritable storehouse of knowledge and trivia and his appealing sense of humour and quick wit are indispensable to any team. On the negative side, he cannot resist the urge to tip the scales in his own favour now and then. He may also be quick to snap up a good offer or take advantage of any brief moment of weakness that he notices in others. Don't expect him to feel remorse for his actions. It is his nature to manipulate situations to his benefit and manoeuvre himself into the best positions if he can, and while you may call him an opportunist, he calls himself the vigilant survivalist. Besides, it is not his fault that he is more alert for opportunities than you are. The Monkey is constantly on the look-out for knowledge or experience, so no one should deny him his just rewards. Yet while he is not a poor loser, nor will he be prone to foolish heroics or self-sacrifice without a good purpose. Calmly and resolutely, he will regroup and return to fight another day.

With his ability to align himself with the powers that be, the Shen personality is skilled at using his influence and expertise in controlling situations, pulling whatever strings are necessary. However, try to pull his string and he may baulk and turn the tables on you. When this person is thwarted or restricted, he can be rebellious and opinionated. When he is out to prove that he is right about something, he will leave no stone unturned, and he does not care how long it takes to make his opponent eat his words. Clever and brimming over with nervous and excitable energy, he likes to grab hold of things and will not let go until he is satisfied. This person is most likely to patent his inventions and copyright his work before exhibiting it to the public. He possesses good foresight and can view the whole picture with its long-term overall impact. A great tactician, he is bound to be astute in business and politics and an audacious over-achiever.

Instead of following consensus and doing things traditionally, the Monkey type tends to question and debate. He likes to experiment and test things from all angles. Never one to accept things at face value, he will always have his own questions and suggestions. It will be worth listening to him, for he often has very novel and workable ideas. The only problem is that he can be overbearing and critical when one does not want to do things his way. Often he is over-anxious, suspicious and may jump the gun when he is impatient, thereby making imprudent choices. Complicated and mischievous, he could be spiteful and destructive when he is negative or when his ego is hurt.

The native of the ninth branch must above all believe in his own power to pull a single strand from a knotted mass to untangle the entire spool of yarn. He is able carefully to separate fact from fiction and apply himself diligently to solving baffling mysteries with amazing clarity of mind and purpose. Of course, this could also mean that at times he will overinflate his self-importance and expect a lot of support and obedience from those around him. But his enthusiasm is always contagious and inspiring and he views hard work as child's play, nor does he seem to tire of challenging his own abilities. An invaluable adviser in times of trouble, he refuses to take no for an answer and will search endlessly to resolve problems in a practical way. Like the first and fifth branches, a person of the ninth branch is a Doer and a self-starter, an extrovert who will need little encouragement. Indeed, he knows exactly what he wants and how he will go about getting it. If you won't be around to cheer him on and applaud when he succeeds, the least you can do is get out of his way.

An avid sportsman, public speaker, media person, marketing expert, lawyer, teacher, politician and inventor, a person of the Shen branch is the innovator of the twelve earth branches. He constantly measures himself and his progress and performance; trying to skip a few steps of the game, he often complicates his own life by overdoing things and taking on more than he can handle. Yet it will be hard to persuade him to concentrate on a few choice projects instead of taking the world by storm as he would like to do. A master of self-motivation, he will have his schedule crammed full of things to do and will make a point of knowing exactly what is on your agenda, too. One is likely to find him lamenting the lack of time to attend to everything and be in all the places where he wants to go.

The Monkey personality is gifted with good, clear judgement and a charming disposition, especially when he is after something. He instinctively knows the value of developing good relationships and will try to get on the good side of people who can help him. Using honey instead of vinegar, he will smile sweetly and be most amicable when he wants to sell his ideas and pet projects. Of course, he will have prepared by doing more than just his homework. He will have charts, statistics and future projections with reams of computer printouts and confidential reports to support his case. It would be difficult ever to disagree or reject his presentation as he can be one of the most convincing people around. And, if you do, rest assured he will be back with a better plan, a new, improved version, and you will fall under his spell sooner or later.

His personal magnetism stems from his confidence and ability to find the right answers if he doesn't already have them. A gatherer of information and processor of important data, the Monkey type's memory banks are always full and well documented. He can cross-check and verify anything, so don't bother to fool him. There is also that streak of vengefulness in his nature that gives him sadistic glee in turning the tables on his enemies. He is not likely to let a big injury go without putting up a good fight, and if he loses, one can be sure he will have the audacity to demand a rematch at his convenience. Concede defeat? 'Unthinkable,' says the Monkey.

In spite of his outgoing, fascinating and sophisticated personality, the Monkey of the Shen branch is secretive and keeps his own motives to himself. His suspicions usually hold water but he will always be careful never to accuse anyone openly until he has the whole proof. He will only let his guard down and relax with people he can trust implicitly. His best partners are the Dragon and the Rat. He will see the Rat as the initiator and competent performer that he is and these two can become an unbeatable team. The Rat will gravitate towards the intelligent and success-orientated Monkey person and they could work with one mind. The Monkey will also quickly realise the Dragon's bright potential and strength. Together, these two will excel and capitalise on their assets and ingenuity. The illustrious Dragon may lead the way symbolically, but the Monkey could be the real power behind the throne.

The Ox of the second branch, the Snake of the sixth branch and the Rooster of the tenth branch are able to work well with the Monkey to a fair degree, provided they are not turned off by his occasional high-handedness and argumentative ways. The Rabbit personality of the fourth branch, the Sheep type of the eighth and the Boar person of the twelfth branch may often need the superior wits of the Monkey, but these peaceful and sensitive types may not welcome his controversial ideas and unconventional solutions. They must understand that the Monkey type does not like to do things the old traditional way and may turn over a few carts to bring his point home. The triangle of the Tiger (third branch), the Horse (seventh branch) and the Dog (eleventh branch) may be where the Monkey will encounter considerable resistance. These outspoken Protectors will not be intimidated easily and will openly question the Monkey's motives and intentions or check his credit rating. Naturally, the Monkey will be outraged and offended that they do not jump at his wonderful suggestions and solutions and he will refuse to deal with such persons of little faith.

Some famous personalities belonging to the Monkey type are: Leonardo da Vinci, Joan Crawford, Bette Davis, Paul Gauguin, Elizabeth Taylor and Queen Sirikit of Thailand.

Remember, the Monkey or Shen type of the ninth earth branch is the Innovator of the cycle and is ruled by the key words: 'I think'.

TRIANGLE OF AFFINITY

The Monkey type is the last member in the First Triangle of Affinity which produces a group of three positive Doers of the Twelve Earth Branches. There are four Triangles of Affinity in which the personality types are grouped and there is one Circle of Conflict in which all opposite branches are incompatible. In this First Triangle we have the Rat, Dragon and Monkey, respectively the first, fifth and ninth branches.

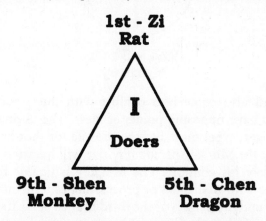

1st - Zi
Rat

I

Doers

9th - Shen   **5th - Chen**
Monkey   **Dragon**

The three who make up the First Triangle of Affinity are a group of positive people who are identified as Doers. They like hands-on activity and are performance- and progress-orientated, adept at handling matters with initiative and innovation. These three players prefer to initiate action and clear their paths of uncertainty and obstacles, and do not hesitate to forge ahead. Restless or short-tempered when hindered or unoccupied, they are fuelled by dynamic energy and ambition. The occupants of the First Triangle are the ones who produce revolutionary ideas and like to make great things happen, and they can team up beautifully since they have a common way of understanding and doing things. Consequently these branches will certainly appreciate each other's way of thinking.

CIRCLE OF CONFLICT

The ninth earth branch will encounter his strongest opposition and personality clashes from persons belonging to the third branch or natives of the Tiger sign. Anyone with his ascendant in the hours of

3rd - Yin
Tiger

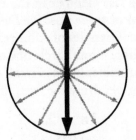

9th - Shen
Monkey

the Tiger will also come into conflict with this personality type. They tend to have opposing points of view. The unpredictable and irrational Tiger type may be too hostile or hot-headed to be enchanted by the Monkey personality. He will question and criticise him too closely for comfort. The Monkey is unable to work well with someone who challenges or procrastinates if he finds things not to his liking, and the person of the third branch is far too daring and independent to follow the Shen or Monkey type without considerable resistance. These two cannot see eye to eye and will not keep quiet about their misgivings. It would be best for them to work through intermediaries and mutual friends. At best, there will be many ups and downs in their rocky relationship, unless they share the same birth hours or the Monkey has the Tiger's hours as his ascendant or the Tiger has the Monkey's.

RELATIONSHIPS WITH THE NINTH EARTH BRANCH—THE MONKEY

Within the Family

Playful, uninhibited and always candid and relaxed at home, the Shen or Monkey type may insist on being taken seriously while lightly taking others for granted. Unless other members demand equal treatment, the clever Monkey personality will just let things slide to his advantage without comment. He can brush off criticism and will take on many commitments. Aggressive and competitive, he often volunteers for community tasks which the rest of the family would rather not do. But he likes to keep a high profile and loves to organise group events, parties and form collective bargaining groups.

As a parent he will groom and coach his children well and teach them to excel early in life. Neighbourly and quite involved in his community and politics, he will also expend a good deal of energy helping his family get ahead—the best schools, a good career, the right kind of contacts and clubs to join to advance in society.

As a child he is inquisitive, precocious and highly strung. He will find it difficult to contain his own enthusiasm and nervous energies and may have outbursts of temper when not given his way. He will do well in school or in sports as he gravitates towards challenges and will be able to concentrate on his own advancement without much outside assistance. Ambitious and charming, he knows how to get along and link up with the best group when it is to his advantage. A self-centred child, he tends to be materialistic (he can play with your toys, but you can't play with his) and he can be possessive with friends as well. He must learn early in life to see the value of sharing and cooperating fairly with others. By and large, he will mature early and show his superior intelligence in his many accomplishments.

As a Teacher

The Monkey type makes a wonderfully imaginative teacher since he enjoys shaping fresh young minds, pushing them to excel and exceeding set limits. Full of tricky questions and little quizzes that could make the students ponder long and deep before answering, he can be an excellent mentor as well as a tormentor. With this person, students must prove their worth and show their true mettle through a series of challenges. Pass this teacher's tests and one truly has merit. Just remember he has mastered the finely calculated art of baiting people to test their skills and endurance. Just when you think you have mastered his game, he could come up with a new one. His students will admire and fear him at the same time. Gifted with a superb memory, he will also have a good sense of humour and allow everyone to skip classes and do something adventurous or experimental to break the tiresome monotony of routine. But he also knows how to enforce his authority and can organise and control his class well. Although he can be aggressive and egotistical, he likes to support his proactive and outspoken students who are not afraid to strike out on their own.

As a Lover and Spouse
A busy life filled with laughter, humour, passion, quarrels, tears and reconciliation will be the standard fare in a romantic liaison with a person of the ninth branch. Restless, thoughtful, imaginative and amusing, the Monkey type can wreak havoc on one's heartstrings if one lets him. Hard to control or predict and difficult to suppress, he must learn to take the middle of the road and trim his sails.

Guilty of sometimes using a double standard, the Monkey type will try to get away with responsibilities while putting his needs and desires first. Of course he will know how to disguise them as mutual goals. Besides, one can hear him rationalising, if someone loves him enough, then he can naturally assume that that special person will want what he wants. Nonetheless, he can be honest when confronted with his faults and make sincere efforts to improve his relationships. Yet he is unconsciously manipulative and adept at controlling things—even affairs of the heart. He can't help himself as he is constantly trying to improve situations. At heart he is always child-like in his sincerity and curiosity. When he feels insecure, he will often try to sell his wonderful image and qualities to his love because he fears losing her if he does not keep reminding her what a terrific person he is. On the whole, this personality type has a great capacity for love despite his many faults, and he will be devoted to those about whom he cares.

As a Business Partner
'Whatever they can do, we can do better' will be his maxim. A go-getting partner, the Monkey person of the ninth branch will be a special asset to have on one's team. Hard to keep up with or keep track of, he is a good negotiator, a skilled coordinator and an excellent manager. The problem is, there may not be anything left for the other partners to do after he has done everything. He needs a lot of independence and may opt for passive partners who finance his ventures with little or no questioning. Advice may not be too welcome either, unless one is the world expert on a subject. But he is very capable and will insist on showing a profit if only to prove his great worth.

If his money is at stake, one can be sure he will be frugal and inventive in making it stretch. He can be tight-fisted and shrewd in business and will leave no stone unturned looking for ways to cut expenses and mislead the competition at the same time. Outwardly he is able to remain cool and focused on his goals. He always has his long-term objective in sight but may grab immediate advancement if he can play both sides of the bargain. This person takes a long time to develop complete trust in his partner or partners. He will not be negligent in his duties but will expect a lot from others, or will tend to nag or supervise excessively if things are not being run to his satisfaction.

As a Boss

The personality of the ninth branch loves to direct others. He realises the significance and synergy of joint forces and will motivate his team with all kinds of inducements. Although he is intense and demanding, he can be generous with rewards and praise so long as everyone does his job. The Monkey type is likely to break up jobs into smaller components and devise shortcuts and checklists to improve efficiency. He is very particular about responsibilities, too, and will carefully monitor productivity and profits; he can be exploitive and unreasonable when expectations are not met.

On the whole, he is not difficult to work for because he is always clear about what he wants and how he expects things to be accomplished. Energetic and confident, he will delegate once he has trained his subordinates and set priorities for them. With his vibrant leadership qualities, he will allow others to learn from their mistakes but will not tolerate laziness or sloppiness. He expects initiative, intelligent questions and lots of brainstorming. When he is overambitious, his chief shortcoming may be that he will allow the means to justify the end or will play one group against another with ruthless efficiency.

As a Friend and Colleague

There will never be a dull moment with the native of the ninth branch. As a very amusing, captivating and spontaneous friend, he will always have some little mischief or plot cooking. Although he may get you into more predicaments than you bargain for, he will be just as quick to get you out of trouble. One dizzy ride after another is what one should expect from an exuberant friend or colleague of the Shen branch.

Sociable, charming and hard to resist, this improviser will not hesitate to try new things or look for adventures. He tends to take control of situations and make decisions for the group without consulting others. Actually, he thinks he is doing everyone a favour by making up their minds and schedules for them. Sometimes it works out well, but on other occasions people may find him presumptuous and too assertive. He enjoys planning group activities and will display originality and enterprising resourcefulness when he is running the show. Just remember, the more he cares about you the more he will want to shape your opinions to align with his. The Monkey type must learn to resist the urge to remake others to his own specifications and allow them to make their own choices once in a while. But then there are those who will always be dependent on him for his invaluable leadership and advice.

As an Opponent

The native of this earth branch can be a difficult and cunning opponent. A good bluffer, he knows how to plant rumours, create doubts and construct some real or psychological bombs under your seat if you are not careful. He may also be unscrupulous in his drive to get even, so be ready to expect the unexpected. The Monkey type will want to win at any cost and may be more destructive than constructive when he is angry. Yet he will never lose his tactical skills and will plot many different strategies to bring down his opponent. He will play mind games and use smokescreens to shield his true intentions. Secretive and vindictive, his mind may work overtime with plots and he will be careful never to drop any hints or spill the beans. Why spoil the surprise?

If one is to work out a good compromise with this personality, one must bargain from a position of strength and show him that one can be more useful on his side than against him. Be self-assured and brave. He respects the bold and strong and will relate well to those who show no fear of his threats. Being a good mind-reader and a skilful negotiator, he will know when the game is up. Then again, he may be too overconfident and overestimate himself while underestimating his enemies. On the whole, the Monkey personality is practical and extremely bright. You won't find him stupid enough to be banging his head against a brick wall in frustration; he will rather explore the alternatives such as climbing over it or digging a tunnel beneath it. But rest assured he will find a way out—his way.

As the Mediator

The Monkey person's bargaining skills will come to the fore when he is a mediator. He can exert a great deal of influence on both sides because he will research the subject beforehand and be able to rattle off statistics and important examples from memory. After brilliantly showing all the pros and cons, he will proceed to prescribe the right medication for the problem in hand. Both parties will then be sufficiently impressed by his quick ability to grasp the vital points of their dispute. The person of the ninth branch is adept at synchronising efforts when he is looking for consensus. He will be able to show each side previously unrecognised benefits to a peaceful settlement and he is also someone who does not believe postponement will help a volatile situation. Acting quickly, he is capable of defusing both sides if he is given the authority. An energetic and excellent problem-solver, he will consider it a personal tragedy if he is unable to resolve a case, and we all know he will never accept failure graciously.

RELATIONS WITH OTHER BRANCHES

With a Rat—First Branch

The Rat personality will find the clever Monkey fascinating and both parties will be drawn to each other by mutual interests, goals and priorities. This pair of Doers is resourceful, energetic and very progress-minded. The Rat will be the innovator while the Monkey is the shrewd tactician. Because they understand each other so well and share the same values and winning attitude, they will rarely let anything get in the way of their compatible partnership. The Monkey's ingenuity and problem-solving techniques will impress the intelligent Rat person who will back the Monkey wholeheartedly. Both will choose not to see each other's faults but will rather capitalise on their enterprising natures and gain much satisfaction and achievement in doing so.

With an Ox—Second Branch
The positive Monkey personality will cooperate with anyone if it will be to his benefit and he will be amenable to working with the Ox. However, it may be the Ox who has reservations or questions the Monkey's methods of doing things. The Ox may have difficulty understanding the Monkey's complicated and intricate schemes and choose to do things in the old conventional way instead of taking any risks. The Monkey may view the Ox as over-cautious, unimaginative and pessimistic. If the Ox can learn to work with the Monkey, he will learn a few short-cuts and may be able to lighten his load, but the traditional Ox may resist any changes in his life. The Monkey will not care to wait around for the Ox to change his mind because, knowing the Ox's inflexibility, it may never happen and the Monkey is just too practical to stay where he is not wanted.

With a Tiger—Third Branch
Both the Tiger and the Monkey types are competitive and not very gracious losers. These negative traits come into play when they work or play as both these aggressive people will be determined to have their own way. The Monkey is the intellectual while the Tiger is a dramatic but emotional personality. The Tiger should understand that if the Monkey matches wits with anyone, he really does not mean to humiliate the other person or show off, but is merely making logical and astute scientific observations to prove his point. Often, however, the Tiger is offended and will take the Monkey's remarks to heart, so creating conflict. Both tend to be paranoid when they are suspicious and in this combination they are constantly on guard and ready to retaliate at the slightest provocation.

With a Rabbit—Fourth Branch
The Monkey may share the same intellectual and artistic preferences as the Rabbit, but the Rabbit does things for pleasure while the Monkey must see some financial results or tangible gains if he is to expend effort. Unless this pair have a common ascendant and mutual interests to work for, they may have only a cool to moderate relationship. The Monkey may find the Rabbit too shrewd and noncommittal in a partnership while the Rabbit could find it hard to trust the elusive Monkey completely. However, both sides tend to be cordial and will not go out of their way to create conflict. They firmly believe

in leaving the door open and never burning their bridges, so one can be sure they will negotiate skilfully if they need anything from each other.

With a Dragon—Fifth Branch
The Dragon may be a powerful engine, but he needs the Monkey to be the driver in order to use his enormous potential. With a strong combination of power and ingenuity, this pair will make a team to contend with. Both parties here know instinctively how to handle and please the other. They communicate on the same level and reinforce each other's ambitions. Energetic, driven and very achievement-orientated, the Monkey and Dragon will create wonderful synergy and have much to show for their successful partnership.

With a Snake—Sixth Branch
The Snake is an intense and resolute loner who cannot compromise easily, especially with the clever Monkey showman. Likewise, the Monkey finds it hard to relax in the Snake's company and will have difficulty in trusting the enigmatic Snake type who keeps his thoughts to himself and does not exchange ideas with the inquisitive Monkey. This is probably because the Snake senses that the Monkey is equipped to outwit or outrun him in the event of any contest and so the Snake is defensive and uneasy. Both may spend too much time looking for faults or focusing on each other's shortcomings instead of building a workable relationship based on mutual interests.

With a Horse—Seventh Branch
The Monkey and the Horse will be able to cooperate and work well to a fair degree as they do not hesitate to use someone when and if it is convenient to achieve a common objective. Neither side will let the other down and will cheerfully do his or her share. Both personalities know how to keep their side of the bargain, fulfil their responsibilities and get things done with a minimum of fuss. Even if they do not agree on some issue, they will each defend the right of the other to disagree and not take things personally. Because they are both flexible and quick to grasp new ideas, they could find much to admire in each other. However, the Horse is the impatient and restless one in this combination and the Monkey may need more commitment from him than the Horse is prepared to give.

With a Sheep—Eighth Branch

The Monkey finds it hard to bond with the retiring and indulgent Sheep person who is often too dependent yet possessive. The Sheep may have need of the Monkey's didactic skills and ingenuity, but feel threatened by the Monkey's bold and complicated ideas. If these two decide to work together, the Monkey will no doubt have a good strategy and be able to fend for both of them with little or no trouble at all. The Sheep will be the more generous and less aggressive partner in this combination and will largely have to accept that he can trust the Monkey to protect their mutual interests. The Monkey will know how to encourage and help the Sheep to give of his best. So long as there is something to gain, these two will not be likely to cut their ties even if they do not fully appreciate each other's way of thinking.

With another Monkey—Ninth Branch

Two Monkey personalities could team up if they have common foes or similar interests. It will make good strategy for them to combine their resources and defeat the opposition. However, they may also be prone to rivalry and petty jealousy and will have some struggles for dominance. There is also a danger of overexposure as they keep seeing their positive traits and irritating faults mirrored in the other. Both will dislike following rules and will not take 'No' for an answer. There will certainly be a good deal of debate and criticism between this two, but the good part is that neither side will be first to cut off the dialogue. So long as they keep on communicating, they will work together.

With a Rooster—Tenth Branch

The Monkey will never be able completely to understand the Rooster, and vice versa, but he could develop immunity to the Rooster's caustic criticism and love of perfection. This is because the Monkey knows he can always change the odds and obtain the results he wants if he puts his mind to work and never gets upset when he fails to get it right the first time. The Rooster may come to respect and admire the Monkey's ingenuity and savvy and listen to his evaluation, no matter how farfetched he may think it is initially. In the end, these two could develop a workable relationship based on similar interests. The Rooster is logical and hardworking, so the Monkey can be sure that the Rooster will do his share and act with integrity.

Both parties here are extremely result-orientated and will certainly strive to have their balances on the plus side of the ledger.

With a Dog—Eleventh Branch

There will be no struggle for dominance between the Monkey and the Dog type as the Dog is good-natured and easy to get along with if the Monkey does not trample on his rights or take undue advantage of him. These two can learn to share if they have mutual friends, interests and objectives. The Dog is a realist but also a bit of a pessimist. The Monkey will certainly try to liven things up with his optimistic, never-give-up attitude and will prove that he can accomplish what others think impossible. However, the Dog will expect loyalty and honesty in their relationship and may be disappointed when the Monkey exaggerates or sometimes stretches the truth.

With a Boar—Twelfth Branch

Monkey and Boar could team up and work towards mutual objectives as they are both outgoing and optimistic personalities. Once each realises how much the other has to offer, they will opt to support one another. The Boar also needs the Monkey to curb his overenthusiasm and extravagance while the Monkey benefits from the Boar's many contacts and the good will he naturally generates. Hopefully, the generous Boar will not mind if the manipulative Monkey pulls the strings, because the Monkey will constantly innovate and look for better opportunities while the less ambitious and scrupulous Boar type may think of ways of spending or enjoying their profits.

10

THE YOU BRANCH
TENTH LUNAR SIGN

The Administrator's Song

I am on hand
to herald in the day,
and to announce its exit.
I thrive by clockwork and precision.
In my unending quest for perfection
all things will be restored to
their rightful place.
I am the exacting taskmaster,
the ever-watchful administrator.
I seek perfect order in my world.
I represent unfailing dedication.

I am You, the Administrator

Theodora Lau

THE TENTH EARTH BRANCH: YOU
THE SIGN OF THE ROOSTER

THE ASSIGNED LUNAR YEARS OF THE ROOSTER

January 22, 1909	to	February 9, 1910
February 8, 1921	to	February 27, 1922
January 26, 1933	to	February 13, 1934
February 13, 1945	to	February 1, 1946
January 31, 1957	to	February 17, 1958
February 17, 1969	to	February 5, 1970
February 5, 1981	to	January 24, 1982
January 23, 1993	to	February 9, 1994
February 9, 2005	to	January 28, 2006

If you were born on the day before the lunar year of the Rooster, e.g. February 16, 1969, you belong to the previous earth branch or animal sign which is the ninth branch (the Monkey).

If you were born on the day after the Rooster's lunar year ends, e.g. February 6, 1970, you belong to the next earth branch or animal sign, which is the eleventh branch (the Dog).

THE TENTH EARTH BRANCH
THE SIGN OF THE ROOSTER

The tenth character profile of the twelve earth branches is that of the Rooster whose branch is called *You* in Chinese, characterised by precision and perfection. The You or Rooster type sees his world as a huge, well oiled, highly efficient factory running like clockwork under his direction—everything in its appointed place and nothing out of place. Efficiency, of course, is at its peak in this environment under the Rooster's sharp eye, not a nanosecond is wasted on anything unnecessary or superfluous. The super-conscientious and diligent Rooster personality is at his best when he is performing exercises of the mind. Although he is not inflexible, he tends to adhere to tried and true hardline principles and does not appreciate changes or deviations even if they are for the better or get the job done faster. Meticulous in the extreme, he tends to nitpick and split hairs to no end.

This personality has a splendid image of himself, so don't bother to ruffle his feathers. He'll brush off your criticism with scorn and disbelief as pure nonsense. He exists to perform his duties and he needs to exercise complete authority or he cannot function at all. No matter how small or insignificant his role, he will follow through admirably. He does not take his responsibilities lightly; on the contrary, he tends to magnify them a hundred times and takes offence if anyone should try to supplant his role. Self-assured and absolutely dauntless in the face of adversity, this person of the tenth earth branch is known for his dedication and no-nonsense enforcement of the rules. He will no doubt expect everyone else to have the great self-discipline he practises and cannot understand or tolerate views that oppose his or, God forbid, are against the law. This person finds it difficult to dismiss even the smallest infringement of the rules. To be truthful, he does sometimes have the knack of making simple things complicated by overanalysing and overworking.

The Rooster type is recognised for his merits as his organisational talents and fiscal abilities come to the fore early in life. Consequently, he is one serious person who does practise whatever he preaches. He finds strength for hard work through his ability to concentrate and persevere. Since he is self-sufficient, he will rely on himself to check and double-check all the facts and figures before making a decision. Tact and discretion are two attributes he could learn to cultivate, but he does not feel he needs them because he is not one to mince words, and finds it imperative to come right to the point. With all his other sterling qualities, one shouldn't expect him to be a diplomat, too. Alert, direct and very precise, he can pinpoint your mistakes with unerring accuracy and write a ten-page report on how to improve your performance. Should you object, he will fail to understand why you are angry that he did not sugarcoat his negative comments. Adroit at expressing himself, he will also never pass up an opportunity to recount his accomplishments and his many victories.

Basically, this personality is sincere, helpful and loves to come to the rescue. If you can stomach all the 'I told you sos', you will find his expertise indispensable. What others might consider drudgery, he will look upon with delight. He does not tire of repetitive tasks and painstaking details such as reconciling accounts, balancing budgets or looking for typing errors and misspellings in proofreading manuscripts. He is the third member of the Second Triangle of Affinity—the Thinkers. Like the other two branches who occupy his triangle, the Ox (second branch) and the Snake (sixth branch), the Rooster is an introvert and looks within for solutions to his problems. Gifted with sharp analytical intelligence, he has a clear and logical mind. Imperfections, however slight, may bother him no end and he will find no rest until he is able to correct that tiny mistake that no one else noticed or even cared about. He may be fastidious and fiercely critical, especially when his routine is disturbed or his schedule changed, but he is predictable in that he will always like to do things in the proper sequence, taking no short cuts. Consistent in his many eccentric habits, he is never afraid of stirring up controversy just so that he can put things back in order. At his best he is very dependable, systematic and hard-working. He won't mind helping out and can be found doing more than his fair share without complaint. His stamina is hard to match and he will not hesitate to take those for whom he feels responsible under his wing, with or without their consent. Protective of those he loves and of his own interests as well, this type loves to investigate all possibilities and leave nothing to chance.

Bold, observant and not easily deterred, the Rooster or You type has his very own brand of foresight. A famous native of this branch once compared himself to a bird perched atop the head of a giant. From his superior position he could see farther than the giant. Never underestimate the abilities of the Rooster type as very little eludes his sharp mind and eyes. Sooner or later he will take inventory and find something amiss. The most capable accountants, efficiency experts, scientists, military planners, computer geniuses and proofreaders belong to this earth branch. He is also chivalrous and generous by nature and will give advice freely, whether solicited or not. At times he can be decidedly overambitious and may carry heroism beyond what is necessary or wise. Egocentric and blessed with absolute faith in his own abilities, he tends to place more emphasis on theory than on practical applications. Thus he may get bogged down in simple things after sorting out the most difficult mathematical problems. His merits can become hindrances when he puts everything under a microscope and creates dilemmas that do not exist in normal circumstances.

For all his interfering and questioning ways, this person is most likely to stick to his convictions and keep sight of his goals. He knows how to focus his attention and lock in on his target. From that point on, there is no way to sway him from his plotted course. More often than not, he will be right. His suspicions are usually valid and his exemplary research data will be beyond reproach. Precise, honest and didactic, he will have a point of view for every issue. Meticulous in the way he organises his life and his time, this industrious type cannot stand laziness or inconstancy in any form. Full of good will, he likes to pay attention to details and succeed in the ordinary things that we take for granted. He is civic-minded and will volunteer for thankless tasks that others shun. But, bit by bit, he will reconstruct large projects that others thought impossible. Many industrialists and entrepreneurs belong to the You earth branch because they are able to compartmentalise things into components and then build up a multinational conglomerate by simply putting one building block on top of another, patiently linking up all the pieces and controlling the entire organisation from their power centre.

When the Rooster of the You branch is challenged, he can be acerbic, domineering and pompous. With or without meaning to, he can also be insensitive to the feelings of others. Competent and competitive, the You personality may be impatient and unforgiving with those less perfect than himself, and that covers nearly everyone. He considers himself in a class all by himself so it's best not to take him too seriously when he starts to pat himself on the back and show off all his medals and awards. His harmless need for attention and acknowledgement of his abilities is just his way of basking in self-manufactured limelight. Be assured, he will not let his delusions of grandeur interfere with his work or duties. Somehow he is able to separate things into their proper priorities and categories.

With his confidence rarely clouded by doubt or insecurity, the native of the tenth branch is a great positive thinker. He does not like to procrastinate or look for consensus; nor does he need a vote of confidence from the majority. Acting on his own belief and being armed with knowledge of the facts are enough for him. Yet when you delegate a task to him, he is one of the most obedient of subordinates and will admire and even revere authority figures who provide good leadership. Power and wealth represent control to him, and control and discipline are things he can fully comprehend and support. Any break in the ranks means failure and a loss of authority and he cannot live with chaos. With this personality type, one must be fully committed, because if you are not 100 per cent for him, then he will conclude that you are against him. His exacting nature does not buy him a lot of friends, but those he does retain will be more than loyal to him and meet his stringent requirements. He will not make any excuses for who he is or what he stands for, so it is relatively easy to take him at face value.

To work effectively with this type of personality, one must first be reconciled to the fact that to know him is not immediately to love him. However, one does not even have to like him to recognise his many abilities and contributions. He is able to do his job efficiently and quickly without ever becoming too personal. He is entirely objective and does not need bonds or close relationships to function well. Actually, he may even prefer to remain businesslike, professional and aloof so that he can disengage himself quickly from any further association once the job is over and done with. All he wants is your trust, cooperation and respect; there is no need to be familiar unless he warms to you first. When he succeeds he will do so by sheer dedication, diligence and tenacity. When he takes it upon himself to pursue power, he will reach the pinnacle and build his nest there. Of course it may be quite lonely up there on his high perch, but from his point of view that is the best place for him to oversee his empire. So don't bother to feel sorry for him: he doesn't need your sympathy at all.

Particular, unyielding and courageous in his arrogance, the Rooster type will bond well with those who share the same analytical outlook on life. His best partners will be the Ox of the second branch and the Snake of the sixth branch. He will also get along with the members of the Triangle of Doers—the Rat of the first branch, the Dragon of the fifth and the Monkey of the ninth. There will always be arguments, debates and long-winded discourses on semantics and logistics wherever the Rooster personality presides, but the Doers are able to work well with him and not lose sight of their own objectives. The members of the Triangle of the Protectors, the Tiger of the third earth branch, the Horse of the seventh and the Dog of the eleventh, will also accept the eccentric and critical You person for what he is and see beyond the brash packaging to the real talents and indispensable contributions he could make. The most difficult relationship for the Rooster will be with the Rabbit type of the fourth branch. Likewise, relations with the other two members of the Rabbit's Triangle of Affinity will also be frosty and strained by the Rooster's love of precision and quest for perfection. The Rabbit, Sheep and Boar trio care more about how a message is delivered to them than the actual content. The Rabbit is soft-spoken and polite but can be very tough and uncompromising in his quiet way. The Rooster type, on the other hand, is full of good intentions and sincerity but somehow comes across as high-handed and abrasive. He tends to present his views in an argumentative and dogmatic tone and this irritates the sensitive Rabbit type who will reject this approach, even if it is the best one.

The You type's problems in life will not stem from his ability to communicate. He is able to do that well and he is adroit in presenting his views and solutions with great clarity. He would make his life easier and smoother if he could cultivate his listening skills and refrain from being too judgemental. If he can realise that it is not necessary for him to like or approve of others but merely to accept them as they are, warts and all, and resist that urge to polish their performance, get them to stand up straight or salute when he comes into the room, then others will also learn to tolerate his idiosyncrasies and pedantic behaviour.

In praise of the achievement-conscious Rooster personality, one can say he is never ambivalent about what he likes or wants. Ask him what he wants for Christmas or his birthday, and he will whip out a list from his pocket and ask you to pick an item. Then he will tell you in no uncertain terms where you could buy it at a discount (he never likes to pay full price) and the size and colour he prefers.

To perform at the peak of his powers, this type needs similarly devoted souls like himself to bond valuable skills together and focus their strength like a concentrated laser beam on a single objective. No doubt, if anyone can achieve such single-mindedness in turning his dream into reality, the dynamic Rooster person can and will.

As the Administrator of the cycle, the You or Rooster personality operates with this key thought in mind: 'I count'.

TRIANGLE OF AFFINITY

The Rooster or You personality is the third member of the Second Triangle of Affinity which produces a group of three introspective Thinkers of the Twelve Earth Branches. There is a total of four Triangles of Affinity in which the personality types are grouped and one Circle of Conflict in which all opposite branches are incompatible. In the Second Triangle we have the Ox, Snake and Rooster, respectively the second, sixth and tenth branches.

This trio occupying the Second Triangle of Affinity is a group of purposeful Thinkers who like quietly to compose their thoughts and

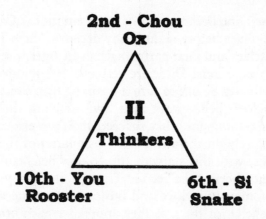

2nd - Chou
Ox

II

Thinkers

10th - You
Rooster

6th - Si
Snake

strategy before taking any action. They are the planners, the schemers and the meticulous decision-makers who base their actions on statistics and information. They are unlikely to need the approval of others once they have made up their minds as these personalities only need their own validation to do the right thing and follow the correct course. In general, these planners prefer to observe, ponder and investigate before making any judgement. You can be assured that they will check out facts, look closely into details and have all the available contingencies thoroughly explained before making their move.

The three Thinkers tend to have introspective and egotistic characters. Secretive, reserved and often stoical, they are also consistent, tenacious and gifted with foresight and fortitude. They will be recognised for their dedication to duty, patience and ability to inspire others by their example. Able to outwit and out-think the competition, the Ox, Snake and Rooster personalities reach their goals through calm resolution and determination.

To work well with them one must have the facts and figures ready and be prepared to appeal to their superior intelligence and analytical capabilities. Be sure to explain how they will benefit both in the long run and the short term. Show how you intend to plough back the profits and how things will pay off in stages, allowing stockholders to profit slowly but surely. They tend to avoid taking risks and dislike gambling or speculative ventures. They can be ruthless in their quest for power and will not hesitate to eliminate those who block their path. This is because power translates into control. Intelligent, practical and calculating, they are systematic in dealing with their problems and with their enemies. Cautious, deliberate and industrious, they will follow their intellect instead of their emotions. Careful about addressing all issues before making any decision, these Thinkers are hard on themselves and their partners when an enterprise or business venture stumbles or fails. These are very business-minded personalities who will always be out to turn a profit or reap some reward for their efforts. Great believers in their own abilities, they will work tirelessly at something until they succeed and their efforts bear fruit. Others tend to rely on them to be the visionaries of the future and will hitch a ride with this stalwart trio to new heights of success.

The three members of the Second Triangle of Affinity will be able to get along famously in love and business. Working as a team is easy and beneficial for them as they appreciate each other's way of thinking. In marriage and business they will find understanding and work productively towards common goals since they value stability and long-term relationships and will have the endurance and confidence to support one another in their endeavours.

People with their ascendant signs belonging to this Second Triangle of Affinity, those born during the hours of the Ox branch, the Snake branch or the Rooster branch, will also be able to establish close ties with the natives of this group and find much in common.

CIRCLE OF CONFLICT

The Rooster personality of the You branch will encounter his biggest clashes and opposition from people belonging to the fourth branch or a native of the Rabbit sign. The Rabbit personality will find the

4th - Mao
Rabbit

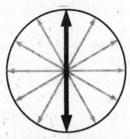

10th - You
Rooster

Rooster much too serious and abrasive for his liking. He feels that the Rooster never learns how to enjoy life, and won't allow others to either. While the Rabbit is guided by instinct and discretion, the Rooster's penchant for controversy and criticism scandalises the well-behaved Rabbit and causes him to distance himself from this trouble-maker who could turn his world topsy-turvy.

From the Rooster's perspective the Rabbit can be inscrutable, unpersevering, docile and indulgent. In the Rooster person's eyes, people of the fourth branch never seem to be worried about anything in life except their own pleasure and interests. Actually, both types are introverts, but while the Rooster is outspoken and direct with his displeasure, the Rabbit may brood and plot ruthlessly in secret. These two occupy their minds and energies on opposite sides of the spectrum and cannot appreciate each other's way of thinking. The You or Rooster person is careful with his finances and lives in an orderly, functional world, while the Rabbit moves in elegant circles, surrounds himself with comfort and affluence and is not likely to bother with too many duties that eat up his playtime. The Rabbit will not hesitate to spend on his own comfort and enjoy expensive toys, clothes, jewellery and gourmet meals in fancy restaurants. In contrast, the spartan Rooster or You personality prefers to lead a busy, involved life and worry about all his responsibilities and commitments before he can relax or even enjoy himself. Frugal and cost-conscious, he does not spend frivolously and, to the Rabbit's dismay, may even consider work as a form of relaxation.

RELATIONSHIPS WITH THE TENTH EARTH BRANCH— THE ROOSTER

Within the Family

The Rooster loves his home and family because this is where his support group and cheering squad reside. A lovable tyrant or organised disciplinarian, he will be responsible and dutiful, always running on schedule or even ahead of it. Making lists, checking appointments and having separate timetables and calendars for everyone in the house posted in visible places, he will take it upon himself to supervise, supervise, supervise.

As a parent he can be demanding and critical. He enjoys his

position of dominance and expects everyone to look up to him for guidance and protection. He makes sure that his children know his rules and can be strict and uncompromising when someone breaks them. But he is a good provider and will try to ensure that his family lacks for nothing. He will blame himself if he is unable to live up to their expectations and will certainly make every effort to anticipate their needs and provide all the essentials.

As a child, the person of the tenth branch can be exemplary in school work and responsible at home. Always eager to excel and please his parents and teachers, he will be diligent and competitive. Busy making the most of his time and handling difficult tasks with perseverance, the Rooster type child can be particular and extremely determined in establishing his own standards and schedules. Didactic, careful and precise, he will want to dissect things and categorise endlessly. Sorting out the pros and cons also makes him opinionated and meticulous in the eyes of others. But he is ever vigilant to assist those who may need him and he is ready to make extra efforts to go beyond the call of duty.

As a Teacher

The Rooster type as a teacher cannot and will not lower his high standards. Either one perseveres or one is out of favour with him. Things must be done precisely his way. He loves charts, graphs, progress reports and passages from the Bible or other favourite texts that will broaden the minds and hearts of his charges. Famous for his deadlines and inflexible opinions, the Rooster type demands respect and unquestioning loyalty from his students. In return, he is a good mentor and a patient, factual instructor who will not tire of guiding his students. His endurance is only matched by his industry and attention to detail. A dedicated teacher, he will strive gallantly to be available to help each and everyone in the class; he can be found staying after school hours to help those who need to catch up in the lessons. Of course, he will criticise small infractions and give rambling lectures, but he does get the job done and will insist that nothing is out of place or amiss. The one good thing about this type of teacher is that he will view things in an objective way and not bear grudges or be vindictive. He may make an issue out of one assignment that is done incorrectly, but he will forget about it once he has set a person on the right course. Analytical and observant, he does not like emotions to distract his objectivity or that of his students.

As a Lover and Spouse

Love to the Rooster type is another kind of responsibility and challenge. He will view it as something to analyse and organise if he can. This person can be intense and very devoted to his loved ones, and no one can accuse him of being unworthy or unreliable, but sometimes he does tend to be domineering and puritanical. He also gets caught up with his own views and forgets to ask others if he has their consent to run the whole show. Often he fails to read people well and may be hurt when they are disappointed in him or do not share his enthusiasm. One must be blunt and specific with him when it comes to affairs of the heart. He cannot read between the lines or take gentle hints. Unfortunately for him, logic won't help: feelings cannot be analysed and structured as he desires, and although he may think that he has the perfect 'formula' for a love potion that no one could resist, he may be set for a rude awakening. His lover or spouse cannot always be a reflection or an extension of his image and the sooner he accepts this fact, the better for everyone concerned. He is bold, ostentatious and self-assured in love and romance. Armed with all the positive answers, he will convince his beloved that he can conquer the world with her by his side.

As a Business Partner

The You or Rooster personality will never want to be the silent partner. He may be uncommunicative, but he will still want to make inventories and balance the cheque book. This person will have the dedication and stamina to take on a venture and nurture it to be a success. He could wear out the other partners with lots of meetings, detailed reports, checks and balances. Quality control, inventories, delivery schedules and alternatives for all contingencies must be addressed to put him at ease. He would like to be prepared for the worst and will buy insurance for protection. Cautious and conservative with finances, he has foresight and likes long-range planning. His fastidious record-keeping will also keep the tax man at bay.

On the negative side, he cannot tolerate opposing views or different ways of doing things. It would be wise to establish rules and divide responsibilities early in a business relationship or the Rooster will feel unstable and insecure about his position in the company.

However, once the partnership has been well established, the Rooster will give all his energies to doing the best he possibly can. It is unlikely that this personality will ever be ambivalent about how the business should be operated and who should be in charge. Under his auspices, a partnership will flourish or be beset with many petty arguments and power struggles, so it is important that the lines be drawn clearly right from the start.

As a Boss
As a boss, the person of the tenth branch will never be unsure of his distinguished role. He may often overstep his authority, but who will have the courage to confront him? Yet even if he does tend to be a little pompous, he is hard-working and tireless in looking for ways to move ahead. His need for order and regularity could be a strain on his subordinates and some may even consider him a control freak, but there will be many who admire his leadership and organisational talents. Dynamic, competitive and astute in money matters, he will expect everyone to pay attention to detail and check the work carefully. His office will be neat and efficient and he will not accept excuses or tardiness.

Expect rules and regulations to be posted on the board and weekly charts and newsletters on your desk as regular as the sunrise. Very little goes on without his knowledge or gets past his scrutiny, so it would be best to apply oneself instead of trying to outwit him. His main problem will be getting bogged down in details and ignoring the large picture while he is busy tying up those odds and ends. As a boss, this personality is protective of the interests of his group and will value team effort and support common goals wholeheartedly.

As a Friend and Colleague
Solicitous and honest in his friendships, the Rooster type is helpful and giving. Always ready to update and inform those close to him, he can also be direct and forceful in pushing his opinions on his friends and associates. He likes to be involved in social functions, sports and competitive activities, and will impress his friends with his natural competence and skill. Steadfast and dependable in times of trouble, he can be counted on to fly to the assistance of his friends when they are in trouble. Of course there is bound to be a scolding

or a long speech once the crisis is over, but this person is worth his weight in gold and is kind-hearted and forgiving whatever other faults he may possess.

As an Opponent
It will be hard for others, especially his foes, to ignore this personality's authoritarian outlook and rigid adherence to the rules. He may be unbending and fastidious in a conflict and accelerate disagreements unnecessarily. Although his complaints or arguments may be justified, he must allow the other side to save face or at least have their say. Patient though he is in studying matters that interest him, he can be intolerant in allowing others to speak out or expound their opposing views. The native of the tenth branch could take lessons in listening before forming his strong opinions and locking himself in an inflexible stance.

One must enlist the help of compatible friends and associates to work out problems with this type of person. He cannot be intimidated, but he can be reasoned with if you find the right ally. Nor will he leave quietly when he finds out that he is wrong or that the cards are stacked against him; he will want faithful supporters to be on hand to nurse his battered ego and comfort him. Yet he will be practical enough to accept a workable solution if he is allowed to participate in its discovery. In other words, if you can possibly make him believe that the solution was his idea, it would be so much easier to resolve the dispute. Indeed, he will take the credit and insist that he was the genius and the peacemaker.

As the Mediator
The Rooster of the tenth branch has unimpeachable honesty and integrity, but his in-depth analytical prowess and intellectual hairsplitting could interfere with his effectiveness as a mediator. If he questions both sides like the Grand Inquisitor, he will overdo things and wear everyone out. On second thoughts, it may be a good ploy because they will beg to settle fast just to get him out of their hair! He may be like someone you have invited to help you organise an event, but who decides to run the entire show and starts ordering you around. All the precision and regimentation will no doubt spoil the mood of the event and eventually you will regret asking for his help in the first place. Of course, now that he has gone to all that

trouble and spent all his time working for you, he will resent your ungratefulness. However, he is not a quitter and, come what may, he may insist on staying and finishing the job he was given. Whether or not you will recover is another matter.

In his role as mediator, the Rooster person must be given strict guidelines and a rigid timetable. He must not be allowed to stray into areas not within his authority. No doubt he can and will be most fair and efficient. Let's just hope the warring parties in the dispute survive his meticulous intervention. One can be sure the You type will not abandon his post as mediator and will see things through successfully if the rules are set and understood beforehand.

RELATIONS WITH OTHER BRANCHES

With a Rat—First Branch
There are bound to be some difficulties in communication between these two types as both dislike listening, are opinionated and have a tendency to argue. They will test each other's patience with their nit-picking and petty debates. The Rooster may be critical and unco-operative if the outspoken Rat elaborates his shortcomings and they will need mutual friends to referee their partnership as both are competitive and will be reluctant to back down. This relationship could work well, but only if the Rat has a Rooster ascendant or the Rooster was born during the hours of the Rat branch. Their points of mutual interest could be that both are family or home orientated and both have the same frugal habits and respect for money.

With an Ox—Second Branch
These two personalities belong to the same Triangle of Affinity, and as Thinkers they will be very deliberate and methodical in their approach. Both are time- and money-conscious and do not like to waste either of these commodities. You can be sure that they will cooperate and support one another faithfully. The Ox will admire the sterling qualities of the well organised Rooster type, who in turn will certainly understand the industrious Ox's need for security and order in life. They will bond easily and establish a long and lasting relationship as they have so much in common and do not have to make many adjustments to work harmoniously with one another.

With a Tiger—Third Branch

The Rooster and the Tiger are both colourful and performance orientated. But that is where the similarities end. The Rooster may find the Tiger's lack of discipline and rebelliousness difficult to accept, while the Tiger will not appreciate the Rooster looking at petty details through a microscope and magnifying the Tiger's faults. However, the Tiger must realise that although he is a subjective personality and prefers to assess things with the heart and ego, the Rooster person is basically very objective and feels compelled to have everything tabulated into pros and cons before he can make a logical assessment. The Rooster will not go out of his way to offend the Tiger, but neither will he be prepared to make any changes in his way of doing things. After all, he is the perfectionist who can do no wrong. The Tiger will either love the dauntless Rooster or find him unbearable, depending on how they interact at their first encounter.

With a Rabbit—Fourth Branch

The Rooster will not be attracted to the well-mannered but introverted Rabbit personality because they have so little in common. The Rabbit loves harmony, while the argumentative Rooster thinks nothing of making a big fuss such as demanding an immediate audit and report of every penny spent. The Rooster also rubs up against the Rabbit's delicate sensitivity and love of discretion. Actually, they may have the same interests and goals, but they handle problems and conduct business in opposing fashions. The Rabbit will work quietly to defuse controversy and resistance, while the Rooster may be heavy-handed and inflexible even when there is no need. Unless this pair shares a mutual ascendant or is obligated to work together, they will opt to avoid the stress of each other's company.

With a Dragon—Fifth Branch

The Dragon is drawn to the Rooster's competence and expertise while the Rooster is impressed by the Dragon's high-spirited outlook and dynamic strength. However, both have large egos and may have inflated expectations. If they hope to find success and happiness together, they will have to be more realistic and less optimistic. Yet their arguments will be objective and even productive as neither is afraid of criticism or hard work. Both are fighters, although the Dragon is physical and emotional in his approach while the Rooster is obsessed with perfection and accuracy in his life. Once each realises that the other has the half of the equation that he himself lacks, these two practical souls will want to join forces and work out their differences amicably.

With a Snake—Sixth Branch

The Rooster is drawn to the quiet but intense Snake personality because the Snake is able to comprehend how the industrious Rooster ticks. Both members of this team are introspective and tenacious although the Snake can be reserved and cultivated in his wisdom while the Rooster feels he must impose his views on others, with or without their consent. The charismatic Snake is able to brush aside the Rooster's eccentricity and many faults and see him for the helpful and invaluable ally he is. The Snake is passionate, decisive and constant and the Rooster will have no trouble in forming a close and lasting partnership with him.

With a Horse—Seventh Branch

The Rooster will admire the speed, agility and intelligence of the Horse but be dismayed by his impulsiveness and lack of consistency. The Horse finds it hard to identify with the intense Rooster's particular and controlling ways. He operates by instinct, whereas the Rooster must do detailed research and analyse everything down to the last molecule. Naturally, the Horse will become restless and impatient with the hair-splitting Rooster's need for perfection. If these two are assigned the same task and not permitted to meddle with the way each goes about accomplishing his objective, they may discover that there are different ways of doing things and that they may both be right. But, on the whole, the Horse likes to be adventurous and unconventional while the Rooster will stick with the traditional and well-proven route.

With a Sheep—Eighth Branch

The Rooster will have great difficulty establishing rapport with the passive and pessimistic Sheep personality. The Sheep needs to be wooed and complimented to bring out the best in him, but the Rooster will do just the opposite and so alienate the peace-loving Sheep. Neither can appreciate the other's view in this combination and they may shun close relations unless they have no choice. The

Sheep will perform and give his support to any cause provided he is allowed to do so on his terms and in his own time frame. However, the Rooster is meticulous and regimental and will not comprehend the Sheep's lack of stamina and inability to function exactly as he dictates.

With a Monkey—Ninth Branch
The Monkey is adaptable and likes to improvise, whereas the Rooster is inflexible and cannot tolerate changes in routine or schedule. Both are efficient and competent and could work well together if the Rooster allows the Monkey some room to express his ingenuity. The Monkey will not take the Rooster's criticisms to heart and will know how to get on the right side of him if he wants anything. However, the Monkey must exercise patience as the Rooster may want to check everything over and over. Their moderate relationship may hit a snag if the Monkey should take a short cut or invent a new way of doing things while the Rooster resists or insists on doing things the conventional way.

With another Rooster—Tenth Branch
The Rooster could have a good relation with another Rooster only if they belonged to the opposite sex. Otherwise, they could suffer an overdose of their own positive and negative traits and find each other insufferable. It would be like having two efficiency experts doing the same job twice. However, one partner may also be extremely quiet, but efficient and observant, while the other may be loud and critical but likewise not miss a single detail. Although these two energetic and egotistical personalities may get a lot done, there will still be a lot of discussion and criticism going back and forth before they agree on the right way to tackle their problem. Yet these two could have a good relationship as they both take responsibility very seriously. Their main problem will be that they do tend to complicate or over-analyse simple things.

With a Dog—Eleventh Branch
The Dog is a realist and the Rooster the high-flying optimist. They could work well together although the Rooster may worry the Dog personality with his lofty ambitions and his need to have everything done just right. The Dog is level-headed and practical and takes the

Rooster's dogmatic opinions with a pinch of salt. After all, what seems to work on paper and in theory may not always turn out the same way in actual application. In this relationship the Dog will be able to hold his own ground, and he has the patience and good will to support the controversial Rooster because he knows that although the Rooster is eccentric, he is honourable and will have good intentions.

With a Boar—Twelfth Branch

The Rooster will get along with the chivalrous Boar personality because the latter is not bothered too much by the Rooster's controlling and particular ways. But the Rooster will try to refine and remake the Boar into someone more disciplined and organised. This could be a losing venture, but the industrious Rooster will still take on this thankless task, much to the despair of the Boar. However, the kind and generous Boar will defuse controversy with the Rooster by his affable nature. The Boar may be receptive to the Rooster's advice and admonitions if he is so inclined, but he also has the habit of hearing what he wants and then doing as he wishes anyway. These two do not deal with conflict in the same manner and may not appreciate each other's approach.

11

THE XU BRANCH
ELEVENTH LUNAR SIGN

The Guardian's Song

Truth and loyalty are my only guides.
Trust is forever by my side.
Humanity has entrusted me
to hear your sorrows,
still your pain.
I am the protector of Justice,
Equality—my stalwart friend.
My vision never blurred by cowardice,
my soul never chained.
Life without honour
is life in vain.

I am Xu, the Guardian

Theodora Lau

THE ELEVENTH EARTH BRANCH: XU
THE SIGN OF THE DOG

THE ASSIGNED LUNAR YEARS OF THE DOG

February 10, 1910	to January 29, 1911
January 28, 1922	to February 15, 1923
February 14, 1934	to February 3, 1935
February 2, 1946	to January 21, 1947
February 18, 1958	to February 7, 1959
February 6, 1970	to January 26, 1971
January 25, 1982	to February 12, 1983
February 10, 1994	to January 30, 1995
January 29, 2006	to February 17, 2007

If you were born on the day before the lunar year of the Dog, e.g. February 5, 1970, you belong to the previous earth branch or animal sign which is the tenth branch (the Rooster).

If you were born on the day after the Dog's lunar year ends, e.g. January 27, 1971, you belong to the next earth branch or animal sign, which is the twelfth branch (the Boar).

THE ELEVENTH BRANCH
THE SIGN OF THE DOG

The eleventh character profile of the twelve earth branches is that of the Dog whose branch is called *Xu* in Chinese, to symbolise integrity and loyalty. A person of this personality type loves companionship and needs to be needed. Although he may seem like a revolutionary with pacifist's views, he sees his world as a vulnerable place that requires his protection. As a result, he must constantly patrol his domain and defend every corner of it from harm. To feel comfortable, the Dog or Xu personality must have an invisible fence around himself or his environment. When someone or some place is under his protection, he cannot abide disturbances, invasions or interference from any source. Watchful and restless by nature, he sounds the alarm without hesitation when he is suspicious, as this personality type can be hostile and uncompromising when provoked. But if he is left undisturbed he is quite peaceful and will not go out of his way to court trouble.

Even when he appears docile and friendly, one cannot easily earn his trust. He finds it hard to open up to strangers or anything unconventional. This is because the Xu is a conformist and traditionalist and hates upsetting the status quo if he can avoid it. Although he is slow to warm up, he does form lasting relationships and makes a loyal friend. Responsible in his duties, he is also very responsive to love and will give unselfishly of himself without expecting much in return. He is kind, caring and thoughtful to those close to him, but he tends to be uneasy outside his territory or circle of friends and family. While he is loyal and reliable to the call of duty, he can also become prejudiced, guarded and defensive when he is besieged. For all his positive and endearing qualities, this personality can be unreasonably paranoid and obstinate when he feels wronged. Outspoken and unyielding to opposition, he is like a one-man army on a crusade when he takes up a worthy cause.

Generally, he is willing and able to forge strong bonds of love and friendship based on mutual loyalty and truthfulness. But he makes a poor liar as he does not like deceit and will be willing to suffer to remain faithful to his promises and principles. Blessed with stamina and resilience, he fights to win and will not back out once he has decided to get involved. For all his charming and affable exterior, the Xu or Dog type also has a pensive and apprehensive corner in his heart. He is always on the look-out for silent or lurking dangers, and although he acts in good faith, he does have a tendency to question the motives and intentions of others. Unbending and self-righteous, he will pick a side and defend it stubbornly. When he is cynical, he has a dour, dismal outlook on life and will pour cold water on the aspirations and ideas of others. As a natural-born fighter, he may have a sharp, sarcastic tongue, and acid wit to go along with it. Militant and ever watchful, he will challenge others single-handedly if he feels he is in the right or if he sees them encroaching on his territory. When the Dog person suspects that something is wrong or that someone is cheating him, he will follow the trail of his suspicions to the very end. Sooner or later, he will find the culprit. He relies on his unerring instincts as they serve him well.

In general, this type is modest and does not like to call attention to himself. Peaceable, likeable and sensible, he prefers to be left alone to attend to his duties. As a rule, he acts with honour and altruism and is not aggressive or power-hungry. He understands that power and clout bring heavy responsibilities and sometimes he will pass that burden to others if he feels he cannot handle it. Rational and brave, a person of this earth branch has a good solid sense of values and stability and possesses unwavering fealty and patriotism. He won't want to change sides and will stalwartly fight on against all odds. Above all, he values his own integrity.

A good team player, he can also be rank-conscious and judge-mental; nipping at the ankles of anyone lagging behind in perform-ance and barking at those who fall short of the mark. Because adversity sharpens his resolve and he is undeterred by difficulties, the native of the eleventh branch is a survivor who remains confident and constant when things are at their worst. However, when he is disillusioned or worried by failure, he will have a siege mentality and distrust or question everyone about him. Of course he is already sceptical by nature and has a habit of checking up on others or asking for a second opinion.

Yet a native of this branch is conscientious and will make the efforts needed to get the support he desires. He is able to communi-cate well with others, and because he is cooperative he can usually get what he is after. Efficient and honourable in conducting himself, he understands quickly what is required or expected of him and will do his part generously, although he is at times overly candid and frank with his opinions. His quick reflexes give him a volatile temper and he will retaliate quickly when angered or annoyed, but he also has a sense of humour and can forgive easily. He admires fairness and appreciates the good use of power. The Dog type can often be found doing volunteer work and involving himself in many charitable functions, but he is hardly docile or easy to push around as he will insist upon mutual respect and sharing in his interpersonal relation-ships. He enjoys consoling others in times of distress and boosting their confidence by his sunny optimism and his faith in their ability to prevail against the forces of evil. It is wonderful and reassuring to have him on your side as he is never half-hearted about his feelings and commitments. His top priority will always be the welfare and safety of his family or group. Although he does not venture out to look for trouble, he will stand firm if it comes looking for him. This personality type is able to put his needs on hold and attend to urgent matters without concern for his own self or safety. At times he is foolishly gallant and will suffer quietly while risking his own interests to rescue others. He just cannot stand idly by without coming to the aid of anyone who may need him. But above all, remember that the Dog of the Xu branch must always be able to justify his actions or choices to his own conscience. Otherwise, he will be guilt-ridden or have a masochistic desire to punish himself.

The resident of the eleventh earth branch is sportive and will need exercise and challenge, both physical and mental, to burn up his immense energy. Most of all, he gravitates towards team sports and close-knit circles because he needs a sense of belonging. Comradeship and camaraderie are important to him and he will be happy in relationships where he works for the good of all. People value his contributions and commitment and will appreciate his readiness to help, but he may secretly suffer from the anxiety of being separated or alienated from his loved ones or team. He does not like to break off relationships, even when they are not working or are detrimental to him; he will keep hoping and praying for a change, even though he knows it could be futile. The Dog personality does not know when to cut the links. He may even think his goodness, unselfishness and fine example will eventually show deserters the errors of their ways and bring them round. He will hold out his hand in friendship and forgiveness and make the first move towards a possible reconciliation. If all this fails, this personality may turn into the worst cynic and irrational foe.

The Dog personality of the Xu branch is passionate about his ideals. It does not take much to keep him happy for his tastes are simple and his needs few, but trample over one of his commandments and he will come after you mercilessly. He gets fixated on certain issues and can be pugnacious and dogmatic—indeed, he could bring new dimensions to the word 'dogmatic'. Yet the egalitarian Dog personality makes an excellent judge, a capable lawyer, a good psychologist, teacher, military man and sportsman. He is not too materialistic and does not need possessions or an expensive lifestyle to validate his worth. Quite content with the simpler things in life, he will only enjoy luxury if he shares it with his friends or family.

Good at bringing understanding and happiness into group relationships, this person is always willing to work for the benefit of everyone. At times he will protect the interests of others more avidly than his own, but if he does not get the appropriate gratitude and affection he deserves, he can be hurtful, resentful and vocal. Even so, he will not desert the group or leave in the midst of a battle—if that is any consolation to those who have suffered his tongue-lashings and temperamental outbursts.

The amiable Dog person is generous and acquiescent towards friends but can be cold, distant and forbidding to outsiders until they have passed his inspection. He prides himself on always being available to those who need him but dislikes imposing on others when he needs a favour in return. This type tends to keep secrets well and will also strive to keep his promises. Although he may be quarrelsome, critically harping and moralising on issues he champions, he gets over his tantrums easily and returns to his normal equilibrium after he has let off steam.

Because he is basically unmaterialistic and does not have the great accumulative urges of the Rat, Rooster or Monkey branches, the Dog is one who can turn his back on success or power if he feels that the price is too high. He is difficult to bribe or corrupt as he places more importance on his values and reputation than on his bank account. Some examples of famous persons born under this earth branch are: Sir Winston Churchill, Victor Hugo, Vladimir Lenin, Voltaire, Ralph Nader, Brigitte Bardot, Judy Garland, Golda Meir and Sophia Loren.

A person of the eleventh earth branch is deeply spiritual and likes to question his own self-worthiness. Often, he feels he is not doing his best or is not doing enough for others. He may even show his deep concern for his family, friends and associates by constantly moralising and criticising their shortcomings. Impatient and irritable at delays and setbacks, he grumbles, writes long letters of complaint and otherwise makes life miserable for those who cannot do things his way or support his causes. However, he does not baulk at discipline and respect for authority. He will be more than ready to work long and diligently, provided you recognise him as a model and learn from his example. After all, he will expect you to follow in his footsteps and duplicate his splendid record—so pay attention.

In relationships, the native of the eleventh branch will give others little breathing space and tend to crowd his loved ones by his need for affection and companionship, regardless of what they may want. He finds it difficult to tone down his emotions or fake what he is feeling. While he makes an excellent and selfless leader, he must learn to take a back seat at times and let others take over the driving without any interference or intervention. His feelings are always genuine and he despises falsehoods, but he must accept the fact that not everyone will appreciate being on a short leash, no matter how close he is to that person.

In his life the Dog person makes unconditional commitments. When he gives his word of honour, he will follow through with determination. Consequently, should he ally himself with criminal forces, he will be just as devoted to his partners. If a person who is regarded as unlikeable has only one friend in the whole world, more often than not that friend will belong to the Dog personality type, who perhaps may see some shred of goodness that everyone else has missed. Or the Dog person may feel that he owes allegiance to his loveless master because of some good deed in the past that was done for his benefit. The Dog feels tremendous obligation to repay favours.

A native of the Xu branch tends to be direct and forceful in his actions and lacks the guile to camouflage his intentions. Uncomplicated in his demands and upfront with his requests, he gives simple orders which he expects to be followed without question. He may be curt and sarcastic when slighted and will not hesitate to take others to task. Most of the time he will fight for his principles or to right some wrong. His ego is not overinflated and usually does not come into play. If one insults him personally, he will just shrug it off goodnaturedly, but if one insults his team, his school, his country or his religion, he will retaliate violently or demand a public apology. In his modest heart, the Dog person does not need to gather praise and recognition to boost his self-esteem. He is reassured by the warm knowledge that he has served well those he loves and done his very best for what he believes in. This is the essence of his nature.

The Dog of the eleventh branch is the third and last member of the Protectors' Triangle of Affinity and he, like the other two residents, is largely guided by instinct and emotions. Armed with his noble intentions, he appoints himself the guardian of justice and equality. Always trying to balance the scales to help the underdog along, he can be aggressive and unyielding in the face of oppression. He will not back away from danger or give in to pressure or public sentiments. In general, a native of this triangle is true to his conscience and acts on his gut feelings. He will be loved for his courage and ability to act on his convictions.

The personality of this branch will face his strongest clashes with persons of the fifth earth branch or the Dragon sign. The Dog is sensible and strives to maintain order and justice, while the Dragon considers himself above the law and may find the Dog's need for obedience and discipline very restrictive to his royal style. The Dragon is magnanimous and adventurous while the Dog type is sensible and loves to stick close to and protect his turf. In the final analysis, these two types will find each other working from opposite sides and will not like to support common causes as they cannot agree on what approach to take. The native of the fifth branch will resent the Dog of the eleventh branch, pointing out his mistakes and urging him to take a more reasonable and conservative stance. The Dog is not a disbeliever, but he distrusts lofty predictions and will prefer to see action rather than just plain words. At best, these two types must work through mutual friends and associates who can insulate their quick tempers and stubbornness.

To get along with the Dog personality one must understand that he does not care more what others think of him than he cares about doing the right thing. He must stick on the righteous path come what may and will not compromise himself or he could not live with his conscience. Open and honest in his relationships, he does not understand or forgive deceitfulness. Forceful and positive, he tends to be level-headed and assured of what he is supposed to accomplish and does not tolerate others who get in his way. The Xu branch is a masculine sign and can be demonstrative and intensely passionate. Realistic and intelligent, he knows how to anticipate how others think or what they want. Not one to abandon his post, this person will show patience, perseverance and above-average tenacity when dealing with adversity. Inspiring when he is bold and decisive, he can also turn negative and be intensely unapproachable, cynical and pessimistic. But he generally stays away from unfamiliar places and faces and keeps close to the home fires. He is happiest when he is able to take care of those close to him and enjoy his leisure with people he trusts and gets on with.

The Dog type of the eleventh branch is not especially competitive but he cannot easily be intimidated. Push him and he is very liable to push right back—harder. He builds useful alliances and most people find his straightforward manner and integrity very appealing. They will relate to him easily and put their trust in his words. By nature, he is not calculating or complicated. He has a talent for making things simple and easy to understand and deals only with the issues in hand. This type has no difficulty working alone or with a team: just be clear what you want him to do and leave him to complete his duties. Make sure he understands that he is an important member and that others rely on him to do his share. He will not want to let others down or be accused of negligence.

In life his most important goal will be his devotion to duty, his indispensable presence when he is needed to provide assistance. His priorities and values are of the best quality and he is capable of eloquently distinguishing right from wrong.

True to his nature, the Dog or Xu type is identified as the Guardian of the cycle and his mind is ruled by the key phrase: 'I watch'.

TRIANGLE OF AFFINITY

The Dog or Xu personality of the eleventh branch is the last member of the Third Triangle of Affinity which produces active, likeable and compassionate people, indispensable to the well-being of social life. The trio in this triangle is composed of the Tiger (third branch), the Horse (seventh branch) and the Dog (eleventh branch). This group of Protectors advocates fairness and opportunity for everyone, especially those who are most disadvantaged. Guided by their unselfish and extrovert natures, they seek to serve others by promoting understanding and peace if they can. Unorthodox, energetic and often acting with missionary zeal, they are aggressive in their idealism and democratic principles. Although they may display short tempers and impatience, generally they are kind, sociable and very helpful. Loyal and selfless, persons of this triangle are staunch and fearless fighters, reputed for their courage and aggressiveness. While they may be rebellious and stubborn at times, their negative qualities are balanced by their innate charm and generosity. Confident, outspoken and never afraid of controversy, this band of Protectors will charge to the rescue of anyone they feel is in need of assistance.

3rd - Yin
Tiger

III
Protectors

11th - Xu
Dog

7th - Wu
Horse

To work well with residents of this Triangle of Affinity, one must appeal not only to their sense of honour and fair play, but tug at their emotional heart strings, too. Honest and open in all their dealings, they will gladly make sacrifices for the good of all. They love personal contact and will go out of their way to bond with others. Not calculating, small-hearted or vindictive, they can assess situations relatively quickly and accurately and make fast and accurate judgements. Gifted with magnetic and captivating personalities, they have no problem persuading others to see things their way. These types know how to project themselves to the public and will often have careers or opportunities in communications, sales, promotion, on-stage or film performances and in the sports, political or military arenas where sharp reflexes and genuine combative passion are required. They believe in themselves with unshakable confidence and will show unerring loyalty to their team, family, friends and country.

The three branches of the Third Triangle of Affinity will be able to get along well in love and business. Working as a team is second nature to them. Capable of intuitively anticipating each other, they have a common way of thinking and reacting. As marriage or business partners they will have no difficulty supporting each other or identifying common goals.

CIRCLE OF CONFLICT

The Xu personality of the Dog branch will find his greatest opposition from the branch directly facing him in the Circle of Conflict,

5th - Chen
Dragon

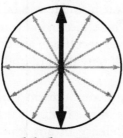

11th - Xu
Dog

which is the Dragon of the fifth branch. The Dog type has an entirely different outlook from the Dragon type of person, and the difference in their perspectives often causes them to be unreceptive to each other's ideas. The Dragon type is known for his daring and love of ambitious action and can be inflexible and tyrannical when provoked by the Dog personality who may be too critical and outspoken for his tastes. The Dragon is at his worst when he is baited by a logical and fearless critic and will react with anger and resistance.

On top of these incompatible traits, both these types tend to be argumentative and contentious when angered. Their militant natures require them to prove to themselves they are right. In fact, the best advice for these two protagonists is to steer clear of each other and deal through intermediaries or mediators. Somehow, the message will always sound better and be more acceptable when delivered by a neutral party. Direct dealings between them are highly likely to lead to bruised egos and irrational competitiveness that are unproductive.

RELATIONSHIPS WITH THE ELEVENTH EARTH BRANCH— THE DOG

Within the Family

In his family, the Dog type is well liked and respected for his impartiality and sound counsel. He takes his duties as a parent seriously and may be domineering and strict with the children. However, he does know how to have fun and will encourage his offspring to participate in active sports. Openminded but practical, he does not stress materialism at home but would rather develop strong values for the family as a unit. A person of this earth branch will find a lot of fulfilment in family life as he is willing to invest of himself in close and beneficial relationships. He will be an efficient and devoted parent who will not spoil his children but teach them to be self-reliant and independent. Yet his expectations are down to earth and he can accept others for what they really are and not push them beyond their natural capabilities.

His own dedication and commitment will serve as fine examples for the younger members of the family, yet he will never hesitate to rush to their rescue or defence in any kind of attack. He puts his family's interests and welfare above his own and will guide and guard them faithfully with his love.

As a child, he is gifted with a great zest for life and surplus energy which could be directed to sports and group exercise. Enthusiastic, playful and happy, he would like to be involved in many activities, yet he can be reliable when given responsibilities such as caring for younger siblings or pets. He will worship his parents unabashedly and have many role models such as his teachers and sports heroes. Idealistic but well adjusted and realistic, this child will not be selfish and will be easy to reason with. Because of his democratic ways, he will have many friends and be able to get along well with his siblings and schoolmates. He enjoys teamwork and being part of the group.

As a Teacher

The Dog or Xu type makes a teacher of great example and integrity. He will of course expect two key things from his students: respect and obedience. A good listener, counsellor and fair-minded mentor, he is able to inspire and instruct wisely. Practical and realistic, the Dog type is a pleasant and efficient teacher. There may be occasional bouts of cantankerous behaviour when he is frustrated, but his devotion far outweighs his faults.

Although he may appear easy-going on the surface, one quickly learns that he will not compromise on certain principles and that his strong temper will erupt when challenged. He is anything but a docile fence-sitter. He usually supports strong views (which he will air frequently) and his loyalty and dedication to a cause are unquestionable. With his students he will work hard to instil ideals and worthy ambitions. An excellent coach, he will always be on hand to cheer them on in victory or console them in defeat.

The Dog personality tends to react quickly when irked, and he does have a sharp tongue. He will not hesitate to use his biting criticism and sarcasm when he feels people are performing below par. However, once he has re-established equilibrium, he will return to his normal level-headed self. Just remember that his intentions are always noble and one way or another he will want to push everyone or even carry them to the finishing line. This person will use every means on hand to motivate those in his charge.

As a Lover and Spouse

A person of the eleventh earth branch values true companionship and treasures those he loves. He is understanding and supportive although it may take him time to warm up and make a binding commitment. Once he has made up his mind, he will stay close by your side. A warm and demonstrative lover, he will want to share all his interests with his partner and will like to be involved in very personal ways. This is because he strives to please and is often anxious for the approval of his loved one. He can be vulnerable in affairs of the heart as he will give much more than he receives and still feel it was not sufficient. A person of this earth branch is intuitive in reading the thoughts and feelings of those to whom he is attached and can sense important vibrations even before they become aware. A worthy partner, he forges long-term alliances and will cherish those he loves. Often he can become possessive and protective, but generally he is open and trusting of his mate. He may only be able to let down his guard in private, so it may take some time to bond well if he is cynical because of previous involvements that have caused him pain or disappointment. By nature, this personality is generous, uncomplicated and very easy to love. He is not prone to complaining or comparing in his romantic relationships. In his eyes, the person he loves can do no wrong. All he wants is to be by your side—through all the good times as well as the bad.

As a Business Partner

The Dog type will be the strong right arm in a business relationship as he tends to be reliable and confident. He prefers to have 'hands on' involvement and can be wary of strangers and distrustful of new or untried methods. It will take some convincing to get him to let down his guard and relax. He must be able to resolve all his suspicions and feel comfortable before he makes a firm commitment, but once he throws his hat into the ring, he will stick with it through thick and thin.

He may or may not keep a close watch on his partners, but he must be assured that he will be fairly dealt with or he can be difficult to manage. He views partnerships as alliances based on mutual trust and he will also support his affiliation wholeheartedly. Do not take advantage of his kind nature and generosity. He could turn on you if you try to cheat or mislead him and he will never give you another chance.

The native of the eleventh branch is not afraid of hard work but will hold everyone accountable for doing their share. He is often beset with secret scepticism and will try to anticipate weaknesses or forecast all the things that could go wrong. It would be best to address his concerns early in the game and not allow his worries and fears to grow. Once this person pledges himself to a venture, one can be assured he will show the discipline and commitment required. One shouldn't blame him if he needs to constantly look over his shoulder or check the lock on the door once more each evening. He just needs to be reassured that his domain is secure.

As a Boss
Friendly and optimistic on the outside, the Xu or Dog personality is not easily drawn into playing favourites. He will rate subordinates strictly on performance. Fair-minded but demanding and inflexible where his priorities are concerned, he is still able to weigh situations carefully and work out problems objectively without too much fuss. Of course, he does not like debate and will not tolerate talking back or opposition. He will nip any rebellion in the bud and insist that everyone follows his instructions without question.

The Dog personality type does not like to tiptoe around to solicit solidarity. He charges about with all his flags unfurled and will not think twice about doing what is on his mind or voicing his opinions. He expects subordinates to back him up and staunchly defend the company or he will brand them as traitors. A resident of this earth branch wants nothing less than total commitment. He has complete faith in his ability to protect the interests of the company or sound the alarm if he senses any danger, and everyone must do the same if they work for him.

As a Friend and Colleague
A native of the eleventh branch will be liked for his nice disposition and ability to relate to his peers. His sociable and outgoing nature will make him popular and much sought after. He is able to share and look after the interests of his friends and associates at work, and as a champion of peace, harmony and friendship in his environment, he will listen impartially to the woes of others, offer them his shoulder to cry on and commiserate with their problems. He should be careful not to take the problems of others to heart and go out of his way to help them if the consequences of doing so are detrimental to his own well-being. Generally, the Dog personality does not judge his friends and colleagues and will accept them with all their imperfec-

tions. He is only critical and outspoken when friends break their promises or deceive him. Then he will break off the relationship completely, without any warning. If anything, this person must be sure who is his friend or foe and cannot tolerate indecision or deceit.

As an Opponent

A person of the eleventh branch is always a worthy and fierce opponent. He does not look for fights beyond his territory and will only retaliate when attacked, but once he goes into battle he can be fatalistic and oblivious to all the dangers of future repercussions. He will sacrifice himself and endure great hardships to prove he is right. Determined and ferocious in battle, the Dog personality will not do things halfway, so if he gets started it will be hard to pull him away from the conflict. He may even turn on the person who tries to intervene. The best way is not to provoke open confrontation. Insist on dealing through intermediaries and let him have the choice of whom he wishes to be named as the arbitrator. Make sure everything is above board and allow him to have his people check the facts and figures before entering into meaningful negotiations. This character type is reasonable once he is convinced the opponent is willing to be fair and is sincerely looking for a solution. A personality of this earth branch will place great faith in what his adviser recommends and it is important that neutral ground is agreed upon to resolve the conflict. It is not advisable to enter into lawsuits with the Dog as he will take off his gloves and fight long and hard in a dirty, drawn-out case which could eventually have no winners.

As the Mediator

While he may turn into a hot-head when he is your opponent, as a mediator this personality type is level-headed and calm. He will look upon his role as a sacred mission to be accomplished without fail. Rational and respectable, he will lay all the issues on the table and allow each side equal time and opportunity to present their arguments. The Dog personality can be relied upon to be fair and sensible in salvaging or repairing relationships. He will not negotiate or try to make any agreement behind someone's back. One can depend on him to be impartial as he has a keen sense of fair play. His natural sense of propriety and ability to relate to people will draw opposing sides together in a spirit of reconciliation. The Dog type will not tolerate unreasonable or unruly behaviour or any hitting below the belt. Optimistic and resolute in his determination to find a happy ending, he will use all his skills to bridge outstanding differences with his positive attitude and peaceful intervention. It would take a horrendous amount of provocation to make the Dog personality abandon his post as a successful mediator.

RELATIONS WITH OTHER BRANCHES

With a Rat—First Branch
The Dog is competent and fair-minded and has a healthy respect for authority. He will find the Rat an industrious and affectionate charmer. The Rat type is the more crafty and possessive of the two and may be manipulative in this relationship. However, the Dog is not as materialistic as the acquisitive Rat, and so long as the Rat stays loyal and close to home, the Dog will let his Rat partner run the show. Both parties here are responsive to the needs of the other, and although the Dog may resent the Rat's calculating ways, he knows that they both have the same practical aims and that the frugal Rat has their mutual interests at heart. A working relationship is possible if both stay true to the Dog's principles.

With an Ox—Second Branch
The Dog will find the Ox person reliable and hard-working. Both parties here will find the other honest and respectable and will work well together. These two are realistic and have no difficulty making commitments, although the Ox can be uncompromising and inflexible in his views. The Dog is more concerned with protecting their mutual interests and will be able to make some adjustments to the Ox's stubborn outlook. However, the Dog could also rebel if the Ox is too domineering and decides to go his own way. On the whole this pair has no great struggle for dominance. Both will attend to their duties and feel assured that the other will fulfil his share of the responsibilities.

With a Tiger—Third Branch
The friendly and protective Dog knows how to handle the impetuous Tiger type. The Dog will allow the Tiger to go his way until he runs out of steam and then rein him in gently without any 'I told you

sos'. The Tiger appreciates the Dog's understanding and rational mind and finds it easy to support the Dog's outlook without any hesitation. In this combination, the Dog is also more alert and defensive and will feel obliged to protect the curious and adventurous Tiger. Both types have strong tempers and sharp tongues but do not like to bear grudges. They can put aside their differences after they have vented their anger. The Tiger will also respect the Dog for standing his ground and not allowing himself to be intimidated by anyone.

With a Rabbit—Fourth Branch
The Dog and Rabbit personalities could find common interests as they have compatible temperaments and can establish a good level of understanding. If both do not take the other for granted, they could have a good relationship. Neither in this team is unreasonably demanding or controlling. The even-tempered Rabbit is the more tactful of this partnership and should be in charge of their public image. The Dog may have trouble holding his tongue and may be more aggressive and hardworking than the Rabbit. However, they will both strive to help and support one another and not let petty differences get in the way. The Rabbit is the more calculating and materialistic partner but the altruistic Dog does not mind the Rabbit's quiet shrewdness as he needs the latter's intuition.

With a Dragon—Fifth Branch
The Dog personality could have serious communication problems and differences with the high-powered Dragon. Both may have difficulty in establishing a meaningful dialogue because they find it hard to trust or read the other's intentions. The Dragon will find the Dog critical and cynical about his overinflated self-image. The Dog prefers to be down-to-earth and conservative and will mistrust the Dragon's bright ideas and grand plans. These two will not work to bring out the best in one another and the friction they create by rubbing each other the wrong way could result in personality clashes in which both sides lose. It would be advisable for them to deal through intermediaries if they do not share a common ascendant to ameliorate their vast differences.

With a Snake—Sixth Branch

The Dog and the Snake have a mutual respect for each other and do not create conflict if they can avoid it. They will be compatible and amicable to a fair degree, as the Dog is trustworthy and the Snake's ambitiousness could benefit this relationship. The reliable Dog will stay loyal as long as the Snake is persevering and steadfast. This should prove no problem as the Snake can be tenacious and constant to their mutual goals. These two could share the same philosophies in life and remain guarded and suspicious of outsiders. The Dog is not overly possessive and will understand the secretive Snake's need for privacy and meditation.

With a Horse—Seventh Branch

The Horse will not seek to control or dominate the Dog person but will rather work alongside him as an equal partner. He finds the Dog's loyalty endearing and will be able to relate to the latter's sensible and rational outlook. Of the pair, the Dog is the better listener and will strive to communicate and cooperate with the Horse who may be restless and independent when the mood strikes him. But they are equally matched in temperaments and do not have possessive and competitive natures. They can bond well and still retain their own individualism. The Horse may be the more aggressive and positive of the two, while the Dog tends to worry about their mutual interests and will be more anxious and vigilant.

With a Sheep—Eighth Branch

The Sheep and the Dog may not have much in common but they will share goodwill and friendly relations if they can. Their outlooks on life predispose each to be attracted to different things and have different goals. The Dog is brave, hard-working and not too influenced by public opinion so long as he does his duty. The Sheep needs approval and consensus before he can make up his mind and may sometimes be unduly influenced to take the easy way out of a predicament. The Dog is stern when it comes to fulfilling responsibilities and may be hard on the Sheep, although he will do all in his power to protect and guide the Sheep type if they are in the same team.

With a Monkey—Ninth Branch

There should be no large clashes between the Dog and Monkey as they are ruled by different priorities and tend to have different sets of values. The Dog is easy to get along with so long as the Monkey does not try to take advantage of him, and the clever Monkey will soon realise that the Dog can be a dangerous foe. These two can learn to combine their strengths if they share mutual friends and interests. The multifaceted Monkey is the optimist who could liven up the cynical Dog's views and banish his pessimism, but the defensive and protective Dog will stay in this relationship only if the Monkey is loyal and stays true to his promises.

With a Rooster—Tenth Branch

The Dog may be able to identify with the hard-working and analytical Rooster type, but will always be worried about what the Rooster could be up to next. He may find it hard to comprehend the Rooster's love of controversy and his exacting ways. The Rooster knows the honourable Dog personality will be a loyal friend and fair-minded partner, but he may sometimes be too demanding of the Dog and may offend his need for equilibrium by his own constant harping on the tiny details. Fortunately, both sides here are not easily influenced or intimidated and will be able to make up their own minds about where and when to compromise, although the opinionated Rooster is less flexible than the Dog in this partnership.

With another Dog—Eleventh Branch

Two Dogs will achieve a good level of compatibility unless they have conflicting ascendant signs. Both are congenial, reasonable and can establish their respective position in a hierarchy rather quickly. These two work well together because each knows what is expected and will be happy to cooperate as a team. No doubt there may still be struggles for dominance and flared tempers, but common goals or enemies will keep them alert and united. The Dog personality is relaxed in the company of others of his type and will not go out of his or her way to look for conflict. Although they may be argumentative and outspoken at times, they can put aside any differences when it comes to attending to their duties and protecting mutual interests.

With a Boar—Twelfth Branch

The sincere and honest Boar will have no serious conflicts with the agreeable Dog person so long as they define their responsibilities and the Boar does not impose on or take advantage of the Dog. The Dog may find the Boar's lack of moderation and sensual appetites a little unsettling and so be guarded in this gregarious personality's company. The Dog never leaves his realism or cynicism at home, so one can be sure that he will admonish the Boar for running risks by failing to be careful and conservative. While the Dog is more loyal and duty-bound in this union, the sociable Boar could be the tireless promoter and public relations man who will exploit opportunities and enrich their partnership. If these two share the same objectives and loyalties, they will not allow their differences to ruin their relationship.

12

THE HAI BRANCH
TWELFTH LUNAR SIGN

The Unifier's Song

Of all God's children
I have the purest heart.
With innocence and faith,
I walk in Love's protective light.
By giving of myself freely
I am richer and twice blest.
Bonded to all mankind
by my fellowship
I strive to unify.
My goodwill is universal
and knows no bounds.

I am Hai, the Unifier

Theodora Lau

THE TWELFTH EARTH BRANCH: HAI
THE SIGN OF THE BOAR

THE ASSIGNED LUNAR YEARS OF THE BOAR

January 30, 1911	to	February 17, 1912
February 16, 1923	to	February 4, 1924
February 4, 1935	to	January 23, 1936
January 22, 1947	to	February 9, 1948
February 8, 1959	to	January 27, 1960
January 27, 1971	to	January 15, 1972
February 13, 1983	to	February 1, 1984
January 31, 1995	to	February 18, 1996
February 18, 2007	to	February 6, 2008

If you were born the day before the lunar year of the Boar, e.g. February 7, 1959, you belong to the previous earth branch or animal sign which is the eleventh branch (the Dog).

If you were born on the day after the Boar's lunar year ends, e.g. January 28, 1960, you belong to the next earth branch or animal sign, which is the first branch (the Rat).

THE TWELFTH EARTH BRANCH
THE SIGN OF THE BOAR

The twelfth and last character profile of the earth branches is that of the Boar whose branch is called *Hai* in Chinese and represents generosity and good will. A person of this personality type is honest, simple and possesses great fortitude. Strong in mind and body, he hides his intelligence under a modest front. He dominates his world with great zest and tends to overindulge in satisfying his senses. The Hai or Boar sees his environment as a huge banquet with himself as the unsurpassed host. Everyone is welcomed and lavishly entertained. Savouring all that life has to offer and more, the native of the twelfth earth branch could easily carry things to extremes. By nature, he tends to be chivalrous, almost to the point of extravagance, and his goals in life will be to gather people of all types together and find some common goal to bind them.

A person of this type is usually free of pretence. He doesn't like it. So what you see is what you get. His openness, jovial manners and tolerance make him very approachable and easy to talk to. Optimistic and progressive-minded, the Boar personality is lavish with his affections as well as his money. Often, he generates a feeling of abundance and can be complacent about his success and progress. Easily lulled by a feeling of security (often false), he will contentedly bask in his good fortune until he gets the bill or sees the bottom line.

Only then will he roll up his sleeves, take things seriously and buckle down to save the situation.

A person of this branch has a hefty appetite and will advocate the good life for himself and all his friends and family. He plans things on a large and expensive scale and will do a great deal of promotion for his ventures. If his grandiose plans come through he will have a big win and make his reputation, but if he fails he will face piles of debts alone. Yet don't expect him to be easily dissuaded. The bold and boisterous Boar has the vitality and optimism of several ordinary people and will need to work hard as well as play hard. When he becomes interested in something, he will dive in with intensity and enthusiasm to the peril of good judgement. He hears what he wants to hear and will only believe the good and positive side. This person never discriminates and sincerely believes everyone deserves a chance from him—even the undeserving. Consequently, in his book everyone is presumed innocent until proven guilty. He will discover that in real life he does not have to provide himself as the test case, by being the victim, but his main problem is that he tries to please everyone and in the end might please no one at all.

In spite of his gregarious and amorous nature he may be shy and insecure, simply putting up a front to keep everyone at ease. His good old-fashioned help-thy-neighbour policy gains him credibility and many friends. No party or club seems quite complete without his warm and jolly personality. But although he may stay modestly in the background, he does want recognition for his contributions and can be vengeful and morose when denied it. He may be big-hearted but he is not stupid, so he will retaliate in his own way if he is mistreated. In general, however, he will seek to identify with as many people as possible, since their vote of confidence means a great deal to him; he is therefore usually kind even when he should be firm. He allows others to impose upon him and pretends that all is well even when it is not.

Ironically, for all his wonderful traits the Boar could be his own worst enemy as he has a peculiar habit of delaying or deferring decisions in the hope that problems will resolve themselves or fade away. It is not procrastination, but rather wishful thinking on his part. When he must make an unpopular choice, he will look for every excuse in the book not to make it. He will also try to remain neutral when disputes get complicated, and in the end he may be left out in the cold. Because he neglects to take a firm stand on issues right from the start, he may give the wrong impression and get blamed for miscommunication at the very least.

Actually, this person's innate goodwill unduly influences his views and often makes him good but unwise. As the Chinese saying goes, 'The good man is not always wise, but the wise man is always good.' Accommodating the requests of all, he will not hesitate to offer you his home, loan you his car and lend you his money, too, if he can. On the one hand he is naive and presumptuous, thinking that everyone is his brother and that he must treat them with love and respect. Consequently, he often fails to spot deception, no matter how obvious, until it is too late. Unwittingly, he is partly to blame when he is chosen to be the victim.

On the other hand, he may be too dependent on certain people he identifies as his patrons or mentors and expect them to do everything for him, thereby setting himself up for disappointment when these people do not or will not perform as he assumed they would. The Boar's main failing is his inability to say no or turn people down. He makes promises to please others or simply to get them off his back. He may or may not know that some requests are impossible, but he will still hope against hope that a miracle will happen. No one is more sorry than he is when he has to disappoint someone, but sometimes it would be better for him to tell people the unpleasant truth now rather than later.

If calculating people know how to cater to the weaknesses of the Boar person, they will be able to gain control over him. For this reason, the kindly Boar needs to insulate himself with protectors and guardians. Left to his own devices and generosity, he could squander his money or give it to swindlers. He should never make investments alone as he is not one who probes deeply or reads the fine print. He would rather wait for something to go wrong before addressing the problem. Although he may feel he never needs to take precautions or advice, in reality he could be most vulnerable to the very things he dismisses as unlikely to happen. He should be wary of ungrateful people who impose on his kindness and parasites who feed on his generosity.

A person of the twelfth branch is either terribly untidy or extremely neat. His style will be evident almost immediately by the friends he keeps, the places he frequents, the food he likes to eat or the sports he enjoys. He will either be sophisticated or very earthy and uncouth. Take him at face value—he can't and won't change for anyone. If he did he would be unhappy as he would have to behave in a restricted manner which could be foreign to his basic urges. It is best to accept him as a whole package, because he is one who rarely criticises or tries to change others.

Because he is lax in self-discipline as well as in enforcing the rules, the Boar person may borrow things and forget to return them, especially in matters of money. He doesn't like doing the accounts and if he is a bit short, well, he will expect you to close one eye or maybe both when it comes to fulfilling his financial obligations. No doubt he will pay back whatever he owes when he has money again, but his attitude seems to worry certain people, especially those who belong to the Snake, Rooster or Ox branches, and they will call him irresponsible. Consequently, the Boar does not get on with the above trio, and his accountant and banker may have these self-same problems with him.

The sensual and indulgent Boar person can also be thick-skinned and insensitive when it comes to gratifying himself. His tolerant and expansive characteristics hide a fatalistic and self-destructive inclination that surfaces when he is faced with awesome losses or catastrophes. He will blame himself and, instead of seeking a solution, will hole up somewhere and sink into deep depression. Luckily there will always be people who will rescue him and nurse him back to health. With his excellent organisational talents and ability to develop group efforts, he has an influential network of friends and contacts to help him.

However, if the Boar could learn to practise self-control and discretion, he would be invincible. He is one of those rare people who can accept his own faults and take reproach or even punishment without complaint. Yet he often does not know his own limits and tends to overpredict results, even trying to convince himself of the impossible. Miracles do happen, especially to the Boar person who is gifted with unbelievable faith, but he must also realise that he cannot count on miracles to pull him through every time. Besides, one can only be allowed so many miracles and no more.

At heart, this person is helpful, sympathetic and giving, but he finds it hard to suppress his emotions and curb his vast appetites and impulses. He cannot be objective in matters of the heart and will always err on the side of kindness and charity. However, just as every cloud has a silver lining, the chivalrous Boar is blessed with incredible luck and will find fame and fortune when he least expects it. All the good will that he planted will reap huge dividends.

Some famous people born under the twelfth branch are Otto von Bismarck, Henry Ford, Maria Callas, Ernest Hemingway, Georgia O'Keefe, Ronald Reagan and Lucille Ball.

It would be fair to say that the amorous Boar will give up a great deal and sacrifice himself for love and acceptance. If he places his faith in the right people, he will be able to achieve his wildest dreams. Furthermore, he must learn to say no and remind himself that he must do what is right and not just what is expedient.

The most important thing for the Boar person to remember is to be careful where he places his trust. He must learn to be discerning and selective.

As the Unifier of the cycle, the Boar or Hai type strives to live by his maxim in life, which is: 'I join'.

TRIANGLE OF AFFINITY

The Hai or Boar type is the last member in the Fourth Triangle of Affinity which houses a group of three Catalysts within the Twelve Earth Branches. There are four Triangles of Affinity in which the personality types are grouped and there is one Circle of Conflict in which all opposite branches are incompatible. In the Fourth Triangle,

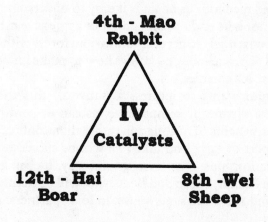

4th - Mao
Rabbit

IV
Catalysts

12th - Hai
Boar

8th - Wei
Sheep

we have the Rabbit, the Sheep and the Boar, respectively the fourth, eighth and twelfth branches.

This trio of the Fourth Triangle of Affinity are Catalysts who serve as useful agents in making relationships work. This group is composed of the intuitive, sympathetic and cooperative personality types who bring about changes in others without changing themselves. Supportive, generous and good listeners, those who occupy the Fourth Triangle of Affinity are keen observers, well-skilled in communication. Artistic, creative and impressionable, they are the guardians of the arts, theatre, publishing and the world of music. Powerful movers and shakers behind the scenes, these types have their fingers on the pulse of society and know how to make things happen in unobtrusive but significant ways. Consciously or unconsciously they tend to dominate the arena in which they are involved and their influence is often well accepted and enduring.

A personality of this particular triangle tends to be insensitive, gullible and self-serving. He can be excessive as well as destructive when he is unhappy or suspicious, making unsound decisions such as throwing good money after bad. In dealing with anyone belonging to this triangle, one must not expect too much or take his promises too seriously. No doubt he will do his best, but he is not as able to control the situation as he believes and he may not want to face reality when things go wrong. It is enough that he uses his influence to bring parties together in a spirit of cooperation and open-mindedness. He does not mind helping others utilise the right contacts and connections, but do not expect ironclad guarantees which he cannot give, no matter how much he professes that he can. True to his nature, he makes a good arbitrator and mediator as he finds it easy to understand and identify with others, nor is he unduly competitive or aggressive in his approach. Hence, he is most likely to get everyone to join forces with him. Sincere, obliging and approachable, he knows how to make influential friends and neutralise his enemies.

Anyone who wants to impress a native of this triangle should emphasise the virtues of compromise instead of confrontation and show him the benefits of negotiation rather than conflict. As the indispensable expert of 'give and take', he will be successful in patching up failed relationships in his own special way, by being the peaceful catalyst. The Rabbit, Sheep and Boar types will be naturally drawn to each other and share the same views. In love, partnerships and business, they tend to understand and support each other with great tolerance and understanding. As a team they will function harmoniously.

CIRCLE OF CONFLICT

The twelfth earth branch will encounter his strongest opposition and personality clashes with persons belonging to the sixth branch or a native of the Snake type. Anyone born with his ascendant in the hours of the Snake (from 9 a.m. to 11 a.m.) will also find conflict with the Hai or Boar person. They will not share much in common and will find their differences hard to understand or bear.

6th - Si
Snake

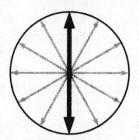

12th - Hai
Boar

The Boar person is trusting, open and honest while the Snake of the second branch can be sceptical, reserved and unsympathetic to the kindhearted Boar. Even if both have a similar destination or goal, they may prefer to use different methods in their approach or travel via different routes. After all, the obliging Boar is decidedly lenient and forgiving to offenders while the Snake person, as the wily Strategist of the twelve branches, will be calculating and punitive.

RELATIONSHIPS WITH THE TWELFTH EARTH BRANCH— THE BOAR

Within the Family
The Boar personality is happy and secure at home where he can be himself and please himself. He will find it hard to deny his loved ones anything, even if he cannot afford it. Good at stretching his

resources, he will always manage to find a way to enjoy life and entertain friends. Socially, he will be a magnet for people from all walks of life as the jovial and personable Hai type is never lacking in friends or events to attend. Eager to participate in charitable functions and sports events, the energetic person of the twelfth branch will be very active in organising and promoting such get-togethers. Not only will he volunteer his own services but he may drag his wife and children into performing charity work, too. Popular and much sought after, he has a good word of encouragement for everyone and people will find him valuable in introducing them around or assisting them in meeting the right contacts. He takes pride in his ability to build relationships and find business opportunities.

Not too particular about who he mixes with, the Boar and his family will allow all kinds of friends into their home and treat everyone equally. His informal style and casual ways relax his guests even if they are from different social classes. Since everyone he knows identifies readily with him, he could be the common denominator to bind everyone together. Good-natured and happy to please those of whom he is fond, the Boar is a thoughtful host, loving parent and supportive friend.

As a child, the Boar character is outgoing but self-reliant. He is easy to discipline and gifted with courage and stamina. His passionate nature may be masked by shyness or a reluctance to offend or challenge others. Respectful and cooperative, he will work happily for the good of all and be unselfish about his own desires. However, he will still seek to satisfy his strong appetites or other indulgences on the sly and will expect his parents to give him a lot of leeway when it comes to discipline or a rigid schedule. This child will not go around picking fights, but he is not afraid of bullies either. He will have the aptitude to persuade others to team up with him instead of being at odds.

As a Teacher
One could not find a kinder, nicer teacher than the Boar person. A native of the twelfth earth branch will use everything in his power to help his students. Selfless and ardent in his desire to teach, this person will go far beyond the call of duty and show genuine interest in the special abilities of each and every child. He runs his class with a minimum of fuss and is not strict or unapproachable; everyone

can speak freely to him and voice their opinions without fear of reproach or retaliation. Indeed, he could be accused of being too liberal and allowing his students to have their way too often. Yet his philosophy will be that although he gives his charges a good deal of freedom, he also places an equal amount of responsibility upon their shoulders. In the end they will do their best to win his respect and affection and, most of all, live up to the Boar's high expectations.

As a Lover and Spouse

Amorous and sentimental, the Boar person is loyal and persevering in love. He will go to any lengths to please the object of his devotion, and if he can move heaven and earth for her, he will. At times it is simply overwhelming to be romantically involved with this type of person. He can be excessive in his display of affection and extravagant to a dangerous extent. When his feelings are reciprocated, he will want immediate commitment from the other person. He cannot do anything half-heartedly, so when he falls in love, you can be sure he will go all the way—with bells ringing and music playing. The main problem may be that he gets carried away and could be living a fantasy with his beloved. He may shield her from knowing important facts about himself or his finances that could affect their relationship later on. The Boar hates to be the bearer of bad news and prefers to defer unpleasant matters until they can no longer be ignored. He must learn that if he has to impress someone so much to gain her affection, then he cannot be sure she loves him for himself. In affairs of the heart, the Boar will be hurt if he does not make sure that he is loved for himself and not for what he can give. It would be wise for him not to give away his heart as quickly as he is apt to do.

As a Business Partner

The Boar of the Hai branch is a promoter *par excellence* and a tireless person to have as a business partner. He will have no problem going everywhere, meeting everyone and organising advertising and media attention for his company. His motto will be: sell, sell, sell. But, although he will definitely generate cash as well as attention, he must be careful to tone down his enthusiasm and not to make promises that are too good to be true. He may unwittingly put the company into a difficult position because of his overoptimistic forecasts. It will also be the responsibility of other partners to curtail his spending and his desire to expand the business at a fast and furious pace. In his assessment he rarely believes anything can go wrong that he could not handle. His confidence in his ability to rally people to identify with his perceptions are often too presumptuous; he must learn to discount good reviews or sales reports and to listen to more conservative approaches.

As a Boss
The Boar person is an energetic and very involved boss, and unlike normal bosses he will be approachable and will openly solicit the opinions of his subordinates. Rolling up his sleeves, he will work alongside everyone and put on no airs about his superior position. He does not lord it over others or intimidate them without reason. On the other hand, he also expects a lot of allowances to be made for his own shortcomings. He may be temperamental and impulsive and not very selective in choosing the right path. Often he may opt for the quick and easy route or purchase something cheap only to discover later that he must replace it with good quality merchandise if he wants it to last. By gratifying his wish for immediate solutions, the Boar boss may prefer short-term repairs to long-term procedures that may be less expensive in the final accounting.

As a Friend and Colleague
The Boar of the Hai branch is everyone's best friend, and indeed he is a wonderful person to know and work with. Eager to be of service and generous to a fault, he is popular and much sought after. However, his views are bound to be liberal; he may support the wrong people and be drawn into undeserving or unrewarding pursuits. Sometimes he prefers quantity to quality and will not be too discriminating in his choice of friends—hence, he could place himself in difficult or controversial positions.

On the whole he is big-hearted and supportive of his friends and colleagues and will usually be elected as their spokesperson or given a position of authority and trust. He will work tirelessly for everyone's welfare without any complaint. Always ready to lend an ear or a hand, he will make himself available to one and all. This person is a valuable and indispensable friend to have as his virtues far exceed his faults.

As an Opponent

A person of the twelfth branch is a formidable opponent because when he goes into battle one can be sure he has exhausted all other avenues of compromise. When the Boar is in the fighting mode, he can be a bulldozer. Armed with loads of ammunition and a legion of lawyers, he can prove intractable. Remember, this person always gives others the benefit of the doubt and allows plenty of leeway for their shortcomings, so no doubt he will be extremely surprised when he discovers he has been duped and he will not take defeat lying down. True, he may have been gullible and appeared an easy mark because of his good nature, but now you get to see the other side of the coin. In his negative state, this previously trusting person views the world as beset with enemies, all out to destroy him. He will rally his forces and his enormous strength to wage a war that perhaps has no winners. The Boar as an opponent can be fatalistic and will destroy himself as well as his opponents rather than surrender. The fall-out and indiscriminate damage that could result when the Boar person is your adversary can be expensive and irreversible.

As the Mediator

The Boar or Hai person is the ideal catalyst. He will perform superbly, patiently going back and forth with messages and proposals. Usually he will maintain an impartial front and be diligent and above reproach in his duties. The person of the twelfth branch does not discriminate and will not take sides as he enjoys being in the middle ground. He sees both good and bad, and instead of judging others he would rather live peacefully with their faults and just capitalise on their positive side. Hopefully he will also make disagreeing parties realise that his outlook is far more preferable and sound than their unresolved conflict. In the end, he may effect a peaceful resolution just by his spirit of good will as both sides may be shamed by his intense faith in the sincerity of their attempts to resolve their problems.

RELATIONS WITH OTHER BRANCHES

With a Rat—First Branch

This could be a happy and workable partnership as the Boar responds to the Rat's need for affection and communication. The crafty rat values self-preservation and could help the Boar to be more cautious and calculating in his dealings. The good-hearted Boar will thrive on the Rat's solicitous attention provided the Rat is allowed to supervise their finances. Neither side is too sensitive or overly demanding, although the Rat tends to manipulate the Boar and tries to influence him in making shrewd choices. One can be sure that the Rat will tone down the Boar's generosity and free-spending habits. These two will have good social as well as emotional ties and create a strong relationship.

With an Ox—Second Branch
The Boar will find the Ox agreeable only to a limited degree as the Ox is basically unbending and unsympathetic to the Boar's ideas of enjoying life. The Ox puts duty and responsibility first and will not tolerate the Boar's disorderly conduct or lack of stoical commitment to high ideals. The Boar enjoys mixing with everyone in a congenial atmosphere and, unlike the Ox, has little or no fixed opinions or prejudices. Neither party here will work hard at finding common ground as each considers the other to have undesirable traits. The Boar does not worry too much about tomorrow while the Ox is obsessed with order, punctuality and consistency in his life. If these two have to work together, the Ox will be very strict and demanding and the Boar will suffer from his authoritarian rule.

With a Tiger—Third Branch
The Tiger will share the Boar's enthusiasm and love of the good life. These two outgoing and gregarious partners will find much to celebrate in each other's company. The honest Boar is the hard worker and scrupulous member of the team, while the Tiger will be the aggressive and optimistic player. These two will love, work and play hard and find good rapport in their partnership. The strong and sociable Boar will find the captivating Tiger as energetic and as passionate as he is himself. Both parties are generous and impulsive, so unless one of them is able to apply the brakes, they are both likely to go overboard in their expenses as well as in their emotions.

With a Rabbit—Fourth Branch
The Boar will find immediate rapport and harmony with the sagacious Rabbit, and the Rabbit in return will share his prudent and observant attributes with the trusting and earthy Boar. The Boar

is the more generous and trusting partner in this relationship and will rely on the Rabbit to direct him behind the scenes. Both know their areas of expertise and will be effective and successful together because they are well tuned to each other. They are able to make allowances for each other's shortcomings and will strive to have close communications. The Rabbit type is skilled in managing the Boar's affairs while the open and adaptable Boar is more outgoing and sociable.

With a Dragon—Fifth Branch
The good-hearted Boar will be impressed by the bright and idealistic Dragon personality who will no doubt want to use the Boar's strength and stamina for his own purposes. When these two form a team, they will both work passionately for their objective without much struggle for dominance. The sincere Boar will give the Dragon his support because the Dragon, too, is never stingy with commitment. If the Dragon is not too domineering and egotistic the Boar will follow him and match him in optimism and energy. However, both parties here are prone to overestimate themselves and love to do everything on a grand scale. One of them must mind the shop and remain objective and realistic or they could be in for a rude awakening.

With a Snake—Sixth Branch
The deep and enigmatic Snake person will have great difficulty in fathoming the honest, too-good-to-be-true Boar type. The obliging Boar is too open, earthy and passionate for the secretive and intellectual Snake who keeps his feelings well hidden. In their assessment of each other, the Snake may be irritated by the Boar's lack of finesse and sensitivity, while the Boar may find the Snake unapproachable and unreasonably suspicious. Neither may want to take a closer look or make the first move towards establishing good rapport or better communications. Their opposing philosophies restrict them from having mutual interests or objectives. In the end they will find it hard to establish the kind of foundation needed for a good relationship.

With a Horse—Seventh Branch
The Boar is usually giving and understanding in his relationships but he will find it hard to appreciate the flamboyant disposition of the mercurial Horse person whose lightning reflexes and restless love of

adventure could spell insecurity for this partnership. If the Horse changes his mind too often and flies off the handle with his infamous temper, the Boar may choose to distance himself from the high-spirited Horse type. Yet, the Horse could benefit if he discovers that he has need of the Boar's strength and good will and seeks to associate with the outgoing Boar for their mutual benefit. Neither of this pair is easily intimidated and they will work together if it is to their advantage. But because of their innate differences, neither may want to make long-term commitments.

With a Sheep—Eighth Branch

The Boar is bold and protective towards the kindly Sheep and will have great sympathy and understanding for the latter's peaceful nature. Together this pair will find happiness and harmony because they will both find it easy to cooperate well and invest their strengths in a lasting relationship. The unselfish Boar is tough and will not mind making sacrifices for the sensitive and well-mannered Sheep type. Both are communicative and as Catalysts will enjoy working with people. The Sheep is skilled in areas where the Boar may lack expertise, while the passionate Boar presents a confident front and a more positive outlook that the Sheep finds reassuring. Together, these two will make an excellent team if they are able to discipline themselves and curb their spending.

With a Monkey—Ninth Branch

The Monkey is a team player and will find the Boar cooperative and optimistic enough in outlook to establish a workable partnership with him. However, the Monkey may also take advantage of the Boar's kind-hearted nature and generosity. On the other hand, the Boar really needs someone like the Monkey to protect his interests and identify good opportunities. The Monkey personality in this combination will likewise exert his influence to curb the Boar's excessive enthusiasm and overindulgence and bring him more in line with realistic goals. The Boar will do well with the Monkey at his side instead of against him, but he will have to be tolerant of the Monkey's manipulative and calculating ways as the Monkey will see and plan farther ahead than the Boar can.

With a Rooster—Tenth Branch

The Boar will admire the hardworking and confident Rooster and seek him out for his many skills. But the Rooster tends to take over the show in this combination and may not stop at giving advice. This very capable fellow will soon be running the easy-going Boar's life and trying his best to polish and reshape the Boar into a well-disciplined and organised specimen like himself. Hopefully, the affable Boar will not suffer too much from the Rooster's valiant efforts. But the Rooster may learn that although the Boar appears to be receptive to his admonitions and recommendations, he will follow his heart in the end and find it hard to deny himself. Both may be frustrated if they cannot find a middle-of-the-road approach. In this union the Boar will probably be the one to bend rather than the inflexible Rooster.

With a Dog—Eleventh Branch

The Dog is sensible and helpful by nature and will not have serious personality clashes with the honest Boar. Their relationship will be agreeable to a large extent provided the Boar displays restraint and does not offend the Dog's love of equality and loyalty. The Dog is protective by nature and will be worried about the Boar's trusting nature and lack of guile. Consequently, he may be the voice of reason in this combination and will appoint himself as the bodyguard of the sociable but unreserved Boar who strives to please everyone. Without the presence of the defensive Dog, the Boar may find others taking advantage of him, and he could be easily cheated by less scrupulous associates.

With another Boar—Twelfth Branch

Two Boars in the same boat could find themselves wanting the same thing and each wanting it all to himself or herself. They find it hard to resolve problems because they are too close to the subject: their own selves. Neither will want to exercise appropriate restraint or discipline as they reflect each other's unflattering traits and provoke each other with contentious behaviour. When the normally obliging, hospitable and unselfish Boar is challenged, he can become destructive, vindictive and unruly. These two like personalities could be the best of friends or the worst of enemies, depending on how much they need the cooperation of the other or how much they view the other as a threat.